ZEV'S CHILDREN

An International Jewish Family

KENNETH COLLINS

VALLENTINE MITCHELL
LONDON • CHICAGO

First published in 2022 by Vallentine Mitchell

Catalyst House,	814 N. Franklin Street,
720 Centennial Court,	Chicago, Illinois,
Centennial Park, Elstree WD6 3SY, UK	60610 USA

www.vmbooks.com

Copyright © 2022 Kenneth Collins

British Library Cataloguing in Publication Data:
An entry can be found on request

ISBN 978 1 80371 007 5 (Paper)
ISBN 978 1 80371 008 2 (Ebook)

Library of Congress Cataloging in Publication Data:
An entry can be found on request

All rights reserved. No part of this publication may be reproduced in any form or by any means, electronic, mechanical, photocopying, reading or otherwise, without the prior permission of Vallentine Mitchell & Co. Ltd.

The book is dedicated to Zev's children whose lives have been recorded here and to our grandchildren, Adi, Matan, Noa, Keshet, Ari, Zev, Eden, Tal, Ella, Libby, Ori, Ariel – the tenth generation of the family story.

Map of the Ukraine: Place names mentioned in the book are **Kagarlyk** 30 kilometres south of Kiev (Kyiv) and **Kovshevata** is 60 kilometres south of Kiev. **Novo Mirgorod** is a few kilometres west of Kirovohrod and east of Uman. **Nikolaev** (Mykolaiev) is north-east of Odessa (Odesa) and **Dnepropetrovsk**, (Yekaterinoslav) lies on the Dnieper River further to the north-east. **Kanev** also lies on the Dnieper River about 150 kilometres south of Kiev and 60 kilometres north of Cherkassy (Cherkasy).

Contents

Map of the Ukraine — iv
Notes on Transcription and Further Reading — vii
Introduction — 1
Family Trees — 7

1. Beginnings — 9
2. Motti the Engineer — 26
3. Zelman the Visionary — 42
4. Ura the Exile — 64
5. The Russians — 83
6. The Siblings — 103
7. Solomon the Businessman — 123
8. Glasgow – Wartime and After — 140
9. The Doctor and Medical Historian — 156

Conclusion — 173
List of Illustrations — 182
About the Author — 184

Notes on Transcription and Further Reading

Much of the early narrative takes place in the Ukraine. I have retained the Russian versions of names and places – Kagarlitsky rather than Kaharlitsky and Kovshevata rather than Kivshevata. I have usually indicated the modern Ukrainian name for places after the first mention of their Russian version – Odessa (Odesa), Kiev (Kyiv) and Nikolaev (Mykolaiv). Zev was usually known as Wolf in Yiddish in Ukraine and was also sometimes called by the Russian Vladimir. However, he was Ze'ev on arrival in British Palestine. I have spelled his name Zev, rather than the more familiar Ze'ev as the former is easier on the English-speaking tongue. His grandson Ze'ev Amzalem has always spelled his name in the regular transliteration while our grandson Zev Sacks uses the shorter form. I have otherwise followed standard practice in transcribing Yiddish and Hebrew words and expressions.

Key works, related to the story, are mentioned in the text at appropriate times and these works can supply more detailed background.

Introduction

This book has a long history. It began when I was a child and my grandfather Solomon would tell me about Kovshevata, his birthplace and where he grew up before leaving Ukraine for London and ultimately settling in Glasgow, where I was born. Kovshevata was a place of rolling hills and fertile wheat fields, with brooks and lakes. It sounded so ideal, this little town, situated about 50 miles from Kiev, that he had to explain why he, and eventually the rest of the large family, had left. A family story never ends but it does have a beginning. Our beginning always started with my grandfather talking about Simeon who, it was reckoned, was born around 1800, and whose move from Kagarlyk gave the family its Kagarlitsky name. Recent investigations of Ukrainian archives by my newly-discovered second cousin, Simeon Briskman, have painted a more complex picture. There was a family link in the early nineteenth century with the *shtetl* of Kanev (now Kaniv), 29 miles to the east of Kagarlyk at an important crossing-point on the west bank of the Dnieper River. Russian registration documents from Kanev, similar to census returns, in 1834 have indicated that Simeon, actually Simeon-Shimmel, was born in 1791 and that his father was named Ilya. This Ilya was married to Sheindel and his father was Mordkha. Simeon also had a son called Ilya named after his grandfather. As Simeon was already known as Kagarlitsky in Kanev in 1834 the move to Kovshevata must have been from there.

As I grew up, other stories of my grandfather followed. His father, brother and three sisters were living in Tel Aviv in the 1920s while the rest of this large family stretched over continents, from Russia through Britain to the United States of America and Argentina. Of course, my grandfather always considered that the most important part was in Scotland and that he was the head of the family. Then I learned about the brother who was an engineer and had become the leading figure in building Pinchas Rutenberg's hydroelectric power station at Naharayim, where two rivers met just south of the Kinneret, the Sea of Galilee. Sadly, this brother had been killed in a work accident at the power station, but I understood that he was a family hero.

Next there was sister Ura (Youra). Ura had lived in Paris after she left Kovshevata and then spent a few years in Glasgow before moving on to Tel Aviv, then back to Paris, before returning to Russia. Many of the family photographs taken when my father was a young child showed Ura with the family. There were also pictures of the period, the early 1920s, when family members from all over the world visited Glasgow and left a trail of photographs behind. As I was growing up, visitors from America and Argentina were part of the family routine.

My grandfather died in 1964, just before I entered the University of Glasgow to study medicine. I was aware of the risks of the family history being lost. Fortunately, my father's London cousins kept in touch with the world-wide family connections. My grandfather's brother Zelman had three children, my father's cousins, Emmanuel and Victor who had been born in Ukraine, and Lilian who was London-born. I remained close to Emmanuel and Lilian to the end of their lives and it was mainly through the activities of Lilian, and her husband, Eric Mendoza, that my first collections of family notes began in the 1980s. Lilian and I kept a correspondence going until her untimely death in 1992 and these notes and cleverly configured family trees, in her meticulous typing from her home in the Old City of Jerusalem, marked the beginnings of this book.

Through Lilian I connected with Sam Altschuler, whose mother Lily Kagarlitsky had come to America before the First World War, and Mervin Bruck, the son-in-law of my grandfather's half-sister Ida. More recently, I have been in touch with Mervin Bruck's nephew, Gary Martel, a dentist who lives in Portland, Oregon and he has helped with information on the family of Ida and Jacob Rashal. Laura Levy, whose family (Roush) are related to Zev's first wife Sarah Milevski, produced material on Zev's son Sam, known in America as Samuel Wolfe Kagar. Much of the early work on the extended family tree was organized with Dick Mannheimer from Los Angeles. Dick's wife Myra was a granddaughter of Feige (Kagarlitsky) Bachelis, who was my grandfather's cousin. Though I have never met a member of the extensive Bachelis family I do have a copy of a poetry book, *Menschen Fun Mein Dor*, in Yiddish, by Barney Bachelis, published posthumously by his widow Elizabeth and son Robert in Los Angeles in 1953, part of the small Yiddish literary legacy from my grandfather.

Emmanuel, always referred to as Cousin Emmanuel, became a leading figure in British industry, as Sir Emmanuel Kaye, but he remained close to his family in Glasgow, visiting regularly, always taking copious notes of what he saw and what he heard. Foreign family members usually began a trip to Britain by visiting Emmanuel and Elizabeth, either at their London home, or their house in the country at Hartley-Wintney. Elizabeth's cousin, Sir Martin Gilbert, was enthusiastic about the Kagarlitsky family project and I expected he would write the Foreword, given his closeness to both Emmanuel and Elizabeth. We met a couple of times in 2011 and discussed the outlines of this story when he received an honorary doctorate from the Ben Gurion University of the Negev, but sadly he died in 2015 when the research for this book was still at an early stage. The only other Collins cousins in Britain who lived near us in Glasgow were Shimmel and Becky Collins. I had great difficulty with great-uncle Shimmel's English. My mother described it as one stage below broken English – completely fractured. Nevertheless, he had managed to build up a successful business in Glasgow.

The family brought more than just themselves to Glasgow. The grown-ups often spoke to each other in Yiddish. We children had no more than a little knowledge of the most frequently-used words and expressions, so we could not understand the conversations when it was נישט פאר די קינדער (not for the children). We heard the Yiddish songs at regular extended family gatherings and tasted the traditional Ukrainian Jewish foods. We saw how it was possible to drink tea through a sugar cube and watched the men playing Klabiash, a complicated card-game with just the higher value cards, and its own internal language. (In the trump suit the jack, known as 'yash' becomes the most valuable card was and the next card was the nine known as 'manel'.) It seemed to be totally incomprehensible. This game was played regularly at my grandparents' house, and in the corner of Jackie Sheville's barber shop in Glasgow's Gorbals.

Our Uncle Sam lived in Winston-Salem in North Carolina, with lengthy spells also in New York. He made frequent extended trips to Glasgow and even started naturalization proceedings on two occasions. However, he always returned to America, his wife and his businesses, both of which we presumed were precarious enterprises. With a brother called Sam it always seemed strange that Shimmel called his textile company Samuel Collins Ltd when his 'proper' name was Simon, and Shimmel was a 'pet' diminutive.

When I retired from my medical practice in 2007 and settled in Jerusalem a couple of years later, I always presumed that I would have time to write, and that the family story would be a priority. This did not happen as I was involved in the production of no less than three books on the history of Jews in Scotland, as well as collaborating with colleagues at the Hebrew University of Jerusalem on a series of books on Jewish medical ethics and leading Jewish figures in medicine. This turned out to be fortunate because over the past few years the various gaps in the family story have closed as we have restored relationships with more and more of the descendants of Zev (Wolf) Kagarlitsky.

Connecting with Simeon Briskman, in Kfar Saba near Tel Aviv, brought details of my grandfather's sister Raisa (Reysie) and his half-sister Clara. At the same time his archival skills and native fluency in Russian have produced new insights into early family history. He also identified and re-established contact with the artist Ze'ev Amzalem, the first family member named after the patriarch Zev. Gary Martel in Portland, Oregon is a descendant of my grandfather's half-sister Ida (Hinde). Agustin Carlinski, Mariela Shujmajer and Gustavo Chocron from Argentina are great-grand-children of my grandfather's brother Shuka (Salomon). The Moscow Kagarlitskys have always been an important part of the family. Anna, my grandfather's cousin, had lived in Glasgow before returning to Moscow to marry my grandfather's half-brother Iosif. Their son Julius (Iuliy) and grandson Boris visited Glasgow in the late 1980s and we have had two visits to Moscow in recent years. François Romagnan proved to be a valuable source on Ura's years in Vichy France and Jon Shore, from Boston, managed to arrange for us to meet his parents over dinner in Wolf and Lamb's in New York and solve the connection between Rose Kagarlitsky, her husband Wolf Antonovski and my grandfather's move from London to Glasgow in 1912. As we entered the restaurant, I noticed an acquaintance from London, who told me with great excitement that he was also meeting with a long-lost relative from Russia.

When Eugene Kogan from St. Petersburg made contact in 2011, after receiving my email address from Boris Kagarlitsky, we were uncertain then about how our families linked up. More recent research has shown that he is a descendant also of Simeon-Shimmel, through his son Menachem, and he had the information which takes us back to Simeon-Shimmel's grandfather, Mordkhe (Mordechai) who would have been born around 1740. Eugene's cousin, Eugenia Mosaleva, from Moscow, has energetically pursued the genealogy of the Kagarlitsky family finding many lost aunts, uncles and cousins who can one day be integrated into the story, but also suggesting that further earlier finds may be possible.

As always, I owe a great debt of gratitude to Zelman's family. Lilian's daughter Rebecca has been a constant source of information, encouragement and advice. Emmanuel's grandson Daniel Harbour manages his grandfather Emmanuel's family archives in London, which are composed mainly in Russian and Yiddish but also in English and Hebrew and has already produced two books of family lore: one mostly of correspondence between his great-grandmother Chassia and her husband-to-be Zelman, while she was in a sanatorium in Switzerland in 1912 and 1913, and a book of Zelman's journalistic articles in Yiddish, Hebrew and Russian written mostly before the First World War. We will visit these in this book.

Boris Kagarlitsky visited Glasgow in 1988 after receiving the Isaac and Tamara Deutscher Memorial Prize, awarded for a book which exemplifies the best and most innovative new writing in or about the Marxist tradition. Appropriately the closing date for nominations is 1 May. In my copy of *The Thinking Reed*, on Soviet politics, he inscribed the words 'from Kagarlitsky to Collins'. That in essence is the theme of this book.

Family sagas, often with dozens of characters spread over many generations and several locations, are popular in fiction. I have not departed from fact in this story, using contemporary documents where possible, supplemented by oral history testimonies and clearly indicating where my own inferences and understandings are drawn. In Michael Weisser's *A Brotherhood of Memories* (1985) he acknowledged, just as I do in this history, that his story of the New York *landsmanschaften* went beyond established archival material, relying also on oral history and family tales, known as *bubbemeises* in Yiddish. He warns his readers that a *bubbe meise* is 'a particular type of story told only to those who understand it even before it is told' which gives it its 'endless variety and vitality'.

As the story progresses, we move from Zev's story to the generation of his children charting their lives in Mandate Palestine, America, England, Argentina, Russia and Scotland. World influences close in on their lives, especially in Nazi Europe and Stalin's Russia. In contrast, the life of my grandfather in twentieth-century Glasgow shows a peace and tranquility that evaded most of his siblings. We will see how his sons served in the British war effort, with the youngest Joseph (Joe) having the most distinguished career and ending the war as acting Brigadier and rewarded with an OBE.

I conclude the story with my own experiences in Glasgow and Jerusalem, a direct descendant of Mordkhe Kagarlitsky who had been born in Ukraine around 1740. This will complete my narrative which flows from the eighteenth century for almost three hundred years. There were other immigrant families in Glasgow where my grandfather's contemporaries had all their siblings in Glasgow, sometimes as many as a dozen. But then my grandfather's path had been different, a young man arriving in London on his own. He had not, like most Jews who settled in Glasgow, been part of the Jewish mass migrations which moved mainly from Poland, Lithuania and Belarus. Their journeys took them to the Baltic ports or to Hamburg and then on to Britain's east coast, at first to Leith and Edinburgh and later to Grimsby. The journey ended with the train to Glasgow, one of the great ports shipping humanity to North America. As we show in *Two Hundred Years of Scottish Jewry* (2019) Glasgow had been a 'revolving-door' community in the immigrant era, growing substantially in size while significant proportions of previous immigrations were moving on.

The strength of the family has been that although only the families of Zelman, Solomon and Shimmel lived in Britain contacts across the world have kept most parts of the family in contact with each other. The Jewish-Gen website has made it easier to establish communication but there was not a time, when I was a child, I was not aware of the family's almost global reach. Our Kagarlitsky legacy is also very diverse but is also real.

Finally, I owe an immense debt to my wife and life-partner Irene. She has come with me on almost all my historical trips abroad and especially on our two visits to Russia and Ukraine. We have continually discussed the developing text and she has helped me find solutions to puzzles in the family narrative.

Finally, I would like to thank Professor Aubrey Newman for his help, support and careful proof-reading, and Toby, Lisa and Jenni at Vallentine Mitchell, whose professional approach has made the production of this book such a pleasure.

The Family Trees

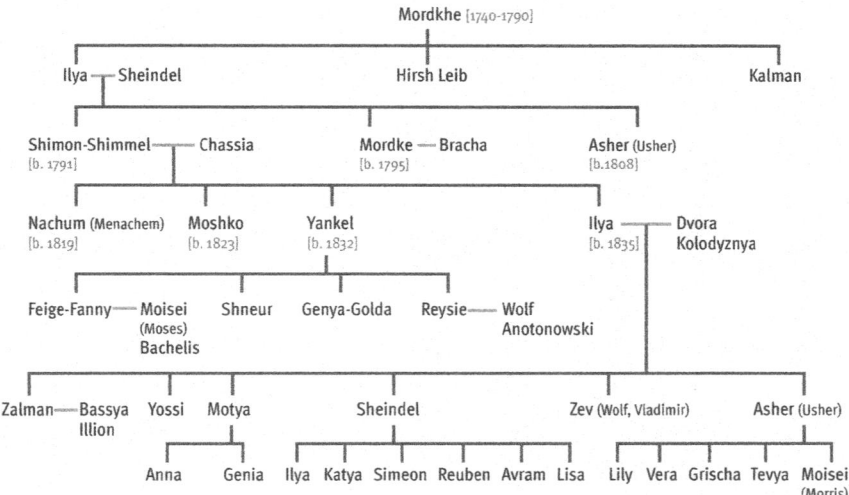

The historical Family Tree – from 1740 down to Zev's generation.

8 · *Zev's Children*

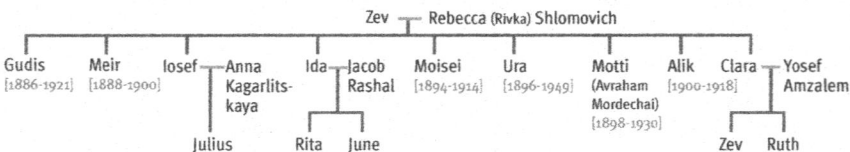

The two family trees of Zev's Children and Grandchildren (first and second marriages).

1
Beginnings

I grew up in Glasgow the child of two very different Jewish families. My mother's parents grew up in Glasgow, always part of its lively religious, cultural and social life. My mother knew her grandparents, who had come to Glasgow from Poland, and who lived most of their adult lives in Glasgow and in turn they were part of her life for some decades. My father's family were different. Although his parents were born in the Ukraine, they came to London as teenagers, settling in Glasgow some years after their marriage. They never saw their parents again. They represented a living connection to what was called in Yiddish *der heim*, literally 'the home', the Eastern European Jewish heartland where Jews formed a substantial part of the urban and village landscape.

Besides their Yiddish language my grandparents brought their Jewish Ukrainian cuisine to Scotland. *Holishkes, knishes* filled with kasha or mince, *p'tcha* and many other items supplemented the more usual parts of the Scottish diet. The family were extrovert and addicted to Jewish music. Festive meals usually ended with singing of a wide medley of Yiddish folksongs so different from the more sober atmosphere of my mother's family. All my father's generation have now passed away, so while much of their heritage survives in the memory of the next generation there is so much that needs to be recorded.

We have been fortunate to be able to have so much information on some of the key members of the family from the first half of the twentieth century and this forms the core of the family story. Collectively, they demonstrate the trials of modern Jewish history, the Holocaust, the Stalinist terror, the rise of Zionism and in contrast the comfortable Diaspora life that Scotland provided for us. My grandfather and his numerous siblings were born into a world that is hard to imagine today and understanding its context and wider background is an essential part of the story.

To explore this world we need to go back more than two centuries when Simeon Kagarlitsky married, moved to Kovshevata and produced a family that would in a few generations span the world and encounter challenges, threats and opportunities that could not be imagined in the Ukraine of his day. As Simeon's family was growing in Kovshevata his sons remained in the area, some moving to neighbouring villages like Lysyanka and Luka or the town of Boguslav. It was his son Ilya, born around 1830, whose seven children and their progeny form the mainstream of the family history. Zev's father Ilya seems to have established the family's prosperity. Ilya rented farmland in Kovshevata and sold its produce. When restrictions were placed on Jewish landownership he branched out into trade, as a timber and wheat dealer. He also had a business making the agricultural machinery that was used in the mid-nineteenth century as well as maintaining a liquor store. He travelled abroad, to France and Germany to buy fine goods, such as porcelain, silver and furniture. Some of these goods survived into modern times in the family ownership, even during the Soviet era. He had been unwell with cancer of the tongue and went to Berlin for surgical treatment, which could only have been palliative. Ilya and Devora then went, as usual, to the Black Sea spa where the family often took holidays, and it was returning from there that he died in Kiev in 1895. A telegram to Kovshevata was received by my grandfather's brother Sam and he delivered it to the family home. Ilya's home was still remembered by locals and could be pointed out to family members, sisters Anna and Genia, who visited from Moscow in the 1960s.

Jews in these small *shtetls* were, in the main petty tradesman and merchants. Crafts included work as tailors, cobblers, blacksmiths and carpenters and there were many shop keepers selling foods and textiles and innkeepers selling alcohol. The needs of the religious community meant that there was a need for teachers, *shochtim* (ritual slaughterers) and butchers. Traditional occupations included water carriers and waggoners while there was a large network of traders and dealers in horses and cattle, wheat, flour and timber.

As the family name is geographical many others, who had moved from Kagarlyk to the area around Kovshevata, or to other places within the Russian Empire, around the same time as Simeon and family did, adopted the same surname. Most of these are not related, but a few years ago we worked hard to establish connections with some Kagarlitskys who had arrived in Israel from nearby Boguslav (Bohuslav) and whose ancestors had very similar first names to those of our own family. We met David Kagarlitsky in Tel Aviv and went with him to the grave of Zev in Rehov Trumpeldor. The cemetery had opened in distant sand-dunes in 1905 during an outbreak of cholera in Jaffa and now is enclosed by the centre of Tel Aviv, close to the Dizengoff Centre. Zev is buried close to the graves of Mayor Meir Dizengoff and national poet Chaim Nachman Bialik, but on the opposite side of the graveyard. We stood in silence in front of Zev's tombstone. David explained that during the Soviet era his family was aware of ours and had even visited our family graves in Moscow, thinking there must be a connection. However, they were afraid to show themselves as too close to a family whose members were 'wealthy and lived abroad'. We compared family trees and discovered that both families claimed an Ilya, born in the nineteenth century who had a son living in Boguslav. 'Our' Ilya did have a son, Yossi, who had settled in Boguslav, but we had no knowledge of David's Kagarlitsky's Ruvim, a son of 'his' Ilya. Ruvim does not appear on our family tree and Ruvim's mother was called Esther while 'our' Ilya's wife was Dvora. David speculated that that Esther might have been a second wife and the oldest daughter, Dvora, could have been named after the first wife. We have found no evidence for this, so the link remains unproved.

Jews began moving to western Ukraine in the sixteenth and seventeenth centuries when the area was under Polish (or Polish Lithuanian) rule, and they were encouraged to help the Polish nobility manage their estates. By the end of this period Jews were settling in areas further east. When the family left Kagarlyk, taking the name Kagarlitsky with them, they settled first in Kanev, before moving on to Kovshevata. Kanev was a small market town on the Dnieper south of Kiev and the fertile inland area around Kovshevata may have offered better access to trade in timber and wheat. They found a group of around a thousand Jews with all the facilities expected in a small *shtetl*. At the end of the eighteenth century the whole area became part of the Russian Empire and after the Russian Revolution it was the Ukrainian Soviet Socialist Republic of the Soviet Union. Ukraine did not achieve independence until 1991.

The complex story of Jews and Ukrainians has a troubled past. Jews in the Ukraine experienced two cataclysmic events in the seventeenth and eighteenth centuries. The first was the devastation of the Khmelnytsky massacres in 1648 when as many as 100,000 Jews lost their lives. Ukrainians point to the control that Jews had over the nobles through their management of their estates and their ownership of the most of the country's inns and alcohol as issues that caused resentment, but no defence can excuse the butchery of these years. Khmelnytsky remains a hero in Ukraine, where a city and a region are named after him and his image appears on Ukrainian banknotes. Indeed, the Order of Bohdan Khmelnytsky is one of the highest decorations in the country, as it was in the former Soviet Union. He also pursued the union with Russia, probably dictated by contemporary political necessity, and his leadership presaged the decline of the Polish Commonwealth which a century later culminated in the partition of Poland with the division of the country between Russia, Prussia and Austria. His legacy in the Jewish world is completely negative. The stories of violence and destruction still resonate in the Jewish world today and Jewish visitors to contemporary Ukraine are shocked to find that the author of one of the most traumatic periods of Jewish history is celebrated through the statues such as the monument in central Kiev (Kyiv).

Jewish life was sharply different from that of the neighbouring peoples. They were distinguished by their clothing, their religious practices, which impinged on their kosher food and wine, their Shabbat observance, their high level of literacy and respect for learning. While Jews were literate in Hebrew and Yiddish, and the more skilled, in the Aramaic of the Babylonian Talmud, most had some level of fluency in Russian and Ukrainian for communication with the authorities and the local peasantry.

The Jews who survived the turmoil of the Cossack rebellions, and the widespread depression caused by the fervour that surrounded the failed Messianic pretender, Shabbetai Zevi, needed solace and this they found in the revivalist and pietist Hasidic movement. The founder of Hasidism was Rabbi Israel ben Eliezer, known as the Baal Shem Tov, or Master of the Good Name, or simply as the Besht. He taught the importance of the connection of the individual with God as he went through the towns and villages of Podolia and Volhynia. His encouragement of Jews to seek joy in their religious life contrasted with the more austere practices of existing Jewish communities and their religious seminaries, or *yeshivot*. He was a mystic but was not ascetic, bidding his followers to worship God in all the mundane aspects of their daily lives. His message quickly spread from his home in Medzibodz, (now Medzhybizh), and became the predominant form of Judaism throughout Ukraine.

The movement grew through the eighteenth and nineteenth centuries through the Besht's disciples who formed many different, and often rival, dynasties based in the villages, shtetls and towns through Poland and Ukraine. Kagarlyk and Kovshevta lay just to the east of these vibrant Hasidic centres, and families would attach themselves to the authority of one of the Hasidic leaders, or *rebbes*. The Kagarlitsky family found their way to the radical and controversial *Rebbe*, Menachem Mendel Morgenstern of Kotsk (1787-1859). He had been a brilliant student and his sayings and behaviour attracted considerable attention and a wide following.

One of the most beautiful descriptions of Menachem Mendel's life and philosophy can be found in Elie Weisel's *Souls on Fire* (1972), which tells the story of the early Hasidic leaders, showing how they built shelters with words and silence and gave hope and fervour to their followers. Weisel describes Menachem Mendel as 'the angry saint, the divine rebel' and the absolute pursuer of truth, declaring that:

> Every fragment contains him, but he is more than the sum of all fragments. He is the flame that draws the sparks, a free and powerful flame that rises and carries the world along. Alive, people dared not look him in the face; dead, but strong in his legend, here he is still, judging as if he were our contemporary.

For the last twenty years of his life Menachem Mendel secluded himself from his followers, living a solitary life in just one room of his home. Many theories have been given for this withdrawal. Weisel, in poetic prose, gives many – including the possibility of depression – but the paradigm of the lonely man of faith has many followers. Abraham Joshua Heschel's book *Passion for Truth* compares Menachem Mendel with the contemporary Danish Christian existentialist philosopher Søren Kierkegaard, who also dealt with how one lives as an individual. While Kierkegaard's antisemitism has been widely acknowledged, his philosophic message giving priority to the importance of personal choice and commitment to concrete and demanding uncompromising honesty and self-scrutiny was something both could share.

Although many of his personal followers joined other Hasidic *rebbes*, especially during the years of seclusion, some of his descendants continued his legacy in succeeding generations. Zev's father and grandfather were alive during the lifetime of Menachem Mendel and they passed on to their children the reverence of Hasidim for their *rebbe*. Photographs of Zev, taken in his last years in Tel Aviv, show him dressed in the traditional Hasidic garb. My grandfather supported emissaries of the Kotzker *rebbes* when they visited Britain from Poland in the inter-war years seeking funds to support the Morgenstern family and their religious networks.

This connection was to lead to the arrival in Glasgow of Rabbi Shlomo David Morgenstern, the sixth Kotsker *Rebbe*. He became the rabbi of a small Hasidic synagogue, the Beis Yaakov, in the Gorbals for a few years just before the Second World War. His brother also came to Glasgow with him to work as a *shochet*. Rabbi Morgenstern's son, Israel Chaim, celebrated his *barmitzvah* in Glasgow on the eve of the Second World War and the event attracted many *rebbes*, dynastic leaders of the various sects, to the city. Followers of the Kotskers, my grandfather likely amongst them, had managed to bring Rabbi Morgenstern first to London in 1936 and then to

Glasgow at a time when entry permits were becoming more difficult to be obtain. This link between Kagarlitskys and Morgensterns was renewed as recently as 2018.

I had been at the morning service at our synagogue, HaTzvi Yisrael, best known as Hovevei from its address in Rehov Hovevei Tzion, in the Talbiye neighbourhood of Jerusalem. I struck up a conversation with an American visitor who asked where I was from and he immediately volunteered that his grandfather had been a rabbi in Glasgow. I quickly established that our visitor, Rabbi Jonathan Morgenstern, could be the eighth Kotsker *rebbe*, though he described himself as modern Orthodox rather than Hasidic and was the rabbi in what is described as the 'upscale' neighbourhood of Scarsdale. We exchanged emails and I was intrigued that his email address began with 'kotskertruth'!

The story continued during a visit to Krakow in July 2018 where I was attending the conference of the European Association of Jewish Studies held every four years and on this occasion was taking place at the Jagellonian University. The conference hosted an amazing collection of Jewish studies scholars, not just from Europe but also from Israel and America and we had time to see the old town and the Jewish area of Kazimierz. Entering the Izaak Synagogue on Friday evening I was quickly aware of a large group of American visitors in the crowded building. It turned out that they were from Scarsdale and their leader was Rabbi Jonathan Morgenstern!

Tisha B'Av that year fell on Shabbat and the fast was postponed to the next day. Tisha B'Av, the ninth day of the Hebrew month of Av, commemorates the day when the First and Second Temples in Jerusalem were destroyed, the First by the Babylonians (587 BCE) and the Second by the Romans (70 CE) but many other dark days for the Jewish people occurred on that day: the expulsion of Jews from Spain in 1492 and the earlier expulsions of the Jews from France (1391) and England (1290). Germany entered the First World War on Tisha B'Av in 1914, which led to the political instability in Europe which produced the Holocaust.

The fast begins with the reading of *Eicha*, the biblical *Book of Lamentations*, attributed to the Prophet Jeremiah. Rabbi Morgenstern invited us to join his group for the reading which they had planned at the site of the Plaszow Concentration Camp. Not much of the camp remains today. What had not been cleared by the Germans was removed by the Russians and the area grassed over. We climbed to a hollow behind a Soviet era memorial where, aided by insect sprays and torches, we followed the ancient text. Before the reading began, Rabbi Morgenstern set the scene and mentioned that his grandfather and great-uncle had only survived the

Holocaust because people like my grandfather had been there to help them enter Britain and find work in the religious community for them in London and Glasgow. It was a very moving evening.

Ukraine was a major centre of Jewish life in the nineteenth century. Cities like Kiev and Odessa (Odesa) were prominent in the enlightenment era of modern cultural life, nurtured by writers like Sholom Aleichem, I.L. Peretz, and Mendele Mocher Seforim as well as important Zionist figures such as Leon Pinsker, Ahad Ha-Am and Vladimir Jabotinsky. By the beginning of the twentieth century, Jews lived in almost all the towns of Ukraine, making up about a third of the total urban population and in many places actually forming a majority.

The brutal pogroms of 1881-82 were carried out mostly in Ukraine, and these atrocities, allied with economic hardship, stimulated substantial Jewish emigration mainly westwards to Western Europe, Britain, the United States and South America. Anti-Jewish violence continued over the next decades and the pogrom which attracted most world headlines occurred in 1903, in Kishinev, now known as Chisinau, the capital of Moldova. The *New York Times* reported:

> The mob was led by priests, and the general cry, 'Kill the Jews', was taken-up all over the city. The Jews were taken wholly unaware and were slaughtered like sheep. The dead number 120 and the injured about 500. The scenes of horror attending this massacre are beyond description. Babes were literally torn to pieces by the frenzied and bloodthirsty mob. The local police made no attempt to check the reign of terror. At sunset the streets were piled with corpses and wounded. Those who could make their escape fled in terror, and the city is now practically deserted of Jews.

I have chosen to call the village they settled in Kovshevata, but my grandfather always called his birthplace Kushovata, following the Yiddish pronunciation, while in today's Ukraine it is known as Kivshovata (Ківшовата) and in Soviet times it would have been the Russian Kovshevatoe (Ковшеватое). There the family prospered, earning a living from trading in the wheat and timber of the area. One of Simeon's grandson's, my grandfather's cousin, went to Switzerland to study medicine. The records of the University of Zurich confirm that 'Schliom' Kagarlitsky, born in 'Koschowetto' in 1874, had graduated MD in 1906 with a thesis on tuberculosis, while his wife Bassia Illion had graduated at the same time with a thesis on tuberculous meningitis in childhood.

I have tended to call Kagarlyk and Kovshevata villages rather than shtetls. The shtetl, like a village, would have a population from a few hundred to a few thousand inhabitants and perhaps a higher proportion of Jews than the approximately 20 per cent of Kagarlyk and Kovshevata. The shtetl has been idealised as a fictional utopia, as in the Anatevka of Sholom Aleichem portrayed in *Fiddler on the Roof*. Sholom Aleichem was the pen name of Solomon Naumovitch Rabinovitch (1859-1916), and he was a visitor to Kovshevata during the summers from 1876 to 1879, when, just out of high school, he was tutoring for a wealthy family in a neighbouring area.

There are many accounts of shtetl life. My favourites include I.J. Singer's *Of a World that is No More: a Tender Memoir* (1970) and Eva Hoffman's *Shtetl: the Life and Death of a Small Town and the World of Polish Jews* (1998). Singer, the brother of Nobel Laureate Isaac Bashevis Singer, had family roots in the Polish shtetl of Leoncin, and his memoir of people and places, contrasts with the more scholarly approach of Eva Hoffman, showing the Polish shtetl of Bransk in its historical context. Sholom Aleichem was born in Ukraine, south of Kiev so his fictional *shtetl* of Kasrilevke cannot be so different from Kagarlyk or Kovshevata.

A more recent publication, *The Golden Age of the Shtetl: A New History of Jewish Life in East Europe* (2014), by Yohanan Petrovsky-Shtern, defines the *shtetl* as 'an East European market town, in the private possession of a Polish magnate and inhabited mostly but not exclusively by Jews' but admits that 'we do not know what makes an Eastern European locality a *shtetl*'. He describes a Golden Age of the *shtetl*, extending from 1790 for half a century, around the time that Simeon was born, grew up and started his family. Of course, the partition of Poland brought the Ukrainian *shtetls* under the control of Russia, but Petrovsky-Stern hastens to point out that the *shtetl* decay as described by Sholom Aleichem and others is not how the inhabitants saw it, describing 'the Jews who walked through history without leaving a footprint', and he delineates its vitality and resilience in the way that my grandfather, and other family members, recalled. Financial stability came from trade rather than small-scale artisanship, especially the liquor trade, much of which was in Jewish hands and the areas around Kagarlyk and Boguslav produced high volumes of alcohol. Jews were literate and supported printing presses such as those in Boguslav which specialised in religious and mystical works.

Kagarlyk is barely 25 miles from Kovshevata and the two places were similar in population size at around 7,000 with around a fifth of the inhabitants in both being Jewish. A Jewish community was formed in 1744 in Kovshevata, attracted by the possibilities in the rich farming area and the extensive network of local towns. In 1914 Jews owned a mill, a pharmacy and 37 shops there. There were larger Jewish communities near Kovshevata, Tarascha, a few miles to the west, where almost half the population was Jewish, and the more substantially Jewish town of Boguslav, a few miles to the east, where the Jewish community was about two-thirds of the total. The population movement was significant. The growing Kagarlitsky family occupied a row of houses making up the inhabitants of a village street, with Ilya's home the most prominent.

The family still had some members there till the beginning of the First World War, but most of the remainder had left during the unsettled period of the Civil War. Despite the family's increasing geographical distance from Kovshevata, and the fact that the family name came from Kagarlyk, the village was still considered to be the place of origin of the family story and carried a huge emotional attachment that family members remembered with affection for many decades. Zev's brother Asher had settled in the nearby smaller village of Lysyanka, less than twenty miles away. Business directories indicate that he ran a grocery store and also sold hardware goods. His youngest child Lily settled in America just before the First World War, but had a clear memory for distant events until her nineties. She told Lilian and Eric, who were visiting America, that she had once been suffering from toothache and it had been decided that she should see a dentist in Kiev which in those days was some hours away. They set off on 14 September 1911 but were overtaken by events.

There was to be a performance that day of Rimsky-Korsakov's *The Tale of Tsar Saltan* at the Kiev Opera House in the presence of the Tsar and his two oldest daughters, the Grand Duchesses Olga and Tatiana. Pyotr Stolypin, Prime Minister and Minister of Internal Affairs, was also present and while his personal bodyguard had stepped out to smoke, he was shot twice, once in the arm and once in the chest by a left-wing revolutionary. Stolypin remained conscious enough to tell the Tsar to leave, but his condition worsened and he died three days later. There was chaos in Kiev, and it was not the time to be looking for a dentist. Lily remembered the events of the day until extreme old age, especially the assassination of Stolypin, one of the most effective of Tsarist politicians, but not well enough to recall what had happened to her tooth. They retreated to Kovshevata, spending the night there before returning home.

My grandfather described Kovshevata in glowing terms. The fertile fields, the orchards and the village stream always stirred nostalgia in his reminiscences. My aunts and uncles were not convinced about this idyllic spot that he had left as a teenager until a visit by family members from Oregon, Nathan Carl, the surname another variant of Kagarlitsky, confirmed my grandfather's story. Nathan Carl had grown up in the village and its beauty had remained with him. I was able to see it for myself during a visit in 2004. Contact with the Carl branch in Oregon is maintained today with Sheila Matthews.

The Russian Revolution and the ensuing Civil War of 1918-21 brought further devastation to Ukraine. The country was filled with warring factions. There were the Reds, the Communists who ultimately became dominant, the Whites, Russian nationalists who wished to return to the fractured status quo and the Poles, whose majorities in the cities of Western Ukraine allowed them to hold onto much of the country in the post-war settlement. For a time, there were Western troops who wanted to see the defeat of Communism. Wearied by the war with Germany they proved particularly ineffective. There were also bands of irregular militias who often owed allegiance only to themselves. It was a perfect recipe for chaos and disaster.

Around 35,000 Jews lost their lives and many more became homeless. Much of this slaughter occurred during the brief life of the Ukraine National Republic of 1918-1921 which was headed by Simon Petlyura. Jews hold Petlyura responsible for the pogroms and the mass-murders while Ukrainians consider that he had been sympathetic to Jews and had issued orders to stop the attacks. While it was true that all participants in the Civil War had been guilty of murdering Jews, most attacks were carried out by troops nominally under Petlyura's control and he failed to control their excesses. Petlyura was eventually killed in Paris by Sholom Schwartzbard, a Ukraine-born Jewish anarchist who claimed that he was avenging the deaths of all those murdered in the Ukraine, including close members of his family. After a trial lasting for eight days Schwarztbard was acquitted.

While the Ukrainian Diaspora see Petlyura as a hero who tried to establish Ukrainian independence, his violent legacy has meant that inhabitants of Ukraine today see him as much more of a controversial figure. Consequently, he does not represent a fault line between Jews and Ukrainians in the way that Khmelnytsky does. By the time that the Civil War was over, most of my grandfather's immediate relations had left or were planning to leave Ukraine. Zelman was living in Dnepropetrovsk while Zev and Clara waited in Odessa to join Motti and Ida in Tel Aviv.

Zev had relocated to Novo Mirgorod after leaving Kovshevata around 1900, and it is this town which is mentioned on his tombstone in Tel Aviv. His first wife, Sarah Milevski, had died in around 1885 and he married his second wife, Rebecca Shlomovich, the following year. It is likely that he was in Novo Mirgorod for some years as his daughter Ida (Hinda), who had been born in Kovshevata in 1896, married Jacob Rashal, who lived in the nearby *shtetl* of Zlatopol, in 1918. Jewish settlement in Novo Mirgorod, in the Kirovograd District, south of Kovshevata had begun in the 1770s, though they had been expelled from the town in 1821 and only allowed to return nearly 40 years later. During this period of exile Jews relocated to the nearby *shtetl* of Zlatopol, just a mile away and today Zlatopol lies within Novo Mirgorod's municipal boundaries. At the time of Zev's arrival in Novo Mirgorod, the 6,000 Jews in Zlatopol made up four fifths of the population while Novo Mirgorod had just 1,622 Jews (17 per cent of the total). During the pogroms of 1919 more than a hundred Jews were killed and when the Nazis arrived almost a thousand Jews lost their lives, some killed by Ukrainian police but for the most part murdered in the Mezhigorzkaya Ravine.

It is not clear when Zev would have left Novo Mirgorod. We have noted that Ida was married in nearby Zlatopol in 1918, and he likely soon after moved to Odessa from where he was to travel with Clara in 1921 to Jaffa to join Motti and Ida. Motti was studying engineering at a technical college near Odessa so this part of Zev's life is somewhat unknown. My grandfather talked of family living in Nikolayev but never in Odessa, which was likely a short stop on the way out of Ukraine. Following the Russian Revolution Zelman had moved to Dnepropetrovsk, seeing it as a place of greater safety during the turmoil, possibly where his background as a merchant and Zionist leader would be less well known.

The city of Odessa had been a magnet for Jews seeking to leave their *shtetls* for big city life. It was a major cultural centre, in Russian, Yiddish and Hebrew. Haim Nachman Bialik, later Israel's national poet, lived and published there as had the Zionist theorist Ahad Ha-Am; Vladimir Jabotinsky wrote novels based there and the Odessa tales of Isaac Babel were to receive international acclaim. The Zionist movement in Odessa was probably the most influential in the Jewish world and the Odessa Committee included prominent figures such as its chairman Menachem Ussishkin, Meir Dizengoff, later Mayor of Tel Aviv, Leon Pinsker, leader of *Hibat Zion*, and many, many more.

The devastation caused in Ukraine during the Civil War has been described in many different histories, but these mainly describe events in the larger population centres rather than in smaller places like Kovshevata with little more than a thousand Jews. Irregular militias were probably responsible for the murder of Jews between Tarascha and Boguslav, the route which passes through Kovshevata. As Jews were at the mercy of the various sides in the conflict, the rapid changes of occupiers caused additional problems. In one week, Boguslav changed hands no less than twenty times, and Kiev was also captured and recaptured many times. On 3 June 1919, the militias had been in Kagarlyk and two months later were in Boyarke where my grandmother had been born. One hundred and sixty-nine Jews were murdered in Novo Mirgorod. A short publication by the Federation of Ukrainian Jews in London in 1921 detailed the horrors of the murders, rapes and burnings.

I was to discover the tragedy affecting just one Kovshevata family in 1999 from an unusual source. Rachel Lichtenstein, then a young artist in the East End of London, had been creating images of the local Jewish life which had once teemed with an intensity. Indeed, my grandfather had begun his life in Britain in Tenter Street in the heart of the East End in 1898. Rachel's work had taken her to the Princelet Street Synagogue. The synagogue had opened in 1870 in the former home of a wealthy Huguenot silk merchant, but by 1999 it was in a precarious state and no longer used as a synagogue. In a garret above the synagogue Rachel found the abandoned room of David Rodinsky, and this discovery led to her publication, along with Iain Sinclair, of *Rodinsky's Room* (1999) by Granta Books. The book has been described as a personal quest which evolved into a compelling psycho-geographical detective story. It is now considered a classic of its genre and has been translated into five languages.

David Rodinsky's families were refugees from Kovshevata, and the family pronounced the name Kushovata, with the stress on the second syllable, just as my grandfather did. Rodinsky had been born in London in 1925 to a religiously observant family that had suffered in the pogroms which followed the Russian Revolution and his parents had come to London where relatives were already settled from before the First World War. Much of Rachel's account describes David Rodinsky's strange character and behaviour and his room which was abandoned in 1961, at the start of a series of illnesses which led to his death in a psychiatric institution in Surrey in 1969. The room was left untouched, allowing Rachel to create images of the material that the reclusive David had left behind – writings in a multiplicity of languages, kabbalistic symbolism and Hebrew writings.

In her exploration of the Rodinsky story, Rachel discovered that David's mother, Haicka, had been raped in one of the pogroms, which had taken place in Kovshevata during the Civil War and was the likely cause of her nervous behaviour. Her experiences in Ukraine had also taught her fear of authority and the dangers associated with the functioning of state institutions. Suddenly, Kovshevata's troubled past became real. Rachel Lichtenstein had been unable to make the journey to Kovshevata after attending a study course in Poland, so I sent her a letter telling her about our connection to Kovshevata and received a reply on a postcard which had her 'Portrait of Rodinsky' on the other side.

By the late 1920s, the Soviet regime began to confiscate synagogues, while creating a network of Yiddish schools, theatres, newspapers and publishing houses which were devoid of all religious content. A decade later, as Stalin's purges intensified, even these remnants of Jewish culture closed. What religious and Zionist life there was became a risky clandestine activity. One member of the Kagarlitsky family perished during these purges: a cousin of my grandfather's, Mosei (Maurice), the youngest child of Ilya. Mosei had left Lysyanka to study veterinary medicine in Paris after a few years in the United States. During the First World War he had left France and returned to America to complete his studies at the State University of Ohio in Columbus. He returned to Russia after the Revolution and by 1940 was the senior figure at the Institute of Veterinary Medicine in Tbilisi, Georgia. Blamed for problems in Georgian livestock he was sent to the gulag where he soon succumbed, following a confession to the charges to save his wife and children.

A major Ukrainian trauma, the Holodomor or Terror Famine of 1932-1933, hit the rural population, killing at least three million people through starvation. The area around Kiev was especially affected. The famine was a consequence of collectivisation of agriculture and consequent poor harvests but is also considered to have been a direct result of Stalinist policies, a crime against humanity, and enforced by Stalin's associates, including Lazar Kaganovich. Raphael Lemkin, who coined the term genocide, described this as deliberate in his *Soviet Genocide in the Ukraine* (2014). Most of the victims were ethnic Ukrainians and just over one per cent was Jewish, given that Jews were concentrated in the larger towns and cities rather than the countryside. Visitors to Ukraine such as Arthur Koestler and Malcolm Muggeridge confirmed the starvation while others, including George Bernard Shaw, who was given a carefully monitored tour, claimed not to have seen any hunger during their visits.

There had been more than a thousand Jews in the Tsarist Census in Kovshevata in 1897. Thirty years later, at the Soviet Census of 1926, the figure had dropped to 326. Local agriculture was collectivised in the 1920s and a Jewish collective farm, named *Pravda* (Truth) was established in 1928. The last synagogue was closed in 1932, although the Maliar family operated a clandestine prayer group in their home and Leonid Maliar celebrated his *barmitzvah* there in 1938. Jewish businesses, including a pharmacy, remained but only thirty Jews families were left when the Second World War began. Many Jews were evacuated but the remainder could not be persuaded to leave as the Nazi death squads, the *Einsatzgruppen*, approached. Forty-eight Jews were massacred in the picturesque ravine at the edge of the village. About twenty Jews returned to Kovshevata after the war but most soon left and so the two-hundred-year Jewish story of Kovshevata had ended.

During the war, nearly all of Ukraine was occupied by invading German armies. There had been around two million Jews in the current border of the country at the outset of the war, but many had been able to flee eastwards as the Germans approached. It is estimated that up to one and a half million Jews were killed in the Holocaust and hundreds of historic communities were completely destroyed at the hands of the German invaders.

Ukrainian wartime losses were also substantial: Ukrainian nationalists and Soviet prioners of war were shot or starved, and the death toll at Baby Yar (Babyn Yar) included more Ukrainians than Jews. More than a million Ukrainian soldiers died in the fighting and perhaps as many as four million civilians also died. While some Ukrainians tried to save Jews, many more collaborated with the Nazi invaders. These included members of the police forces and ultra-nationalist, fascist groups that celebrated the Nazi presence. This created an extra factor in the mutual suspicions of the two groups.

However, survivors returned from Central Asia and other places of refuge after the war. While small communities like Kovshevata were not re-established Jews returned to the larger population centres such as Kiev, Lviv, Kharkon and Odessa. In the 1959 Census there were 840,319 Jews in Ukraine comprising 2 per cent of the population compared to over 5 per cent before the war. The migration to Israel and other countries after the fall of the Soviet Union and Ukrainian independence has reduced the Jewish presence in the country substantially. However, our visits to the country in 2003 and 2018 show substantial development of a Jewish infrastructure and cultural life especially in Kiev and Odessa, but also in the towns associated with Hasidism such as Medzhibozh, Uman and Zhitomir.

The family story continues in Russia to the present time, through the years of the Second World War, known there as The Great Patriotic War, through Stalin's last years, continuing years of repression followed by thaw, *perestroika, glasnost* and the break-up of the Soviet Union. These years were experienced by my grandfather's sister Raisa (Reysie) and family, half-brother and cousin Iosif and Anna and family and the fateful decision of half-sister Ura to return to Russia after surviving war in Vichy France. We also maintained contact with Dimtri and his sister Alla Linsky, whose mother Eugenia was a sister of Anna, and a first cousin of my grandfather. Anna had returned to Moscow after years in Glasgow and London in the 1920s to marry her cousin Iosif, my grandfather's half brother. Dmitri had managed to leave the Soviet Union for Israel with the wave of emigrants in the early 1970s while Alla had only left twenty years later, around the time that Reysie's family, the Briskmans, had also settled in Israel.

My father's younger sister Anne was only about five years old when Anna returned to Moscow but following my grandfather's visit to Moscow in 1934 she exchanged letters regularly with her aunt for many years. Unfortunately this correspondence has not survived but the publishing of Julius's book on H.G. Wells in Britain in 1966 marked a renewed awareness of ongoing Russian family connections. Much has been written about the last years of the Soviet Union which amplifies the stories told by family members. Two good oral history works cover the ground well. Anna Shternshis's *When Sonia met Boris: An Oral History of Life under Stalin* (2017) covers more than four hundred interviews with Soviet citizens who had moved from *shtetl* life to the big cities, usually leaving behind the simple religious life of their parents but unable to shake off the Jewish identity which affected employment and access to higher education as well as more subtle forms of discrimination. Jeffrey Veidlinger's oral history, *In the Shadow of the Shtetl: Small Town Jewish Life in Soviet Ukraine* (2013), focusses on the experiences of a similar number of interviewees, who had returned to their *shtetls* after the war. Far from the metropolitan areas these areas had been slow to be 'Sovietized' before the war and they were able to maintain closer links with Jewish customs and traditions. The return from the dislocations of the evacuation to Central Asia was not easy, and coming back to their homes they were immediately confronted by trauma of the losses of family and friends. In addition, they were met with suspicion by their neighbours and as Veidlinger noted:

> The postwar era in general gave Jews few rewards for the sufferings they had endured. It is no wonder, then, that when asked to pinpoint the best years of their lives, many of the people we interviewed simply cried and shook their heads.

One example of recent attempts to show Jewish-Ukrainian relations in a positive light is provided by Paul Robert Magocsi, who holds the Chair of

Ukrainian Studies at the University of Toronto, and Yohanan Petrovsky-Stern, who is Professor of Jewish Studies at Northwestern University in the United States. Their book, *Jews and Ukrainians: a Millenium of Co-Existence*, was published by the Chair of Ukrainian Studies at the University of Toronto in 2016, aiming to counter biases and misconceptions by presenting an impartial account of the stories of the two people sharing the same territory for a thousand years.

Writing the family story has been made simpler by the worldwide connections of the fourth and fifth generation of Zev's descendants, faciliated obviously by the internet. The website JewishGen has also been helpful. Many years ago I posted family and location details there and occasionally found people whose family knew Kovshevata. Occasionally, this can yield spectacular results, such as the email I received from Elena Dobrovolskaya in Moscow in July 2013. Elena had suspected that her great-great grandfather Yankel was none other than my grandfather's Feter (uncle) Yankel. The Kiev Region State Archives records of the 1897 Census in Kovshevata mentioned Yankel son of Simeon (aged 62) and his wife Eida (aged 60). Also resident in Kovshevata with them was their daughter Reisya Antonovskaya, (aged 30), with her young children Shlema and Feiga; their son Shneur Kagarlitsky (aged 41), his wife Matlya (aged 41), and their children Ovsiy-Leiser, Leiva, Nyhim-Mot and a 13 day old baby Shifra. It was also recorded that Yankel and Eida had another daughter, who is not listed in the census, and her children were being raised by the Podolsky grandparents.

Allowing for the census recorders mangling the Yiddish names, these matched the family tree precisely. Reisya Antonovskaya (née Kagarlitzkaya) is of course, Rose Antonowski, whose husband Wolf, later Wolf Anton, as we shall see, was the textile trader in Glasgow who brought my grandfather to the city in 1912. The fact that Wolf, whose family lived in nearby Lysyanka, was not present with his wife in Kovshevata in 1897 indicates that he was already in Glasgow and preparing for his wife and children to join him. Rose would have had to wait with her parents until the pregnancy was over and she was fit to travel. By 1913 the only Kagarlitsky listed in the Kovshevata trade directory was the pharmacist Mordko Kagarlitsky.

Simeon Briskman's searches have produced more basic information. Birth records for Sarah's children show that the oldest, Zelman, was born in August 1873 indicating that Zev was just eighteen at the time of their marriage. He was followed by Reysie (December 1874), Shulim (known as Shuka and later as Salomon, born in January 1877), and Shimon (Shimmel, born May 1879). Records are missing for 1881 when my grandfather Shama

(Solomon) was born. The youngest child of the first marriage was Shmul (Sam), born in May 1883. The 1897 Census has further information. It shows Zev, with his second wife Rebecca, living in 'a wooden house with an iron roof' in Pochtovaya (Post Office) Street, Kovshevata with the first six of their nine children. Rebecca was thirteen years younger than Zev, born in 1867 and produced these six children in only eight years. The children's names are all quite recognizable allowing for minor distortion often found in such returns – all except Ura (Youra) whose name was recorded as Channa. She was known as Ura when she arrived in Glasgow in 1916.

Another question mark in the Kagarlitsky family tree was solved in a very unusual way. I was reading a story in the weekly *Jewish Chronicle* in 1986 about a new Jewish school opening in Berlin. The article described the school, the Heinz Galinski Elementary School in Charlottenburg, the first new-build Jewish school in Germany since the war and it mentioned that delicious kosher food was being prepared for the children by Ella Kagarlitskaya from St. Petersburg (Leningrad). I wrote to the journalist asking for contact details, though aware that most Kagarlitskys were not relatives and that time I did not know of family moving to Leningrad. Ella was happy for me to write to her and her family tree was definitely ours also.

It turned out that she was more closely related to Eugene Kogan's branch of the family! She was married to Gennadij Kagarlitsky and his father, Nochum Haimovich, who had passed away in 1965, was born in Kovshevata in 1902. Nochum was a grandson of Simeon-Shimmel and had two sisters, Berta who had settled in Moscow and Raisa in Leningrad. Ella's letter included a short message from Gennadij's brother Alexander, with some copies of photographs of Nochum and his sisters.

The shifting sands of family identity show many influences, linguistic, religious and national. This story tries to sort out the balance between these often conflicting concepts as it moves between Odessa and Glasgow, Marseilles and Tel Aviv, Paris and London and Buenos Aires and Jerusalem. This narrative has been compiled with the help of our world-wide family whose roots lie in Kovshevata and has managed to maintain its links and recognise more than two centuries of its history.

2
Motti the Engineer

Motti (Avraham Mordechai) Kagarlitzky is probably the first of Zev's children to have been schooled outside Kovshevata. Born in Kovshevata in 1898, just after my grandfather left for London, the CV he presented to the Palestine Electric Company confirmed that his elementary schooling had been in Novo Mirgorod. He continued his education in Odessa eventually graduating from the Technical College with a qualification in engineering. He followed this up with work, along with further training in engineering, in what was probably deemed an essential national industry – working as a maintenance engineer in a brewery just outside the city. The skills he gained as an engineer would be required when the more settled times came.

He must have finished his high school studies in 1916, during the First World War. We have no indication that he was called up for military service so he would have been able to proceed to the Technical College. He was in Odessa during the tumultuous events of the Revolutions in 1917, followed by the Civil War. The armies of the Reds and the Whites managed to fight each other and occasionally managed a pogrom as they passed through the heavily Jewish populated countryside. With territory constantly changing hands and the Jews being targets from both sides, life was hard. Bands associated with the Whites wreaked havoc on the physical life of the Jewish communities while the Reds, often led by the Jewish communists known as the *Yevsektzia*, destroyed the precarious religious and economic balance which had existed in the *shtetls* for centuries.

It is likely that Zev was with his children Clara and Motti in the Odessa area during the last days of the First World War and the Civil War. Ida and her husband Jacob Rashal could not have been far away. They had married in Zlatopol, just a mile from Zev's home in Novo Mirgorod in 1918, but must already have been in Odessa as Jacob was involved in making the arrangements for them to leave Ukraine. This was all happening during a period of total chaos as the Tsar's Army was disintegrating and Kerensky's attempts to continue the War were proving disastrous. In the wings, the Bolsheviks were preparing for power.

In Odessa, the Communists seemed to have the upper hand at first. Yet, by the summer of 1919, the 'White' General Anton Denikin, leader of the anti-Communist Volunteer Army, recaptured the city and started a purge of Communist sympathisers. By December 1919 the opportunity to leave the country became real. Just months later, in February 1920, the Bolshevik Army was in Odessa and the port became packed with thousands of residents desperate to sail in the few merchant ships and Allied warships that were still in the harbour. People were trying to board ships while Bolshevik snipers were firing from nearby buildings. Charles King's *Odessa: Genius and Death in a City of Dreams* (2011) gives a lively account of those perilous times.

Odessa was and remained a very Jewish city before and after the Russian Revolution. During the early years of the twentieth century it was in many ways the centre of Jewish literary activity and the leading city of the Zionist movement. The first Jewish periodical in Russian was produced in the city and the list of key figures who lived in the city is quite astonishing. Leon Pinsker was a Zionist activist and the author of the influential pamphlet *Auto-Emancipation: Warning to His Fellow People, from a Russian Jew*. Pinsker was one of the first Jews to study at the University of Odessa, qualifying in medicine, and he died in the city in 1891. Sholom Aleichem, one of the most popular Yiddish writers of all times, lived briefly in Odessa after leaving Kiev (Kyiv), before settling in New York. The great Hebrew poet Chaim Nachman Bialik was there for twenty years writing many of his greatest verses in the city. Bialik founded the Hebrew printing press *Dvir* in Odessa, but facing increasing criticism from Bolshevik agitators he managed to leave the city in 1921.

I learned about some of the Jewish ambience of Odessa in these years through Vladimir Jabotinsky's novel *The Five* (1935) which was finally translated into English in 2005. It is set in the milieu of assimilated Jews, showing that even for emancipated Jews their paths through life would follow ethnic ones. The Odessa Committee was the leading Zionist group in its time and Jabotinsky became one of the leading figures in the Zionist movement. Ahad Ha'am, a leading figure in cultural Zionism, lived in the city for many years as did the Jewish historian Simon Dubnow and the Hebrew poet Shaul Tchernikovsky.

During 1919, the British Military Government in Palestine announced that they were prepared to admit some new Jewish immigrants. The Mandate would not begin for another three years but this initiative gave some hope that the proposals inherent in the Balfour Declaration would be implemented. Motti failed to get an immigration certificate but managed to get a place for himself, under a separate regulation which permitted inhabitants of Palestine who had been displaced by the ravages of war to return. About 150 of those who made it on board of the *SS Ruslan* were genuine refugees, but the others managed to obtain the certificates which indicated that they had been refugees with pre-war settlement in Ottoman Palestine. His brother-in-law Jacob was indeed one of the genuine refugees having been in Palestine from 1912, having to leave when Turkey entered the war on the German side. This made the Russian-born Jacob an enemy alien, who then returned home via Egypt on an American ship. The passengers were finally authorized to travel by the British Consul-General in Odessa who accepted all the passengers, whether genuine refugees or not. In any case, Motti had a certificate that indicated that he had once lived in Petach Tikva, printed in French, Russian and Hebrew.

Motti's certificate indicating 'previous residence in Petach Tikva'.

There were now many thousands of displaced Jews in Odessa, Zev and Clara amongst them. Many had tales of pogroms. There had been violent deaths. There was a preponderance of women and the elderly and the chaos and its aftermath were to give the great Russian Jewish writer Isaac Babel the background for the Jewish characters in his *Odessa Tales*. His stories of the gangster hero Benya Krik were made into a silent film in 1926. Another silent film of the era, Sergei Eisenstein's classic *Battleship Potemkin*, released in 1925, retold the events on the ship in 1905 as presaging the eventual Bolshevik victory.

The *SS Ruslan* was bought for two million roubles and set sail from Odessa on 27 November 1919 with 644 passengers on board. The ship was seriously overcrowded with a lack of food and limited sanitation. With the poor winter weather producing turbulent seas and strong winds the voyage was extremely uncomfortable. The boat had only four cabins and passengers had to sleep on the deck or in the hold. Conditions were very cramped there owing to the personal library of Dr. Joseph Klausner and the large unauthorised cargo of wheat, which the captain hoped to sell in Athens and Constantinople. Klausner was a representative of a passengers' committee which failed to persuade the captain to make directly for Palestine as had been agreed before departure. The lure of the financial gain from the sale of the wheat was just too great. The journey took three weeks travelling via Turkey and Greece. The passengers were not allowed off the ship as the authorities in the two countries suspected that there might be Bolshevik agitators amongst their number.

Some accounts of immigration recognize the arrival of the *Ruslan* as the beginning of a third wave of Jewish immigration to Israel, known as the Third Aliya. However, the *Ruslan* was not the first ship to arrive in 1919 but she had a major distinction lying in the make-up of the passengers. Those on board arrived with a sense of historical mission and many were to become the cultural and political elite of the State of Israel, which was to be established in 1948.

It is worth just considering some of Motti, Ida and Jacob's fellow passengers on their momentous but extremely uncomfortable journey in an overcrowded ship, with only four cabins and little room in the hold as winter storms raged about the vessel. The following are just a small selection of just some of the more prominent passengers and this gives a flavour of the company that Motti, Ida and Jacob had during the voyage. Joseph Gedaliah Klausner (1874-1958), the great-uncle of Israeli author Amos Oz, was on board. He was a professor of Hebrew Literature, a distinguished Jewish historian and author of *Jesus of Nazareth*. He was a candidate for president in the first Israeli presidential election in 1949, losing to Chaim Weizmann. Klausner was a member of the circle of Russian Zionist political activists from Odessa, which included Ze'ev Jabotinsky and Menachem Ussishkin.

There were the architects Yehuda Magidovitch (1886-1961) who was Tel Aviv's first City Engineer and the designer of several iconic buildings; Zeev Rechter (1899-1960) is considered one of the founding fathers of Israeli architecture having designed Binyanei Ha Uma (International Convention Centre in Jerusalem) and the Mann Auditorium (together with Dov Karmi). There were many doctors too. One was Baruch Nissenboim (1886-1971) reckoned to be one of the pioneers of medicine in the country and a founder of the emergency medical service, Magen David Adom, in 1931. Dr. Arye Dostrovsky was the father figure of Israeli dermatology and venereology. He served as the first Dean as well as the first professor at the Medical School in Jerusalem and was Director of the Hansen (Leprosy) Hospital in Jerusalem. Dr. Chaim Yassky (1896-1948) was an ophthalmologist and Director of the Hadassah Medical Organization in Jerusalem from 1931. He was killed in the Arab attack on a medical convoy bringing supplies to Hadassah Hospital on Mount Scopus.

Yaakov Peremen had many talents: poet and philosopher, bibliographer and collector of books and art. He created Tamar, the first artists' co-operative in the country whose modernist art contrasted with more traditional styles, such as that of the Bezalel School in Jerusalem. Pinchas Litvinovsky, who designed the set for the Habimah Theatre production of *The Dybbuk* which took place in Moscow in 1922, was another passenger. The Hebrew language theatre had been established in Moscow in 1918 and Stalin, as Commissar for National Minorities had given it authorization. Harassed by Jewish communists in the *Yevsektsia* the group left Russia in 1926 and arrived in Tel Aviv in 1928.

Joseph (Constantinovsky) Constant gained renown as a sculptor both in France and abroad after the Second World War. Earlier he was part of an artists' cooperative in Tel Aviv with Yitzhak (Frenel) Frenkel, a great-grandson of the famous Rabbi Levi Yitzchok of Berditchev. Frenkel opened the Histadrut Art School in Tel Aviv in 1925 and was the mentor of many leading Israeli artists. In an active career he became one of the founders of the Artists' Colony of Safed in 1949. He is considered one of the most important Jewish 'École de Paris' painters; along with Soutine, Mogdiliani and Manne Katz. Baruch (Kaushansky) Agadati (1895-1976) was a Israeli classical ballet dancer, choreographer, painter, and film producer and director.

Rachel Bluwstein Sela (1890-1931) was a Hebrew-language poet, known simply by her first name, who had previously immigrated to Palestine in 1909. When the First World War broke out she returned instead to Russia. After coming back to Palestine in 1919 she was diagnosed with tuberculosis. Most of her poems were written in the final six years of her life, and she quickly achieved fame 'for her lyrical style, the brevity of her poems, and the revolutionary simplicity of her conversational tone'. Her poems are included in the mandatory curriculum in Israeli schools. Rachel Cohen-Kagan was a Zionist activist and Israeli politician and was a signatory of the Israeli Declaration of Independence in May 1948. (The only other woman signatory was Golda Meir.) Another politician on board was Nahum Het who served as a member of the Knesset for the General Zionists between 1951 and 1955 and was elected President of the World Maccabi Federation in 1957.

Because of the cramped conditions and the lengthy voyage, the passengers had time to get together and form bonds which were to last for decades. Motti met Yoni Tamid, Jabotinsky's nephew, who was being met at the port in Jaffa by his uncle, who was a close friend of Pinchas Rutenberg. The Third Aliya lasted to the mid-1920s and brought around 100,000 Jews to the country. Unlike most of the youngsters on the boat, Motti did not seek to become a rural pioneer and an alternative approach would be required. Yet, through a series of fortunate happenings Motti's life plans were sorted out within a few weeks.

When the boat docked at Jaffa, Vladimir Jabotinsky met his nephew Yoni who, like Motti, had a background in technical work and within a few weeks they were working together mapping out the ground south of Kinneret, the Sea of Galilee, for Rutenberg's proposed hydroelectric power station. The whole story of electricity in Mandate Palestine is bound up in the larger-than-life character of Pinchas Rutenberg (1879-1942) who had been born in Romny, Ukraine. During the First World War he was among the founders of the Jewish Legion with Joseph Trumpeldor and Vladimir Jabotinsky. He was active in both Russian revolutions but, after the 1905 revolution ended in failure, he returned to university to study hydroelectricity and the construction of dams. He backed Alexander Kerensky after arriving in Petrograd in July 1917 and he was jailed by the Bolsheviks but released when the Germany army was approaching the city. He escaped through Moscow to Odessa sailing to Constantinople then going on to Marseille and London. A vocal and committed Zionist, Rutenberg also participated in establishing the Haganah, the main Jewish militia in pre-war Palestine and later founded Palestine Airways.

Details of Motti's appointment came quickly. He met Rutenberg at the Amdurski Hotel in the Old City of Jerusalem on 25 December, barely a week after arrival and was soon on his way to the Galilee with Yoni to begin work. Rutenberg and Motti were both from Ukraine and both had passed through Odessa during 1919. It was a good match. By this stage Rutenberg already had in his mind the plans for a hydroelectric power station using the water flows of the Jordan and Yarmuk rivers and had visited the area. He had immigrated to Mandatory Palestine early in 1919 and through his connections managed to obtain a concession for production and distribution of electric power. His company, the Palestine Electric Corporation, now the Israel Electric Corporation (IEC), was formed as soon as the permissions and the funding were in place. This had not proved to be easy. He had to raise a considerable sum of money and needed to persuade the British government and the Mandate authorities to grant him the electricity concession for Palestine.

The Rutenberg story and the electrification of Palestine has attracted much scholarly attention. Sara Reguer's article 'Rutenberg and the Jordan River: A Revolution in Hydroelectricity', was published in *Middle Eastern*

Rutenberg with his first employees: Motti is at the far left in the back row (10/6/1920).

Studies in 1995. She showed the long tortuous process experienced by Rutenberg in getting Naharayim to production. Ronen Shamir's article 'Electricity and Empire in 1920s Palestine under British Rule' looked at the electrification of Palestine in the German language *Zeitschrift für Geschichte der Wissenschaften: Technik und Medizin* in 2016. Shamir had noted that Germany was much more advanced than Britain after the First World War in electrical technology and that British companies were content to see colonial projects for electrification to be in the hands of locals and thus funded outside government finances. German prices for industrial goods were cheaper than those from British companies and consequently AEG, who had a better knowledge of the climatic conditions their exports would experience, provided the main source of electric equipment in the Mandate's early years.

Rutenberg was convinced that his plans to build a hydroelectric power station with water flowing between the Jordan and Yarmuk rivers were feasible. The Yarmuk flowed through Trans-Jordan and negotiations with the British authorities were necessary to obtain the water rights. He felt that the area had the water both for electricity and for agriculture, collecting the winter rains and constructing dams to hold the water until it was needed. The electrification of Palestine was a massive undertaking but Rutenberg was equal to the task. When Winston Churchill, as British Colonial Secretary, met with Emir Abdullah to remove Trans-Jordan from the Palestine Mandate he was able to assess the project and he gave Rutenberg his backing and obtained the necessary support from Parliament in London. It was decided to situate the power station in Trans-Jordan with the agreement of the Emir Abdullah. Abdullah had taken a benevolent interest in Rutenberg's Palestine Electric Company from the start as it helped to electrify his kingdom too. Rutenberg also had to deal with the French authorities in Lebanon and Syria. One of the sources for the Jordan, the Litani, began in Lebanon and diversion of the Yarmuk would have implications for Syria, as the boundary between Syria and Palestine came almost to the north-eastern shoreline of the Sea of Galilee. This was a large, prestigious and exciting project and Motti was there at its very beginning, even before the formal founding of the Palestine Electric Company.

When Motti arrived in Palestine any local electricity was supplied by diesel generators. Electrifying the country involved massing planning to utilise the output of Rutenberg's power stations. It was likely to take some time and involved the Mandate authorities in plans for its uptake. The British were impressed with Rutenberg and one of their officials commented:

> I am struck with Mr Rutenberg's ability... I do not recall having seen any scheme which has been more carefully presented... there is an almost unrivalled opportunity of obtaining necessary agricultural improvement and initiation of industrial works from the natural power resources of the country.

Historians have noted that most of the improvements in the country in the early years of the Mandate concerned Britain's imperial requirements. The airport at Lydda (now Lod) served to help communication between Europe and India while the development of the port at Haifa helped bring oil from a pipeline in northern Iraq, belonging to the Anglo-Iranian Oil Company, whose stock was controlled by the British Government. Extraction of minerals from the Dead Sea proved to be a lucrative concession. The single largest Jewish project of the period was therefore Rutenberg's electric company and the Mandate authorities seemed to be in no hurry to move it along. Eventually, it was conceded that supporting Rutenberg might help the Jews channel their energies into national infrastructure rather than political agitation.

The wheels of British colonial bureaucracy moved very slowly. Motti's visit to Switzerland in 1926 coincided with the beginnings of construction at Naharayim. Compromises had been reached about the siting of the power station in Trans-Jordan and Rutenberg had kept Abdullah on board. Motti's practical on-site engineering work now began. While Motti, Ida and Jacob, Zev and Clara were adjusting to their new life in British Palestine, they were joined by Ura who must have been attracted by the prospect that Tel Aviv seemed to offer during the 1920s. Tel Aviv expanded rapidly during the first years of the mandate and northern Jewish districts of Jaffa were added to the new municipality. It is in one of these districts, Neve Tzedek, now gentrified and enjoying some of its old ambience once more, that Zev and his family now lived. The socialist ethos of the pioneers, the Mediterranean climate and the pavement cafe culture were a world away from Ura's life in Glasgow, but still gave her a strong family network. So, Zev had four children close to him, but it was Motti who provided financial support for his now ageing father. Conditions at Naharayim were not easy. For Motti, who had grown up with temperate summers and freezing winters the weather in the Jordan Valley was very uncomfortable. Heavy winter rain could cause the rivers to flood and the scorching summer heat brought trouble in the form of mosquitoes and black flies. Accommodation was primitive until proper housing for the workers was ready. We have a photograph of Motti on his motorbike, ideal for traversing the route of the canals bringing the water to the hydroelectric site. Perhaps, it also helped him to visit the electricity headquarters in Haifa and his family in Tel Aviv more quickly.

After just a few months in Palestine, Motti received a *laisser passer* allowing him to visit Britain and to make the trip to Glasgow to visit his half-brothers, sister Ura, his cousin Anna and the growing Collins families. He stayed for several weeks in Britain and again during the mid-1920s he was able to return to Glasgow after travelling on company business to London. While Rutenberg was used to negotiating with figures at the highest levels of the British Colonial Office and Mandate, Motti would have been easily able to discuss the technical aspects of the operation of the power station as it entered the construction phase.

By this time, Ura had left Glasgow for Tel Aviv and he was able to reunite with her there. Despite his warnings Anna was now in Moscow and Gudis had died so only Solomon and Shimmel and their families were still there. With Ura, Ida, Motti, Clara and Zev in Tel Aviv the centre of the Kagarlitsky family now seemed to be in Palestine. Ida had married Jacob before leaving Ukraine and Clara had married Joseph Amzalem, a policeman originally from Morocco now in the service of the British Mandate. Zev was living with Clara and her husband and this provided Motti with a base when in the Tel Aviv area. However, for the most part he was at Naharayim or in accommodation in Jerusalem. He was a regular visitor to Haifa too, where the Palestine Electric Company was headquartered, and where Rutenberg had his very impressive office. We visited Rutenberg's office at a visit to the IEC Archives. It was a very large room and looked as if it might be able to accommodate a tennis court. Rutenberg's desk was situated beside a door at the far end of the room. For a miscreant employee the long solitary walk from the other door to Rutenberg's presence would have been a nerve-wracking experience. Fortunately, Motti was a treasured and influential employee, a senior engineer who was often photographed standing next to his mentor Rutenberg. It was not just the office and the desk that were impressive about the IEC Archives. It was very well staffed and cataloguing and storage facilities were of a very high standard. I could not help thinking that the IEC, less than a hundred years old, had a much large archival staff than the University of Glasgow which dated back to 1451.

Rutenberg has passed into the stuff of legends in Israel. He inspired Mordechai Zeira to compose the song called *Shir Hareshet* although it is better known as *Hazaken Mi Naharayim (The Old Man of Naharayim)*. When the song was composed in 1935 Rutenberg was only 56 years old, so was hardly an old man, but the words stuck. With its simple lyrics it quickly became a favourite folk song of the old man who built the (power) station, before there was nothing – just water and now there is electricity.

מִנְּהָרִים הַזָּקֵן, זָקֵן, הַזָּקֵן –
הַמִפְעָל אֶת הֵקִים הוּא.
כְּלוּם שָׁם הָיָה לֹא,
מַיִם רַק הָיוּ, הָיָה לֹא
חַשְׁמַל לֵב שָׁם וְעַכְשָׁו.

There was a list of Motti's possessions at the IEC Archives. This included a number of technical textbooks on concrete construction and the strength of materials which were in English implying some facility with the language. In January 1929, the Yarmuk dam with a water catchment area of 3,000 square miles was ready, and the canal to bring the Jordan waters to the Yarmuk had been completed and just had to be lined with concrete. High tension lines to convey the electricity were being constructed. Motti remained very busy. He spent most of his time at the power station but still continued to provide support for his father.

Contemporary film of the construction process shows that the construction of the technologically advanced installation depended on many procedures which looked decidedly unsafe. Having seen the old ciné footage of the construction process it was surprising that only four workers lost their lives during the building period. Unfortunately, Motti was one of them, killed when a heavy overhead beam, six metres long, fell from its position from a height of 4.5 metres directly on to his head killing him instantly.

Rutenberg himself was present at the funeral and arranged that a monument be erected in memory of those who had fallen during the construction process. With his attention to detail and style a fine monument was erected adjacent to the power station and designed by the same architects in identical Bauhaus style. The power station was built, as we have noted, not in British Palestine but a few hundred metres over the border in Trans-Jordan to catch the maximum water flow from the Sea of Galilee and to utilise the 50 metres of different heights of the water between the Jordan and Yarmuk rivers. Motti's grave was out of bounds. Lilian and Eric had tried to find the monument from the Israeli side of the border. They had advice from a Jewish former member of the Arab Legion then living in Rechavia and took his advice on where to look. When they knew that they were close a Jordanian army officer noticed them and asked, from the other side of the border, what brought them there. They explained but he couldn't help them.

Motti's death was a tragic blow to Zev. He had lost not just the breadwinner in his home but the son who had been at his side all his short life. Ura had left for France and Ida, Jacob and Rivka (Rita) were now in New York. He must have been inconsolable. Zev immediately sought compensation from the Palestine Electrical Company and in due course after much negotiation between lawyers received £P500 (worth £33,000 in 2020 prices). The news of the death spread rapidly round the family. Iosif wrote from Moscow in May 1930 to press the claim of Motti's full siblings to any inheritance, counselling against any claims from the half-brothers and undertaking to provide all such support as was necessary for Zev. It did not help much as within a year Zev too was dead. The only indication that the siblings did receive a share of the estate is a letter to Ura in Paris from the Electrical Company in 1935 enclosing a cheque for £50.

Abdullah was present, along with the High Commissioner for Palestine, Sir Arthur Wauchope, at the opening ceremony of the Naharayim Power Station in 1932, two full years after Motti's death, pushing the switch to start producing the electricity. Rutenberg had kept in touch with Abdullah as he had the concession to provide electricity in Trans-Jordan too. Despite British misgivings the presence of the Emir at the ceremony was a tribute to Rutenberg's persistence, trying to ensure a role for the Jews east of the Jordan even though the territory had been detached from the Mandate. Abdullah had been a regular visitor to the site during the construction works and seemed to accept the presence of 600 Jewish workers in his territory. The plant worked efficiently through the Mandate years but was destroyed by the Iraqi soldiers during Israel's War of Independence. While Naharayim produced most of the country's electricity needs when it opened, growing population, industry and agriculture reduced this to just 25 per cent by the time of independence. The original hope – for the plant to generate 150 million kilowatt hours of electricity a year – did not materialize; the actual figure was between 50 and 64 million kwh. Today, Israel's power plants generate about 500 times the Naharayim output and in many years the waters of Kinneret are dammed at the southern end, only flowing south into the Jordan in very wet winters. The concept was a product of its time.

When the peace treaty between Israel and Jordan was signed in 1994, David (Gershowitz) Sarid, the son of one of the other three workers killed during the construction period, between 1929 and 1932, succeeded in persuading President Katsav to request that the King Abdullah of Jordan permit the exhumation of the men and their reburial at the Kibbutz Gesher cemetery. The process involved the Israeli Foreign Ministry, the Israel

Defence Forces, the Chief Rabbinate and the Israel Electric Company. The fine new stone monument, like the old one, carries both a Biblical quote and excerpts of a poem by Bialik. David Sarid said that the Bialik quote had been chosen as Bialik had known Motti and that it should be regarded as a tribute to him.

While Rutenberg was not an easy man to work with he was an idealist who saw himself and his workers as national builders, working together in creating the National Home. Housing for his workers was provided and designed by the same architects who created the innovative designs of the power stations. Even the original monument to Motti and his colleagues had been inspired by the architect Erich Mendelsohn.

On 15 July 2001 the new monument was consecrated with many family members present. At the exhumation it was discovered that Motti had been buried with his watch. The watch is now housed in a display case at the Archives of the Israel Electric Company (IEC) in Haifa and shows the weathering effects of being buried for 70 years. There was a story that when the watch was found at the exhumation it was stopped at the right time. However, as the hour hand is missing this would seem to be a bit fanciful. The watch, shown below, is an Omega and had most likely been bought by Motti during one of his business visits to Switzerland.

Motti's watch, retrieved after the exhumation.

Motti's name is also engraved on Zev's tombstone erected on the eastern side of the Old Cemetery in Trumpeldor Street in Tel Aviv. The small cemetery was opened in 1905 in the distant desert to accommodate deaths from a cholera outbreak in Jaffa and remained the official Tel Aviv cemetery until the year after Zev's death in 1931. I suspect that my grandfather Solomon paid for the fine marble tombstone for Zev's grave that was on the other side of the cemetery from the gravestones of the luminaries of Tel Aviv life, such as the famous first mayor, Meir Dizengoff, and the Hebrew poet Chaim Nachman Bialik. With the growth of Tel Aviv, it is now in the heart of the city close to the Dizengoff Centre. I had always been puzzled that the inscription on the stone indicated that Zev was from Novo Mirgorod, rather than Kovshevata, but of course Clara was the daughter on the spot to arrange the wording and she, the youngest of Zev's children, had been born there.

Motti's name is still revered by the IEC as I discovered at a meeting at Bet Ha Tfutsot, the Museum of the Jewish Diaspora in Tel Aviv. I was due to speak at the annual conference of the Israel Genealogical Society whose theme that year was migration to Israel in the pre-State period. The IEC had an exhibition of the archives running alongside the conference and I approached their stall to mention that my presentation made reference to one of their early employees, who was my great uncle. They asked for the name and when I mentioned the words Avraham Mordechai Kagarlitsky the excitement was palpable. All the IEC came round to hear from the 'relative of Kagarlitsky' and I suddenly became the subject of great awe!

We were immediately invited to visit their Archives in Haifa and we chose a time around Chanukkah to see what they had about Motti. They were well prepared for us with a large file and the famous Omega watch which was on display in a suitably inscribed glass case. The documents they held were amazing. There was even his CV detailing his schooling which gave us the clue about when Zev would have left Kovshevata for Novo Mirogorod.

The refugee certificate, in three languages, which entitled him to travel to Palestine on the *Ruslan* was there as well as three reminiscences by former colleagues at Naharayim. One of these accounts was by Jabotinsky's nephew Yoni, who entered Rutenberg's service along with Motti on 25 December 1919 and retired from the IEC in July 1967 just before his 67th birthday. He recalled the mapping exercise that he did with Motti plotting out the ground near where the power station would be built, ensuring that the water flow requirements for hydroelectricity would be met. Yoni acknowledged Motti's skill as a competent engineer. He had also met with Rutenberg at the Amdurski Hotel in Jerusalem and again in the office in Jaffa Road and was present to receive the first equipment from Germany.

Ezra Shemesh, who arrived in the country in 1922, joined the IEC in 1928 just two years before Motti's death. He recalled, in a retirement deposition in 1963, that Motti had been one of the two leading engineers in the company when he arrived at Naharayim, with special responsibility in the construction of the power station building. Shalom Bielski also referred to Motti even though he had only arrived at Naharayim three years after Motti's death, mentioning his devotion to his family. Other items in the archival documents were letters of permission and introductions for him to attend the hydroelectric conferences in Switzerland. However, the larger past of the documents concerned Zev's concern for some financial settlement after Motti's death, given that he had lost his main source of support. There was also a list of his possessions at the time of his death including his engineering texts.

Motti's Funeral: Rutenberg is on the left of the picture wearing a dark jacket and pith helmet.

Even today, Motti's contribution is not forgotten. The booklet of the Naharayim Experience at Kibbutz Gesher, which shows a model of how the power station worked, refers to Motti. In the book which accompanied the exhibition on the architecture of the early Rutenberg power stations, *In Search of Excellence: Building Projects of the Electric Company in the Land of Israel: 1921-1942* (2003) by Gilbert Herbert, Ita Heinze-Greenberg and Silvina Sosnovski, there are several references to Motti. in connection with his hydroelectric work. The group picture of Motti and the other first workers of the Palestine Electric Company, shown on page 32, printed in Rutenberg's biography, is the one that had been presented to Motti as the inscription at the lower right-hand side of the illustration shows.

3
Zelman the Visionary

The last decade of the nineteenth century and the first decade of the twentieth saw a major family movement from Kovshevata, and Zelman's move to Nikolaev (Mikolaiv) was an important part of the relocations. Solomon was in London by 1898, Shimmel was in Paris around 1908 and Shuka reached Argentina in 1906. We have already noted that Zev himself had moved south to Novo Mirgorod where his youngest children had their elementary schooling. Zelman went directly to the city of Nikolaev, certainly by 1900 when he would have been 22 years old, an indication of his rising importance in the world. The family in Glasgow identified with Zelman's move to the city and often, when asked where the family came from, my grandfather would mention Nikolaev as well as Kovshevata. Above all, the move to Nikolaev may have been associated with work in the city, possibly related to its considerable wheat and timber trade. It was here that he met the family of Samuel Imass and their daughter Chassia who would become his wife.

Samuel Imass (1854-1918) was a highly successful wheat merchant. His company dealt with grain production in the south of Russia and its export to a number of countries abroad. He had entered the business after receiving a traditional Jewish education in Biblical and Talmudic studies and with his financial success came the ability to support many Jewish charities in Nikolaev. These included providing the funds for the building of the Talmud Torah, which provided Jewish education for younger children, aid for the poor and the production of matza for Passover. I would presume that Zelman had been working for his company for some time and that his foreign visits were linked not just with his Zionist commitments but included business travel.

Nikolaev was an important Black Sea port city of over 100,000 people, about one fifth of whom were Jewish. It was also an attractive city with many fine parks and grand buildings with tree-lined boulevards at its centre. The city had become part of the Tsarist Empire following the Russian victories over the Turks in the Second War between Russia and Turkey from 1787-1792. Nikolaev was founded by Prince Gregory

Potemkin and named by him after either Tsar Nicholas I or Saint Nicholas. There had been restrictions on Jewish settlement in the town in earlier years, but these were lifted in 1866 and the city grew rapidly.

Besides the physical appearance of the city there were many other reasons for Zelman's move to the city. Nikolaev had become a major industrial city, and its port, the largest grain exporting city in the Russian Empire, was only exceeded in the Russian export trade by St. Petersburg and Odessa. However, as Zelman noted in an article in the Russian language *Trudovaya Gazeta* in June 1911, the port lacked direct trade routes with the Middle East, which Odessa possessed. Jewish businessmen were involved in shipbuilding and supplying the fleets that berthed in the port. The city also boasted a lively Jewish cultural life based around its religious institutions and the Yiddish language. The seventh and last leader of the Lubavitch Hasidic dynasty, Menachem Mendel Schneerson, was born in Nikolaev in 1902, where his father served as the rabbi of a Hasidic synagogue. A sign of the Jewish community's prosperity was the opening of the Choral Synagogue in 1884, one of the most beautiful buildings in the city and a centre for important meetings related to the welfare of the city's Jews. It was closed in 1928, as part of a wave of Russian synagogue closures following the official Soviet anti-religion policy.

Zelman was prospering too. Working for Samuel Imass there were funds to support other members of the family, for example giving Solomon crucial loans as he was growing his textile business. But there was also evidence of serious poverty in the Jewish community and in Zelman's time there was an array of Jewish welfare activities: free loan societies to establish Jews in trades and businesses, help for the sick and poor, pauper burials, a medicine dispensary, alms houses and many more.

Zelman found that the local Zionist movement was especially active and was promoting strong Hebrew cultural activities which included Hebrew theatre. He was a passionate supporter of the new Zionist movement founded by Theodor Herzl and despite his young age he moved rapidly through the ranks of Nikolaev's Zionists, propelled both by his easy personality and his presentational skills which found expression in journalism for the Jewish and Zionist press. By 1904 Zelman was leading a delegation of Ukrainian Zionist to Jaffa where he delivered a significant speech. Though the original text is not extant he refers to it in his newspaper articles. He was to visit Ottoman Palestine regularly, commenting on the development of the Jewish colonies such as Zikhron Yaakov, Rehovot and Rishon Le Zion for the Hebrew paper *Hed HaZman* in Vilna (Vilnius) and a Yiddish paper based in Warsaw, *di Naye Velt*. His Tsarist passport indicates

Nikolaev Zionists c. 1904. Zelman is in the back row third from left..

the breadth of his endeavours, pulled around Europe as a kind of movement ambassador keeping the remote branches associated with the core movement ideals.

Zelman's visit to Jaffa came at a pivotal time in the history of the Zionist movement. Pogroms were frequent. The disastrous attack on the Jewish community of Kishinev (now Chisinau), where 49 Jews were killed, many women were raped and around 1,500 homes destroyed focussed world attention on the plight of the Jewish community in Russia. One outcome was the urgent need to find a safe haven for the Jews at risk. Herzl's discussions with Joseph Chamberlain, the British Colonial Secretary, about identifying an area within the British Empire where Jews could be settled, led to the 'Uganda Scheme'.

Chamberlain's proposal was for a sparsely populated and temperate area, of around 5,000 square miles, called Gwas Ngishu, to be made available to the Zionist movement. Despite the name of the Scheme the area is actually within modern day Kenya. Herzl proposed accepting the British offer at the 6th Zionist Congress in Basle in August 1903. Though it was agreed to set up a commission to examine the proposal there was considerable opposition especially from Ukrainian and Russian delegates, who represented the areas where the bulk of the pogroms had occurred.

Herzl commented: 'These people have a rope around their necks, but they still refuse.' The Zionist movement was seriously split over the Uganda Scheme, which was only finally rejected at the next Congress in 1905. The prominent British Jewish novelist Israel Zangwill then formed the Jewish Territorial Organisation, which spent more than a decade in a futile search to find a piece of land elsewhere in Africa or South America suitable for mass Jewish immigration.

This was a time for calm talk and a healing approach to enable Zionist societies around Europe to focus on what remained the main task, of settling in Ottoman Palestine and trying to obtain a charter to create a national Hebrew speaking society there. Those involved in visiting local Zionist societies, like Zelman, would have had to exert all their diplomatic skills to keep the Zionist movement on track, and avoiding the diversion of British East Africa. The British offer was withdrawn after the 7th Zionist Congress and Zangwill could not resuscitate it.

A collection of Zelman's newspaper articles was edited by his great-grandson Daniel Harbour in a book entitled *Distant Dreams and Hard Truths: Zionist and Other Writings of Zelman Kagarlitsky* (2010). Daniel, Martin Gilbert, Boris Kagarlitsky and I all contributed short introductory essays. The distinguished historian, biographer of Churchill and author of many books on Jews, Israel and the Holocaust, Sir Martin Gilbert, a cousin of Emmanuel's wife Elizabeth, described him as 'a man ahead of his time' and the book as 'rich in [his] experiences, thoughts and wisdom of ideas'. Zelman had been aware of the movement of the children of the early Zionist pioneers to Alexandria, turning their backs on the rural life of their parents for the glamour of a large cosmopolitan city.

He was aware of negative attitudes to Zionism, in his visits to Palestine and Egypt and made the warning in one of his most prescient comments: 'The question is not one of Zionism, but that affairs that are wont to begin at Zionism and end up at anti-Semitism.'

Gilbert picked up on his comments on the need for a contemporary Jewish urban space in Palestine, a role that was to be filled by the growing Hebrew city of Tel Aviv, which had been founded as Ahuzat Bayit in 1909 getting its present name the following year. In Zelman's words about Tel Aviv in 1910:

> .... the place entirely settled by Jews in homes of their own, in beautiful buildings in the modern style [where] the Jewish soul swims in a sea of spiritual pleasure… The crown jewel of the place is the Gymnasium, [built by Jews] without self-aggrandising fuss… the

present Imperial Duma do everything in their power increasingly to close schools off to Jewish children, and for this reason in many families the possibility of sending their children to the Jaffa [sic] Gymnasium is now being discussed... Those in charge of the Hebrew Gymnasium should try to the effect that their high school diploma be recognised for entry into European universities.

During a second visit to Jerusalem, Zelman was uplifted by visiting the newly established Bezalel School of Art in Jerusalem and welcomed the promised establishment of a *Technikum* (now the Technion: Israel Institute of Technology) in Haifa. However, he remained upset that the dire condition of the Western Wall, part of the retaining wall of Herod's Temple on the Mount above, had not changed.

> How great an indignation and how great an insult that the only monument we have in Jerusalem and that belongs to the whole nation of Israel is surrounded by refuse and mire and sullied by hands ingrained with filth and where everyone attends to their 'needs'.

Boris Kagarlitsky noted that Zelman had no illusions about the scale of the tasks ahead. He hoped that Zionist developments would bring benefit to the Arab inhabitants of the country emphasizing the sense of progress he encountered on his visits. I commented on the Zionist aspirations of Zelman's immediate family: Motti, the pioneer and engineer; his father Zev and half-sisters Ida, Ura and Clara living in Tel Aviv; while Zelman was, in my words, '... the thinker, who helped to forge the ideal, and indeed the very language of the future State of Israel, [ensuring that Jews need no longer be] bound body and soul to... a small muddy village in the Pale of Settlement'.

In his insightful Foreword, Daniel Harbour noted Zelman's facility with language. He was fluent in Russian and Yiddish, able to write in Hebrew and to speak good German and French and seems also to have passable Arabic and Turkish. Zelman and his siblings wrote to each other in Russian, and even in the last decades of the nineteenth century the proportion of Jews entering higher education who considered Russian their first language was rising rapidly. Russian was seen as the way into the wider society with all its opportunities. For his later work in London he would also have needed a high level of competency in English, and he may have gained a grounding in the language during an extended stay in Egypt between 1909 and 1910, possibly related to trading links between Ukraine and Egypt.

Daniel also commented on the contemporary respect for his views, such as his inclusion in the Hebrew Vilna newspaper *Hed HaZman* of 2 January 1911 where he is listed as a 'distinguished contributor' along with Ahad Ha'am and Nachum Sokolow and as a notable at a funeral in Odessa. These letters indicate some of his movements during the years before the First World War as we shall see.

Zelman was living in Chelyabinsk, which lies on the Miass River, just to the east of the Urals, during the Russo-Japanese War of 1905. Today Chelyabinsk is one of Russia's largest and most industrialized cities and by 1905 it was growing rapidly following completion of the Trans-Siberian Railway and a train line to Ekaterinberg. As it lies on the border between Europe and Asia it was the main hub for shipping goods to Siberia. A customs point was created in Chelyabinsk, which imposed duties on the shipment of goods between the European and Asian parts of Russia, which led to the emergence of mills and a tea-packing factory. By the time Zelman was there its population was around 30,000 and a fine synagogue had just been completed. The building was confiscated during the Communist era but was returned to the Jewish community in 1992. It was extensively restored and functions again as a synagogue with a Chabad rabbi based there. Chelyabinsk is not much known outside Russia, but it had a short-lived burst of fame when a meteor exploded over the city in 2013.

Zelman recalled an encounter some years before, in an article for a Yiddish newspaper in Warsaw in 1910, with some young Jewish soldiers at the Chelyabinsk Train Station, spending some days in the town before going on their way to serve in the Russian Army in the 1905 war against the Japanese. They correctly identified him as being Jewish and asked if they could see some Yiddish newspapers and where there was a synagogue so that one of them could observe a yahrzeit. Zelman was impressed:

> At that moment I felt myself fill with pride. At the time when others are carousing, the Jewish soldier seeks a shul, a newspaper. How physically fit is yet the Jewish people, that it produces such handsome, healthy soldiers, and how strong it is mentally.

His pride also extended to the Jews he met in Egypt, allowing himself some musings at the mummy of Rameses II, the Pharaoh of the Exodus, while standing with some Jewish tourists from Germany and the Netherlands:

> Three thousand two hundred years beyond Pharaoh's history, we are no longer slaves, but healthy, cultured and educated people. To this

bore witness the small clutch of men who had returned to the land several thousand years later and had stood around Pharaoh's mummy!

His despatches for the Russian press deal mainly with trade matters, while his articles for Yiddish and Hebrew press cover the realities of the problems facing the nascent Zionist movement. We find that his travels through the Middle East were quite extensive. After visiting Palestine and spending a year in Egypt, Zelman travelled on from Haifa to Beirut, Izmir and Constantinople. He made detailed comments on the state of the Jewish communities in each and described two visits to the Turkish Parliament, which did not overly impress him.

He pointed out, in an article for *Hed HaZman*, in December 1910 that the Zionist organisations like Hovevei Zion were failing *olim,* the Jews who were immigrating to Palestine, by not providing the support services that newcomers to the country required:

> However, they have forgotten to create an institution to which the new immigrant can turn, in which he might find a trusty advisor who will try with all his might to persuade the arriving visitor to stay in the country... [so that he] returns to his country, bitter of spirit and brimming with fury at the Land of Israel and her leaders.

Besides the newspaper articles the book contains a speech Zelman made in Odessa in 1905, providing a report of the 7th Zionist Congress in Basle. Beside his report of the technical parts of the Congress his lengthy comments on the remarks of Dr. Hillel Jaffe, as he described life in the Jewish settlements, indicated how they had caught his imagination. Jaffe had been born in Ukraine, studied medicine in Geneva and obtained a license to practice in Turkey. He settled in Tiberias in 1891 but it was his work with malaria in Zichron Yaakov, where he settled in 1893, which established his medical reputation. Jaffe instituted hygienic measures to cut transmission of the disease and promoted the draining of the local marshes, where the malaria-carrying mosquitoes were breeding, by the use of eucalyptus trees.

Zelman's brother Solomon had been in London for a few years by the time of these newspaper articles. It was clear that Zelman had a high regard for British administrative skills, which he encountered on his extended visit to Egypt, then a British protectorate. He noted how Egypt was flourishing under British rule, with industrialization, following major inward investment, and agricultural improvement consequent on better utilization of the Nile waters. He even commented that 'as for taking bribery or baksheesh, this is unacceptable and unmentionable', presumably an aspect of British policy. Zelman noted elsewhere how the Libyans greeted the Italian colonialists with joy following the Italian-Ottoman War of 1911 and was told in Beirut that they too would welcome relief from oppressive Ottoman rule. Another article, probably written by Zelman but not signed by him, referred to the 'Egyptian Peril' and the suggestions there that Egypt should annex Palestine and Syria, then under Ottoman rule. Gilbert considered that Zelman's comments that in Egypt 'could be found a centre of Egyptian nationalism which has a great influence on all Arab tribes' could be a prophetic allusion to the Muslim Brotherhood.

The British, he noted, kept a low profile, as one only encountered Arabs in the normal run of activities though there was an awareness that:

> ... there is an invisible Englishman somewhere, steering all the machinery of government' [while] in areas of life where English influence is lacking and which lie wholly in the hands of the Arab intelligentsia, such as justice and education, there is the stench of rust and rot.

In another article for *Hed HaZman* in December 1911 Zelman described a train journey westward, explaining why the line to Berlin was so much more pleasant than using the Austrian train network through Vienna. In any case he was aware of rampant antisemitism in Vienna, and wondered why any Russian Jew who had their fill of antisemitism at home would wish to spend time in the Austrian capital. Berlin, however, was another story. Zelman had had several extended visits to Berlin too, enjoying its reputation as an international city, both clean and orderly, although he sensed the tensions, especially with Britain, which inevitably were to lead to war. The description of this visit included the Berlin Grain Exchange where Russian wheat was traded. There was a ready market for Russian grain in Germany and the Russo-German Trade Agreement was due to be renegotiated in 1917. Zelman was aware of the issues involved in its renewal. By the time this happened the world was a very different place.

The final article in Daniel Harbour's collection was entitled the 'Ambassador's Balagan', written (anonymously) for the *Russkaya Gazeta* in Paris, and dated 22 December 1924, when he was already based in London. The word *balagan* in Hebrew has the connotation of chaos and comes to the language from Russian, although it actually derives from the Persian

זלמן קאהארליצקי.

פלשתינה ומצרים.

פלשתינה ומצרים — שתי הארצות העתיקות האלה היו כמעט בכל תקופה קשורות זו בזו ע"י אינטירסים חדרים ומשותפים. וכך אנו רואים את הקשר הזה הולך ונמשך גם בימינו אלה, אך קי"ב לעשרים שנה עברו לבן היום שהתחילה פלשתינה להתפתח התפתחות איקונומית, ואנחנו רואים כבר את מצרים מתרפה שהתפסת נברצת בהתפתחות זו. אפשר לדבר, כי לא רחוקה היא העת, אשר דחיים דפוליטים של מצרים יהיו משפיעים על פלשתינה.

למן' היום, שנחיתה אנגליה לאדונת ברצב במצרים, עשתה הארץ הזאת חיל רב בחמר וברוח. מצרים היתה עתה לארץ מציינת לא רק בקבריה הדתחים, בהפי ראמים דפטורסטים שלה וכסגולותיה הקרמונית, כי אם גם בהקילמודה דקרקעית רנבידהה שלר, במברה ובוכלתר, הוולכים הולך ודתפשט, באוכלוסן הסרובים של תוצביה, דברנישים כבר צורך בחיים קולמוריים, בהזי לקסס וכיוצא בזה.

ע"י דרפאקה דטלאכתיה של נהר הנילוס, שהעלתיו עברית על פני כל הארץ ומשפיעות בכל ימות השנה שפעה מי עדיכלייי, אין' המדינה לקיה עיר בשנות־בצורת. כמעט בכל הארץ פורח ומשגשג מטע צמר־הגפן, המוצא למכירה

לחוץ־לארץ וגם לאמידיקה בסכום של שש מאות מיליונים פראנק בכל שנה. מובן מאליו, כי אין הדבר נח למצרים לפתח על ארמתה את אודם דפרודוקטים, שהוא יכולה לרביא אותם אליה בבחירים עולים מארצות אודיות. מארצות פלשתינה, הקרובה אליה ביותר, היא מכניסה אליה יין, ליקר, קוניאק, ספירס, ענבים, נוריח, מאבאק, פולין, רטים, שערון, סיבין', אבטיחים, תפוחי־זהב, לימונים, שקדים וזיתים. עד כמה שהתי פלשתינה מפוחתה ודתפתחה בלכלי וכאיוה מדה שירב פריה, אין היא בכסקת ערין למלא את צרכיה של מצרים. הפרודוק ד היחידי, שפלשתינה מוציאה אותו לעיי בשיעור מרובה מאד, הוא—היין, ומצרים כבר בכסיה אליה ב"דג אהיסד כפרנה ובכלית השנתית.

ה"כרמל" המרחו התחיל מהפתחת במצרים אך זה קרוב לארבע שגום, מן היום שרותיצב בד לומסקין בראשו, ובמשך הקת הזאת הספיק לדתפשם בארץ במדה מרובה מאד, אף עפ"י שהוא פרודוקט של סוהרות, שקשה לפצוא בשבולי בכל שוק חדש, ובפרט כמשאריך להתחרות בעסק זה עם פיוטה ישנה ומפורסמת בפראנציה, אומליה, ויין, בל הין, שפלשתינה מכניסה למצרים, אינו עולה אפילו לעשרה אחוזים מהשיעור הכללי

Article by Zelman in Hebrew from *Hed HaZman* on Palestine and Egypt. His surname is spelt Kaharlitsky in the Ukrainian style (7/4/1910).

word for a balcony. A journalist invited Zelman to this Ambassador's Balagan which took place in Berlin, while Zelman was getting ready to travel to Paris. It was a social event where he could expect to meet Soviet diplomats from around Europe, rather than the events for Russian émigres he had been attending to gain some impressions of their 'moods' and 'aspirations'. The Deputy Ambassador to London, Yan Antonovitch Berzin, whom he described as an 'insignificant taciturn Latvian' was present and as Zelman recorded, 'Any question, even from their own people, about his role in England... was met by Berzin with prevarication and mumbling... all of which gave more the impression of a thick, unintelligent rogue, than a deputy ambassador to London of the USSR'.

Given the opinions which come through the article, including meetings with émigrés, the reference to Stalin as 'bloodthirsty', the 'cheap boorishness' of the Soviet ambassadors and of the 'worthlessness of the Bolshevik gang abroad' it is not surprising that he did not put his name to it. If known, it would have provided ammunition for those who would have wished him harm. Maybe it did, as we consider these last couple of years of his life.

We have some idea of Zelman and his then fiancée Chassia's activities in the final years before the First World War through Chassia's letters to Zelman, preserved in a rich family archive. Sequencing has been complicated by letters which do not indicate date or place, but Daniel Harbour edited a selection of these letters in 2005, in a small family publication extending to 158 pages, which follow a reasonable chronological form. The book, like the later volume five years later, was dedicated to Daniel's grandmother Elizabeth Kaye on her special birthdays. The letters cover everything from the sanatorium treatments and food to Chassia's need for more money and her concern for Zelman's health. During 1911 Chassia developed tuberculosis and had to spend extended time at a sanatorium in Germany before their marriage.

Chassia's academic pedigree was quite outstanding. She had been born in Nikolaev, attended a Russian language high school and had private tutors with French and German. She had studied art, literature and philosophy in Paris but switched to the sciences, botany, zoology and biology, and graduated at the University of Montpellier. While still in France she had considered the possibility of using her knowledge of botany in Palestine and was recommended to contact Aharon Aharonson, the Managing Director of the Jewish Agricultural Experiment Station at Atlit. Aharonson had identified emer wheat, the ancestor of contemporary strains. He was hoping to extend the research at the agricultural site, setting up a company in the United States to provide financial support. We have the letter of reply from Aharonson to Chassia dated 12 August 1910 and written from Haifa. His response is quite frank. He hoped she could come to start work on identifying his herbal collection containing rare species of local plants, but this would have to be on a voluntary basis, although with an accommodation allowance provided. After two or three months she would receive a 'modest salary'. On the basis of this reply, Chassia went for further training, first to the herbarium at the Royal Botanical Gardens in Berlin and then to Berne in Switzerland. From there she was suddenly recalled to Russia where her father had become unwell and the Palestine move never happened. The Aharonson family were to become famous as the Nili spy group, providing vital information for Britain as they fought the Turks in Palestine in the First World War.

Chassia was out of Ukraine for much of the time from March 1911 until the end of 1913. She was in constant touch with Zelman and the delayed wedding must have happened soon after her return, either in December 1913 or January 1914. In March 1911 she describes trips to Baku in Azerbaijan and Tiflis (Tbilisi) in Georgia. At this time Zelman's sister Reysie was living in Azerbaijan, in the town of Lankaran, about 150 miles south of Baku. This was followed by travel in Europe after which she still hoped to move to Palestine and settle there. However, health problems came to complicate things. Chassia was admitted to a tuberculosis sanatorium at St. Blasien in the southern Black Forest, not far from the German border with Switzerland in March 1912. By August, her letters to Zelman anticipate a speedy return to Russia to spend their lives together and indeed she spent some time in Vienna, planned a trip to Paris and was even considering a return to Russia. However, she was back in St. Blasien in September and three months later was still having extended time in the 'fresh forest air' and was receiving injections. An account of an event at the sanatorium to mark the birthday of the Duke of Baden in July 1913 confirms that her stay in Germany was perhaps unexpectedly prolonged. Zelman too was experiencing some health problems and Chassia was recommending that they might meet in Munich where he could see a gastroenterologist. Perhaps, he was having early symptoms of gallstones which was to be implicated in his early death.

Chassia had obviously visited Britain as evidenced by her 'critical familiarity', indicated below in her correspondence to Zelman, with Solomon, his wife and children. I suspect her visit, to London, would have been in the summer of 1911, thus before the birth of David in February 1912 and the family move to Glasgow two months later. Golda and

Solomon's first two children were Sarah (born 1906) and Alf (born 1907) but Golda also had twins born in March 1910. The boy, Jacob, had died shortly after birth but the daughter Rebecca (Rivka) only died in December 1910. If there were two daughters at the time of her visit, she would have been in London a year earlier, in 1910. As she wrote to Zelman:

> Your brothers are good people, but they lack culture. Examples are many. Take for example your Shama [Solomon]. His wife [Golda] has already been ill for several years. All surplus funds go for the enrichment of doctors, while she should have undergone radical treatment and, after several months, would have been healthy. She should be sent abroad for a change of climate, but it would never occur to them to do it. You like his boys and I have a weakness for his girls. Of all Shama's daughters I like Sarah. Perhaps because she looks like you. She is not clever, but a very kind girl. I think that when I have a daughter, she will be like her, only I hope, more clever and better raised.

Around this time, just after Solomon had settled in Glasgow, Zelman loaned his brother 500 roubles (worth around £4,000 today) following a previous loan, while Solomon was in London, of 100 roubles. Chassia was not comfortable with this, but Solomon confounded her predictions by making a success of his new business with the money.

Violence however was never far away from the Nikolaev Jewish community. There was a pogrom in the city and surrounding villages in the spring of 1899. While Jews and their property suffered during the pogrom, self-defence groups in nearby Jewish agricultural colonies proved themselves able to defend themselves and their property. Nikolaev also experienced a further pogrom during a wave of anti-Jewish violence in 1905, but by this time a Jewish defence group had been organised by the local Zionist movement. Further anti-Jewish activity accompanied the unrest of the Civil War in 1919 and 1920.

With the dislocations of the Russian Revolution the Imass family, with Zelman and Chassia, relocated to Ekaterinoslav (from 1926 it was known as Dnepropetrovsk and since 2016 it has been called Dnipro). It was a city some 240 miles from Odessa where they already had business connections as mentioned by Chassia in a letter to Zelman. Ekaterinoslav was named for Empress Katherine the Great and Dnepropetrovsk after the Communist leader Grigory Petrovsky. In any case, the Civil War was a time for being watchful as the tide of victory turned frequently. The city was more heavily Jewish than Nikolaev and Jews constituted around 40 per cent of the population, which numbered about 200,000. The city was briefly under Bolshevik control after the November Revolution and was then occupied by German and Austrian-Hungarian armies followed by periods of anarchist and White Russian rule before the Red Army finally captured the city in 1919. With the anti-Jewish violence during the Civil War Jewish emigration increased until the Soviet authorities were able to stop it. In the meantime, instability in the surrounding regions brought many thousands of Jews to the city. Zionist activities were also gradually suppressed by the Soviets, although the Poalei Tsion Party, which had tried to operate as a Zionist and Communist grouping, survived for a few years. Zelman and Chassia must have been aware that it was time to leave and for their sons, Emmanuel and Victor, to grow up in a freer environment.

Daniel Harbour has noted Zelman's fascination with Italy and his hopes that the Italian occupation of Libya would bring to that country some of the benefits that the British were bringing to Egypt. Perhaps, he indicates, this was why his two sons got their names – after the Italian King Victor Emmanuel III (Vittorio Emmanuele), and even speculates that Lilian was named after the Italian Queen, Elena of Montenegro.

The ravages of civil war and the Bolshevik land policies had severely damaged grain production in the Ukraine and rendered the role of the major grain dealers largely redundant. The Russian financial collapse following defeat in the First World War and the Communist Revolution left the country lacking an industrial base, with little foreign currency and few diplomatic links with other countries. The first trade agreement between the Soviet Union and Great Britain was signed in March 1921, the same month that Lenin introduced his New Economic Plan. The country had not been ready for the wholesale nationalization of all its enterprises and the Plan aimed to give the economy a bit of relief before the Communist economic plans could be implemented in full. Although the trade agreement was only signed in 1921 the All Russian Co-operative Society (Arcos), which would ostensibly encourage trade between Britain and Russia, had been set up a year earlier with its office in Moorgate. It was a strange hybrid; a British company that was operated by the Soviet Union and in control of approved co-operative societies there.

Our understanding has been that Zelman was chosen to head the commercial interests which involved the purchase of British machinery funded by the sale of Russian timber and furs. However, the story proves to be quite complex, full of intrigue and with a tragic ending. Firstly, it is not entirely clear what Zelman's role in the company was. Officially, he was employed by the Soviet Government Trade Department in the White Russian capital Minsk with a supervisory role at Arcos in London. His office was at 49 Moorgate. We have no specific details of his responsibilities in a company which eventually had many hundreds of employees and carried out trade worth £86 million between Britain and Russia between 1921 and 1927 (£86 million in 1925 is worth £5 billion in 2020 prices). The company had a Board of Directors, a management team, a finance team and officers covering each specific area of imports and exports. Zelman could have been in any of these.

Zelman's passport indicates that he paid a trip to Britain in 1922, the year before Arcos formally began trading, to appraise the situation. During this visit Zelman was able to visit Solomon in Glasgow despite the British ban on Soviet citizens travelling more than 50 miles from London. Zelman was given special permission to address members of the Jewish community at a small Hassidic synagogue in the Gorbals. A report in the *Jewish Chronicle* indicates that a 'Mr Z. Collins' from the Ukraine told members of the Jewish community about the suffering of Ukrainian Jewry following the Revolution and the Civil War and some funds were raised for famine relief. It is possible that he felt that the use of his own surname in such a public undertaking could have produced unwelcome attention.

During the first year £5 million of coal, textiles, provisions and agricultural machinery were sent by Arcos to the Soviet Union. As the Russian wheat harvest recovered from the poor crop of 1921 Britain began importing butter, eggs, wheat and flax although much of the trade concerned timber and fur. In May 1923, Arcos established its own bank to handle the financial transactions of the organization, to control all future transactions in the import or export of Soviet commodities and to issue traveller's cheques for visitors to the USSR. Russian fur was a key import, but it never reached more than a fifth of British purchases through Arcos and in any case Arcos did not have a monopoly of the Russian fur trade in Britain. Dutch fur buying from Russia was also based in London, but there were bigger players around.

In her book on her Russian family entitled *The Eitingons: A Twentieth Century Family* (2009), Mary-Kay Wilmers described how Monya Eitingon, who had been arrested in Moscow but arrived in London as a Czech citizen, had set up the Moscow Fur Trading Company in 1921. Acting for his cousin, Motty Eitingon, he had made a trade arrangement with Arcos in 1923 by which time Zelman was in London. This deal allowed Arcos to draw on substantial sums of money to purchase the furs in Russia to be sold in London. Some furs, as part of the deal, would now be sold on to New York rather than traded in London. Motty Eitingon had been known as a major fur dealer in Tsarist times and he would have had the confidence of the Russians in finding the right markets and ensuring that Arcos got a share of the profits. At the same time, his own company Eitingon Schild, registered in New York but with international offices in London and Paris and elsewhere, was making substantial profits. By 1926 this arrangement seemed to be breaking down. There had been disagreements between Arcos and Eitingon Schild but Arcos's position in Russia was weakening and Motty Eitingon landed a huge contract with the Soviet government to sell millions of dollars of fur in America.

On 12 May 1927, a large force of uniformed and plain-clothes police officers entered the headquarters of Arcos and the Soviet Trade Delegation at 49 Moorgate. MI5 had had suspicions that Arcos was acting as a cover for espionage for a couple of years, when one of their agents tailed a suspect back to Moorgate. They then began tapping the phone lines which revealed many calls between Arcos and suspected Soviet intelligence operatives. Interception of its post revealed copies of classified French dispatches. Besides clandestine links with Communist sympathisers there was a suspicion that industrial espionage, sending blueprints to Russia, rather than buying equipment, was also taking place. Harriette Flory described what happened next in an article entitled 'The Arcos Raid and the Rupture of Anglo-Soviet Relations, 1927' which was published in the *Journal of Contemporary History* in 1977:

> The police took possession of the telephone exchange, detained all the employees, and made a thorough search of documents on the premises. Drilling machinery was brought into open locked rooms and strongboxes recovered numerous classified documents in the basement which was rigged with numerous anti-intruder devices. A secret cypher room was discovered where workers were hurriedly engaged in burning papers. A struggle then ensued when police tried to arrest remaining papers from staff. The chief of this room then attempted to pocket a list, which on inspection detailed cover addresses used for secret communication with the communist parties of the North and South American, African and Australasian continents. A considerable number of documents were removed from the building in the course of the investigation. This raid and subsequent diplomatic fisticuffs subsequently became known as the *Arcos Affair.*

Although the information retrieved from the raid was not as conclusive as perhaps British ministers claimed, and MI5 had already been aware of what was going on at Moorgate for some time, papers later found in a raid on the Soviet Embassy in Beijing confirmed their suspicions. However, the dramatic events of the Arcos search publicised unwelcome Soviet deeds. It led directly to the break in diplomatic relations with the Soviet Union, only established by the previous Labour government in 1924. After the raid Arcos was transformed into a simple trading company acting on behalf of a Moscow fur syndicate that now handled all Soviet fur exports.

A similar organization, the Amtorg Trading Corporation, was established in New York in 1924 by the merger of Armand Hammer's Allied American Corporation with Prodexco and the United States branch of Arcos. The United States and the Soviet Union did not establish diplomatic relations until 1933 and Amtorg served as Russia's address in America. It handled almost all the imports from Russia to the USA of lumber, furs, flax, bristles, caviar, and all the exports of raw materials and machinery Soviet industry and agriculture needed. Extensive business arrangements were set up and it was only after 1930 that Amtorg was found to be involved in industrial espionage. In the summer of 1925 Amtorg's first President, Isaiah Khurgin, and his colleague Efraim Skliansky drowned in a boating incident on Long Lake in upstate New York. Wilmers remarked that 'it's tempting to think that his death wasn't an accident' but continued 'in the summer of 1925 the killings hadn't yet begun'. Wikipedia lists many confirmed Soviet assassinations abroad. The first, of a Russian White Army General Pyotr Wrangel, occurred in Brussels in 1928 and another White Army General, Alexander Kutepov, was killed in Paris in 1930 as was Noe Ramishvili, a former Prime Minister of Georgia. However, Wikipedia admits that it does not include suspected assassinations of political opponents who died in suspicious circumstances.

We need to add the death of Zelman to the 'opponents who died in suspicious circumstances'. On 26 June 1926 Zelman, just 48 years old and in previous good health, became ill and was taken to St. George's Hospital where gallstones were diagnosed and an operation was recommended. Zelman did not survive the surgery. There persists a family feeling that there may have been some foul play at work. There is even a story that a surgeon was brought over from Russia to monitor the treatment. There was, however, not enough evidence to require an autopsy. Despite archival searches I have been unable to trace any hospital records to confirm the story. We should probably also note that Zelman's closest colleague, also Jewish and called Aaronson, was recalled to Moscow in 1925 at the same time as Zelman, just as MI5 suspicions of Arcos were increasing. The name Aaronson also appears as a friend of Zelman in one of Chassia's letters. It is possible that when the two men came together to London they were already colleagues. There is a family story that Zelman and Aaronson both received letters recalling them to Russia and giving explicit directions for their return. Aaronson left for Russia and was never heard of again. Zelman thought that there something very suspicious about his letter and remained in London but was soon dead. The mystery therefore remains.

Many Russians, even Soviet officials, faced unwelcome suspicion on returning from postings abroad. It had made sense for Zelman to stay in London. The Russian Trade Commissioner in London at the time of the Arcos raid was Arkady Rosengolts, the son of a Jewish merchant. Rosengolts played an active role in the Revolution of 1917 and was a leading officer in the Red Army. During the Russian Civil War he had worked closely with Leon Trotsky. This was no protection and may have counted against him. He was one of the defendants of the third Moscow Trial, along with other prominent Soviet officials facing a long list of capital charges, including espionage, sabotage and plotting to assassinate Lenin and Stalin. He was convicted, sentenced to death and shot on 15 March 1938 in Moscow. He was only rehabilitated 50 years later in 1988. There are many other examples.

Zelman's older son, Emmanuel, had been born in Nikolaev in 1914. He was only eight years old when he arrived in London and twelve when his father died suddenly. In 1926 his only Kagarlitsky relations in Britain were the families of Solomon and Shimmel in Glasgow, and it was Solomon who registered his father's death. Emmanuel only changed his surname to Kaye in 1933, five years after leaving Richmond High School and becoming a British citizen. He left school two years after his father died to work in a small engineering factory and began engineering studies in the evenings at the Twickenham Technical College.

His Collins cousins had fond memories of his summer visits to Glasgow in the 1930s and remembered that even as a teenager he was extremely focussed on many different topics related to science and health. As the Glasgow family prospered, they were used to an endless supply of fashionable clothing and they noticed that Emmanuel's wardrobe was very limited – a shabby green suit was part of the family recollections. Chassia had to tolerate these family visits but she would counsel him not to spend too much time with his Scottish cousins, lest he lose his carefully-nurtured English accent and end up sounding like an uncouth Scotsman. This is, of course, an echo of a letter from Chassia to Zelman, bemoaning his lack of a proper education and advising him to study syntax and grammar: 'Stop buying unnecessary newspapers and read instead serious books.'

In 1940, along with John Sharp, he set up an engineering business J.E. Shay Ltd (a combination of both their names) making various tools and instruments which were taken up by such companies as Hoover and Ford. I seem to remember my grandfather and uncles talking about buying a share in developing the company in the manufacture of ball-bearings, an essential component of their machinery. Their big break came just three years later when they took over Lansing Bagnall, a small company making electric platform trucks and tractors. However, their work had already gained recognition for its wartime potential with a visit by Emmanuel and John Sharp to 10 Downing Street for a meeting with the Prime Minister, Winston Churchill in September 1942. The company's origins went back to the 1920s when W.G. Bagnall arrived from Lansing, Michigan to be a representative for the Lansing company. In 1930, the company in America ceased making trucks and tractors, so Bagnall decided to manufacture them in Britain under the name Lansing Bagnall.

After wartime production of radio control mechanisms for bomber aircraft, they introduced a new tractor in 1945 and in 1946 became agents for fork-lift trucks. In 1949 they opened a factory in Basingstoke to manufacture fork-lift trucks and the business grew both in the domestic and export markets, eventually with allied businesses in Switzerland and Germany. The company became the biggest employer in Basingstoke, with a workforce of 3,500 at its peak, and was the largest manufacturer of electric fork-lift trucks in Europe winning many Queen's Awards for Export Achievement and Technological Innovation. During a visit to the factory in 1965 the Duke of Edinburgh drove one of the fork-lift trucks. In 1989 Emmanuel sold Lansing Bagnall to the German manufacturing firm Linde, and became Honorary President of what became Lansing Linde Ltd.

Emmanuel was an active member of the Confederation of British Industry and of the Council of Industry for Management Education. He was a patron of the arts, and his beneficiaries included the National Portrait Gallery in London, where he funded a new room, and charities in Israel. He was on the UK Board of Governors of the Israel Centre for Social and Economic Progress (ICSEP), an influential policy think tank, of which he was a founder member, and after the death of his sister Lilian instituted an annual prize awarded by the Department of Jewish History of the Hebrew University of Jerusalem. I have attended many of the award ceremonies in recent years, along with three of Lilian's children, Ruth, Rebecca and Simon, and we bring a personal connection to award winners.

Portrait of Sir Emmanuel Kaye (National Portrait Gallery).

As an opera lover Emmanuel went to the Salzburg Festival every year for over three decades and was a trustee of Glyndebourne for many years. Among many personal awards Emmanuel was knighted in 1974.

Emmanuel and Elizabeth Cutler, whom he married in 1945, often accompanied by their daughters Joanna and Deborah, were regular visitors to Glasgow, rarely missing a *barmitzvah* or a wedding, always making sure that food was not being cooked in aluminium pots and pans. Emmanuel was concerned about the health risks from aluminium although the evidence of human disease from aluminium kitchenware has not been established.

We were to see them on other occasions too, perhaps in London, but our final meeting with just the two of them was in Scotland. I was used to regular phone calls from Emmanuel, often at irregular times, usually very early in the morning. He always had something to tell me about his medical ideas, some based on Indian Ayurvedic principles, along with some more mainstream views on thrombosis. This last had been a particular interest of his and he had donated the money to establish the Thrombosis Research Institute in London. They opened a building named after him in 1990, and he served as its first chairman. He was also quite committed to alternative medicine. He had discussed homeopathic remedies with the Queen Mother in 1991 and some years earlier the Queen had visited the Kayes for Emmanuel's views on homeopathy, one of her rare visits to a private home. He also advised Margaret Thatcher on natural treatments.

He phoned early in April 1995. He and Elizabeth were going to be visiting their 'cottage' in a beautiful corner of Dumfriesshire, on land formerly owned by the Duke of Buccleugh. I had just given my first talk on the life story of Ura, and in the pre-PowerPoint days I had designed a collection of posters to accompany the story. Emmanuel knew that he featured in part of Ura's history and was keen to hear and see what I was doing. We arranged a date during the intermediate days of Pesach, the Passover festival. Emmanuel suggested that Irene bring some of her Pesach baking and the date was set. The setting was delightful, the cottage warm and tastefully furnished and the Scottish weather did not let us down as we walked and admired the scenery. Emmanuel was amazed to see the photograph of himself with Ura at the Dinard seafront in the early summer of 1939 and was intrigued with the way the family story was presented.

Our final meeting with them was under very different circumstances. Our daughter Eve had just become engaged to Joshua Sacks, son of Chief Rabbi (later Lord) Jonathan and Elaine Sacks. Emmanuel had been a supporter of the journal *L'Eylah*, produced by Jews' College when Rabbi Sacks had been the Principal. They were delighted to be at the engagement party in Hamilton Terrace, St. John's Wood and received a warm reception from the Chief Rabbi. After Emmanuel's death in 1999 we met Elizabeth in London and learned for the first time of the family archive he had preserved but not shared over the many decades since Zelman's death. Elizabeth told us of her involvement with the Israel Guide Dog Centre, and her contribution in 2001, which enabled the Society to erect a purpose-built building to house the centre's offices, guest rooms and other facilities.

We were to be even closer to Zelman's daughter Lilian and her husband Eric Mendoza. Lilian and Eric, like Emmanuel and Elizabeth, married in 1945. They described how after the death of Chassia in 1943 Solomon and Golda in Glasgow had been recognized as the heads of the Kagarlitsky family and had to be visited before their engagement could be announced. They spent a weekend in our home in Glasgow in 1987 and we visited them countless times in Israel, ate with them at their favourite Jerusalem restaurants and treasured our visits to their home at Ma'amedot Yisrael in the Old City. There was one Yemenite-style restaurant on King George Street that Lilian particularly liked, and she had recommended it to the *Jerusalem Post* food critic, as a kosher restaurant rather than some of the other places he wrote about in his column. He graciously acknowledged her in his review.

Eric was very knowledgeable about the buildings in Old City and knew which were Roman and earlier. He once pointed out a large wall from a later era, by remarking 'that's not an antique structure, just some Byzantine rubbish'. One Shabbat when there was no service in their beloved Stambouli Synagogue, one of the four in the complex of ancient Sephardi prayer houses in the Old City, we joined them for a service at the atmospheric Italian Synagogue in the city centre. On a recent visit to the Old City, we visited the Stambouli and saw the plaque honouring Lilian and mentioning the contribution to the synagogue that had been made in her name.

Lilian and Eric were devoted to family history and we corresponded regularly. In fact, she was composing a letter to me at the time of her death in hospital in London in the spring of 1992. They had compiled 'Shorashim', the first printed collection of early family history, and Lilian had set out the Kagarlitsky family tree and kept in touch with many family members around the world. It was her contact with the French Ambassador, Alain Pierret, that led to Rosanne Romagnan being recognized as a Righteous Gentile by Yad Vashem for sheltering Ura for three months in wartime Marseille.

Eric was a distinguished scientist. He had been Professor of Physics at Bangor University in Wales from 1963, becoming a science Professor at the Hebrew University of Jerusalem in 1972. He also had spells as a Visiting Professor in Italy and America. Eric had a love of teaching science. He was mainly responsible for reforming the physics syllabus at Manchester University and took on a similar role at the Israel Science Teaching Centre. A simple internet search brought me to his High-Entropy Essays, forerunners, in the 1960s, of computer-generated texts that have been tried to pass as authored by humans. I highly recommend reading Wayne Clements' account of Eric's Little Gray Rabbit stories, in a paper entitled 'Resuscitating a Dead Rabbit'. These stories used innovative programming to compose one of the first examples of a fiction-writing-computer-programme. (Accessible at http://dx.doi.org/10.14236/ewic/EVA2020.45)

Eric even managed to add a word to the Welsh language. Returning to Wales after a sabbatical at the Haifa Technion he described how the ulpan in Israel has been used to teach Hebrew from a basic to proficient level. Eric gets the credit for the Welsh word wlpan (the English letter 'u' is represented in Welsh by 'w'), which is attached to Welsh language teaching centres. It was only after he died that I learned of his highly secret military sphere scientific research – during the Second World War – on radar and later, when living in Jerusalem, for the Israel Defence Forces.

Zelman's son Victor died in 1975 at the age of only 57 years. However, his wife Joyce (Mendoza), the last member of that generation, celebrated her 100th birthday in Manchester as these lines were being written. Victor had spent a year in Palestine in 1936 working in the Post Office in Haifa and became a trained workshop engineer on returning to England. He served in the Royal Air Force during the Second World War but struggled at first with employment in the post-war era. Joyce had been a maternity nurse and later a medical secretary, but together they enjoyed running a gift shop in London's Mill Hill.

Eric and Lilian's daughters, Ruth and Rebecca, remain close friends as well as being second cousins. Ruth was a regular visitor to Glasgow as a student. Our paths cross regularly and our last trip before the Covid-19 lockdown was a long weekend in London, in February 2020, for Ruth's marriage to Terry Sopel. There we reunited with Ruth's brother Jonathan, Daniel Harbour's mother Deborah whom we had not seen for over 30 years, and met Daniel's daughter Romy again. Rebecca Mendoza was there too, of course, and we were able to snatch a few words with her and Daniel about pursuing the family story. We hoped for a meeting. The Coronavirus travel restrictions made us settle for less. During Rebecca's recent years in Israel we met regularly, and she also became close to our daughter Rachel, in the same way as we had with Rebecca's parents.

4

Ura: The Exile

> Ura Collins seemed to have no roots, and Glasgow was just a pause in her travels.
> From Benno Schotz, *Bronze in My Blood* (Edinburgh, 1981), p.66

Ura was born in Kovshevata in 1895 and arrived in Paris around 1912, where her half-brother Shimmel was living. No details of her early life have survived, and we do not even know what she was doing during the few years she spent in Paris. We do know that she arrived in Glasgow with many of the characteristics that she would display later in life – her self-sufficiency, her artistic nature and the socialist principles which would guide her life, even when it took her in difficult directions.

She had arrived from Paris soon after the Collins family were settled in Kennishead, probably in 1916 when Shimmel was also relocating to Glasgow. While in the city she adopted their surname. I never heard that she had worked for my grandfather as Gudis had done or even how she might have spent her time in Glasgow. It was not long before she met Benno Schotz, later to be recognized as the leading sculptor of his generation in Scotland by his appointment as the Queen's 'Sculptor-in-Ordinary'. It is family lore that he had spotted Ura while riding on a tramcar and recognized her special facial features. From such a beginning he resolved to create a sculpture to capture the essence of her restless character. Schotz had arrived in Glasgow from Estonia where he had been born in 1891, so was just four years older than Ura. He had studied at the Russian Gymnasium although the family spoke German at home. Schotz had an older brother in Glasgow who arranged for him to study engineering at the Royal Technical College and by 1912 he was in Scotland. Schotz soon moved to the internationally renowned Glasgow School of Art and quickly achieved mastery in sculpture.

Using a solid piece of mahogany Schotz delineated Ura's features so exquisitely that family resemblances were easy to identify. Moreover, Schotz described the work, the first head he had modelled, as 'The Exile – a Russian émigrée who had lost her roots'. It is the only surviving work from this early period in Schotz' career and remains on permanent display at Glasgow's Kelvingrove Art Gallery and Museum. Schotz, with amazing perspicacity, seemed able to reach into the future and recognize her fate while Ura was still barely twenty years old. My aunt Mona told me that her parents felt that Ura and Benno were living together but Benno specifically denied that in his memoirs, *Bronze in My Blood* (1981), saying that Ura was really too sophisticated for him and she already sensed that life in Glasgow was not to be her destiny.

Given that Ura was later described as a 'liberated woman' perhaps it is strange that the only recorded romantic encounter is the relationship with her sculptor. Emmanuel maintained that she had gone to Palestine in the hope of getting married, but that when she did it turned out badly. Lilian said that she had heard a story that Ura had been married at one time to an English publisher, who killed a man he thought was having an affair with her. Anna in Moscow confirmed a marriage, in France, and added that there had been a child who had died.

Ura decided to join her father and siblings Ida, Clara and Motti in Palestine around 1923. She had seen some of her siblings in Glasgow

Three generations of Zev's family, grand-daughter Mona and great-grandchildren Anita, Jeffrey and Kenneth, with Benno Schotz's mahogany sculpture of Zev's daughter Ura. (Kelvingrove Art Galleries and Museum, Glasgow, August 1996).

during their visit in 1920 and Tel Aviv, where they were living, seemed to be an interesting new stage in her life. The city grew rapidly during the 1920s especially following a significant wave of migration from Poland as a result of increased antisemitism and restrictions on Jewish migration to the United States in 1924. Tel Aviv suddenly grew from just 15,000 citizens in 1922 to 34,000 three years later. Even at that early stage Tel Aviv had all the comforts they were used to in Europe: electric light, clean water, cinema, opera, theatre, as well as busy restaurants and cafés open until late at night. Ura was already interested in left-wing politics and developments in the kibbutz movement, groups such as Hashomer Hatzair, and eventually the Palestine Communist Party would have attracted her attention.

Her Palestine period ended in 1927 when a downturn in the economy was beginning. From Palestine she returned to the Paris she had left a decade earlier. Her choice of Paris as a destination should not be seen as too surprising. She had lived in Paris before coming to Glasgow, and she was able to relocate quite easily re-joining old friends in its lively Russian Jewish émigré community. Ura was interested in socialist politics and among the Jewish refugees there were those who shared her radical views. The family in Glasgow and Moscow had believed that during her twelve years in Paris she was working in a hospital affiliated to the Communist Party, possibly also teaching English. However, as we shall see, she later gave her occupation as couturier on a formal document in Marseille. Given her experience in Paris and Glasgow with her brothers Solomon and Shimmel, who were in clothes manufacture, it would not have been impossible for her to be involved in the design of up-market clothes of the kind that Anna was copying in London some years earlier.

There were enough Jews from Russia and Poland in the French Communist Party during the 1930s to have their own section and from 1934 a Yiddish daily newspaper with a circulation of 5,000. These last years before the war in France were extremely unsettled. The brief premiership of Leon Blum between June 1936 and early 1938 seemed to hold out hope for stateless Jews like Ura, but the level of left-wing agitation continued and Jewish divisions became obvious. David Weinberg describes these ideological fractures in *A Community on Trial: the Jews of Paris in the 1930s* (1977), suggesting that only the increasing threat brought the different factions together. Whether Ura was working in a politicized couture workshop or at a Communist Party-run hospital she would have faced the challenges of antisemitism and the helplessness of European Jews following the failure of the Evian Conference in 1938. This signalled that the doors of the world seemed closed to Jewish refugees. The urgent need was to unite a society that had to confront Nazi aggression.

Meanwhile, the situation on the European continent was getting worse. Jewish antisemitism was rife and Nazi Germany was already waging war against its Jewish community, removing their citizenship and excluding professionals from work. Violence was just below the surface. And then, on one night in November 1938 Kristallnacht happened. Hundreds of synagogues across Germany and Austria were torched by Nazi mobs as police and army watched and the fire brigade only intervened if other buildings might have been affected. Thousands of Jews were rounded up and Jewish shops and businesses were ransacked.

One British response was to open the country's doors to 10,000 children in a programme called the *kindertransport*. In Glasgow, as we shall see, Shimmel and Becky, Alf and Doreen and Sarah and Hymie all fostered children. Solomon was anxious about Ura's fate as she had never obtained French nationality and her status as a foreign-born resident in the event of a Nazi take-over of France left her open to deportation or worse. As 1939 wore on, the news from around Europe was increasingly gloomy. Appeasement was not controlling Hitler's appetite for conquest. Further, the signing of the Molotov-Ribbentrop peace pact between Germany and

Motti with sister Ura and cousin Anna (left) in Glasgow, 1920.

Russia indicated that war with France was increasingly likely with the threat of Russian resistance removed.

By the summer of 1939 Solomon decided that Ura should rejoin the family in Glasgow where she had lived less than twenty years before. Ura was resistant to the idea. Victor, the son of Zelman and Chassia, was despatched to Paris to plead with his aunt to come to Britain, but Ura was determined to stay where she was. The postcard Victor sent his mother indicates only that he toured Versailles with Ura and that he would be flying home a couple of days later. Ura added a brief note at the end of Victor's message in Russian merely commenting that she had enjoyed meeting her nephew but making no mention of a return to Britain. With the failure of Victor's mission, his older brother Emmanuel was sent to France to plead with Ura. Aunt and nephew met at Dinard, a fashionable resort on the Brittany coast. Emmanuel would have used all his skills of persuasion but like Victor he found his aunt to be obdurate. A few weeks later Britain and France were at war with Germany and within months the Nazis were at the gates of Paris.

Ura's wartime experiences were described in a letter, written in faltering English, that she sent to an aunt, Bessie Davidson, her mother's sister, in California in 1945. The letter lay forgotten in a drawer for over 40 years, until discovered by her nephew Mervin Bruck. It is from these pages that we can put together her experiences during the war years. The letter is difficult to understand as the chronology is not always consistent. She had been on the run, spent a short time living rough, been hidden in a village, detained in two different internment centres and befriended by Louis and Rose-Anne Romagnan. As a foreign-born Jew who did not have French citizenship, she was most at risk. About a quarter of French Jews perished in the Holocaust but amongst the large number born outside France the proportion was much higher.

Ura left Paris on 11 June 1940, just three days before the Germans arrived in Paris and began an itinerant life heading south through Vichy France to Marseille. The port city of Marseille had become a magnet as it was the only exit point to the world still open in Vichy France. This brought large numbers of refugees, many of them Jewish, others political, who sought exit visas to anywhere that would accept them. The arrival of so many refugees placed strain on the facilities of the city and caused tensions between the inhabitants and the incomers. Some stayed a relatively short time like Marc and Bella Chagall and many other artists and prominent figures, including some of Europe's non-Jewish *avant-garde* who were able to escape.

Emmanuel and Ura at Dinard, August 1939.

Through books such as *The Holocaust and the Jews of Marseille* (1996) by Donna Ryan and *Jews in France During World War II* by Renee Poznanski (2001) we can have some insight into what Ura endured over these five years. She was arrested and imprisoned at Camp Nine at Argeles-sur-Mer in Pyrenees-Orientale, in February 1941, one of more than 30 such camps in the Vichy Zone. This has been variously described as a concentration camp or as a detention or lodging centre and could accommodate up to 15,000 people. Many of the earlier inmates had been Spanish but this changed as the war continued and it became more of a processing centre for those who hoped or were forced to move on. A very few of those interned were released if they could provide exit visas from France. Based on clues in the letter Ura had sent to her aunt after the war, I had thought it likely that she had been in Gurs, in the Pyrenees, but I was later to discover the true place of her internment. Life was unspeakably brutal at Argeles, just as it was at Gurs. Barracks were overcrowded, unlit, filthy and verminous and there was a significant death rate, with hunger the commonest cause. Although some aid agencies were allowed to bring in relief, by 1943 there had been more than 1,000 deaths in the camps and almost 4,000 prisoners had been deported to Nazi death camps.

After four months she managed to escape in February 1941 and made her way to Marseille, but she was recaptured and returned to Argeles. Inmates who were poorly dressed and lacking money and were without knowledge of local dialects were quickly located and returned to the camp. Donna Ryan describes one successful escapee who had tricked the guards into thinking that he was a German. With help from the outside, escape was possible and in fact there were 755 who managed to evade the guards. However, an internment-camp document suggests that she was merely moved from Argeles to the Hotel Bompard in Marseille on 22 May 1941, awaiting departure in July for Argentina to join her fiancé Cuert Krechmer. Her letter indicates that a French policeman accompanied her to the Hotel Bompard.

We have no other knowledge of the existence of Cuert Krechmer and the document notes that the papers formalizing a visa were with the Argentinian Consulate. We can only presume that this was the only way possible for her out of France and that the engagement to Cuert was how Argentina might have been prepared to extend a visa to her. Yet, there are no further mentions of an Argentinian visa so it seems that it was never granted. She was, however, permitted to visit the Argentinian Consulate in Rue Torte then allowed to return to the Hotel Bompard rather than to places like Argeles or Gurs.

Four hotels in Marseille were converted into refugee hostels and the residents were mainly Jewish women and children. The Hotel Bompard is probably the best known of these facilities, accommodating up to 250 inmates each month in its 25 rooms. In theory, it was a place of rapid turnover as people who were awaiting visas could leave as soon as they were granted. In practice, some stayed on for much longer and school facilities for Jewish children were set up by organisations like Oeuvre de Secours aux Enfant (OSE). Ryan noted that corruption by the hotel's proprietors meant that some of the rations intended for the inmates were being sold for profit.

By August 1942 Vichy France was collaborating in the transport of foreign Jews to Germany and in November of that year the Germans occupied and controlled the Vichy Zone. In January 1943 the French authorities deployed police forces, from the Occupied Zone, as well as Vichy

France, along with reserve troops carrying out mass arrests at peoples' homes, on the streets, cafés and places of entertainment. In October 1943 there was a round-up of Jews and hundreds of women were sent to Drancy and then on to Auschwitz, where all but a handful perished. Some months earlier there had been deportations of Jews to the death camps of Majdanek and Sobibor. One of the worst excesses had been committed by Klaus Barbie, head of the SS in Lyons, who ordered the deportation to Auschwitz-Birkenau of 34 children from the orphanage at Izieu. The danger to Ura was increasing.

Many of those who failed to get visas were moved on to the internment camp at Les Milles in the Bouche du-Rhone which functioned until March 1943. Again, many of the inmates were distinguished cultural figures, including Lion Feuchtwanger, the author of *Jews Suss*, Golo the son of Thomas Mann, and Nobel Laureates Otto Meyerhof and Thadeus Reichstein. This was a time of great danger. The Vichy authorities maintained a semblance of responsibility to French Jews but were willing to transfer foreign Jews to the Germans. Beginning in August 1942 inmates were being deported from Gurs and other camps, and women were being moved from Hotel Bompard to Les Milles, and onwards to Auschwitz-Birkenau. Ryan records a group of 40 who had managed to escape this convoy through the help of a camp guard. The Hotel does not seem to have functioned beyond November 1942 and Ura found her way to the home of Louis and Rosanne Romagnan.

Much of the details about the Romagnan family and their courageous work during the war can be found in their son François' book *Le bureau de l'homme en blanc: Louis Joseph Romaganan – un 'Juste' au conseil municipal de Marseille, 29 Novembre 1940-21 Aout 1944*, published privately in 2018. Louis Romagnon was born in Marseille in 1909 into a family of Italian origin, and after leaving school found work with a painting firm. His father had fought in the trenches in the First World War returning to work first repairing roads, and then from 1935 head of maintenance in the cemeteries of Marseille. His wife Rosanne (Rose-Anne) Macello also had Italian roots, but more recent, from the area of Piedmont-Turin and the family had only obtained French citizenship in 1924. Her mother Emilia was a couturier and her father a bricklayer. Rosanne was born in Marseille in 1913, one of thirteen children but many of her siblings perished in the 'Spanish' flu after the First World War.

Louis and Rosanne were both practising Catholics and religious values and morality were important. Louis had been a chorister in one of the Catholic churches and they were both referred to as Jocistes, members of the young international Christian youth organisation JOCI (la Jeunesse Ouvrière Chrétienne Internationale). By 1935, they had left the family home and were established at an apartment on the second floor at 45 Rue Breteuil, very close to the Great Synagogue along the street at number 117. This was a more prosperous area and Louis was able to establish himself with a better clientele. Rosanne had studied couture after school and with a certificate of studies and an apprenticeship she found a good job in a large department store.

The 1930s were years of political instability in Marseille. The Yugoslav King was murdered in Marseille in October 1934 at the start of a state visit to France, by Bulgarian Vlado Chernozemski. In May 1936 the *Front populaire* (Popular Front) won the national elections. An alliance of left-wing movements, including the French Communist Party, brought Léon Blum to power, but its success was short-lived and despite many beneficial social achievements the coalition fell apart in 1937 as French politics stagnated in the face of the growing threat from Germany.

Because of a sight problem Louis had not been called up to the French Army but he was involved in practical action even before the fall of France in June 1940, when an Armistice agreement was signed by France and Germany. This set up the Vichy regime headed by Marshal Philippe Pétain which operated until November 1942, when the Germans and Italians occupied the zone until the Allied liberation in 1944. In 1940 Louis became concerned about conditions in the city. He had joined the Marseille City Council and was involved in groupings of artisans. At a meeting in the Romagnan apartment in the same year, an organisation called the Provencal Family was formed as a place of resistance and to provide support for people of Jewish origin.

By 1942, Louis and other members of the Provencal Family were sheltering Jews who had escaped from the camp at des Milles or from the various hostels in the city. Ura seems to have found a safe house out of the city but her hiding place was revealed by a collaborator to the Germans. Fortunately, she had a tip-off and was able to hide elsewhere but her remaining possessions were destroyed. At this time, she came to the attention of the Romagnans through a mutual contact in the person of Elie Pardigon, who was Director of the Family Allowance Fund and active in mutual aid networks such as the Association Economie et Humanisme in which the Romagnans were also involved. Louis and Rosanne agreed to Pardigon's request to employ Ura as their housekeeper. Indeed, someone who saw Ura on the stairs of the building had merely concluded that she was the nanny for the couple's four children, and it was long remembered that she had a good relationship with the Romagnan children. After the war Louis and Rosanne would tell their children about Ura's coming to the family home, during the winter of 1942-1943, as a simple act of Christian charity, a principle they followed throughout their lives.

When this became dangerous the arrangement was changed, and she became an employee of the Provencal Family working out of the Louis' rarely-used office in a separate part of the apartment. This was a very serious situation. Louis could not ignore that he should be informing the police and municipality that Ura was in his home. From July 1942 such activity was completely illegal and there were many informers against Jews in the locality. Renee Poznanski has emphasised in *Jews in France during World War II* just how dangerous this period, from November 1942 to February 1943, was for foreign-born Jews without French nationality. Ura spent Christmas of 1942 with the Romagnans but they were clearly concerned about the situation outside with its frequent round-ups. As Ura recalled:

> As long as I was in the house, everything was calm and I was safe, but it was impossible to always stay inside and once I got out, I was never sure I would be back. People were taken from the streets, shops and homes, for days and nights. When I was outside and didn't come back when I had to, I would find them running around looking for me. It was impossible to live such a life and it was decided that it was better that I leave for a safer place.

A major round-up in the Old Port had been carried out in January 1943 by French and German personnel. Rosanne at first had only been prepared to shelter Ura during the day to avoid the day-time patrols, but when she saw the effects of Ura sleeping rough she made up an attic room for her. The Old Port of Marseille was about to be destroyed on Himmler's orders to clear out any remaining illegals. Louis spoke out at the City Council about the destruction of the Old Port and of the restrictions being placed on his fellow artisans and the whole Council officially condemned an action of the German troops.

By February 1943 the situation was untenable. Ura told her hosts that if the police called, she would leave by the window. Plans had to be made for her to leave town. The first thought was for her to head for Nice where the Italian occupiers were not persecuting the Jews, and the Nazi presence there only began with the surrender of Italy to the Allies in September 1943. Given Ura's ability to speak French without a trace of a Russian accent, it was agreed that with good false identity papers she could survive outside Marseille. It is not clear whether she ever got to Nice, as it would only have been a few months before she had to move again, this time on foot to avoid the Germans who controlled the roads and railways.

Ura's letter suggests that she spent the last year of the war sheltered in a village after leaving Marseille, working initially as a cook then as a farm hand. The Romagnans believed that rather than reaching Nice she had sheltered in a rural area and then would have tried to leave the area when the Germans arrived. It was likely, they felt, that at this stage she would have tried to move from a village in the Nice area to one further north which might be much safer. She would also have had to consider distances, the terrain and the possibility of German patrols. Looking at the routes out of the area around Nice and considering the characteristics of the village described in her letter, the Romagnons considered that the small settlement of Braux, near Castellane, was a strong possibility.

Even there, life remained tense as German patrols continued, and she was constantly afraid of discovery. We have no idea of the location of this village although we do know that many Jews were sheltered in the Protestant village of Chambon-sur-Lignon, Haute Loire, accompanied there from Marseille by Ermine Orsi, an Italian Protestant and anarchist/antifascist. Emilie Guth, who had worked for OSE, had brought Jews to Switzerland or to villages in the Cevennes. The story of how the villagers of Chambon-sur-Ligne, but also other villages nearby, saved Jews from the concentration camps is told in Caroline Moorhead's *Village of Secrets: Defying the Nazis in Vichy France* (2014). The Huguenots of these villages knew their Bible well and had seen themselves as a persecuted people in Catholic France. Living in isolated communities, they were ready to extend a welcome to Jews on the run from the Nazis and their French collaborators. Moorhead's book does not mention Braux, so the precise place remains one of conjecture. Some of the residents of Chambon-sur-Ligne were arrested by the Gestapo but the people of the area saved up to 5,000 Jews from certain death.

I tend to believe that the evidence of the letter, which mentions mountains, suggests that Ura had been in the Cevennes. She describes German patrols searching the villages and then moving on. The advantages of sheltering in the hilly region is that patrols could be seen from some way off and it would be possible to hide in an area that the

Germans had passed through before returning to their shelter. It was, as she described, a nerve-wracking time. Ura worked for long hours as a cook but she was still not far from danger and she recorded that 'more than once we had to hide in the mountains during the night'. St. Martin-Vesubie in Alpes-Maritimes was also in high ground and Jews there were safe as long as it was under Italian occupation. When the Nazis arrived in November 1943 after the Italian surrender, a few Jews escaped over the mountains to Italy, but the rest were transported to Auschwitz-Birkenau. Ura would not have survived there. After the war she worked for a time in a hotel and then on a farm before she returned to Marseille 'broken physically and morally'.

Back in Marseille from February or March 1945, Ura came to visit the Romagnans. She worked as a waitress in a hotel until she had saved enough money to pay for passage on a boat from Marseille to Odessa. She noted that she had been happiest in her life while in Glasgow enjoying the companionship of her cousin Anna and she made the fateful decision to re-join Anna in Moscow (Anna's husband Iosif, Ura's brother, died during the war). Now almost 50 years old she could at last begin planning for the future. A major effort was beginning in Marseille to repatriate all the displaced persons making their way to the city. The recollection was that Ura had arrived at the Romagnan home, still at 45 rue Breteuil, dressed in combat gear, armed, accompanied by an officer. It therefore seems that Ura participated in the liberation of France and had possibly been a member of a resistance group in the last year of the war.

The letter to America, containing as it did the address of the Romagnan family, spurred an effort to try to locate Ura and to persuade her to join the family in Britain or America, or at least help her to return to a liberated Paris. Eric Mendoza tried to find her, but it was too late. Ura was in Marseille only long enough to reply to the letter from America and thank her aunt for the food parcel, but she was soon bound for Russia. The route of her travel is also not clear as she wrote that she would leave France accompanied by a Russian government official and might travel through Germany. It had always seemed that a boat from Marseille to Odessa was the likeliest option. As the family in Russia recalled she had indeed travelled to Odessa and was sheltered there by a family she knew. However, the arrangements did not work out and she persuaded Anna to invite her to come to Moscow to stay with her and Julius. This was problematic as there were special regulations related to living in Moscow and Ura did not have permission to reside in Moscow and did not even have a Soviet passport, having left the country in Tsarist times.

When Ura's letter appeared naming Rosanne Romagnon as her rescuer, cousins of Ura in Jerusalem, Zelman's daughter Lilian and her husband Eric Mendoza, made contact with the French Ambassador to Israel, Alain Pierett. Pierett, then contacted the Mayor of Marseille, Professor Robert Vigouroux, who in turn identified Rosanne Romagnan, living in Gignac-La-Nerthe, a residential area just a few miles north-east of Marseille. Rosanne received the Righteous Gentile award of Yad Vashem, the Holocaust Museum in Jerusalem, at a ceremony in Marseille on 18 June 1991. At the ceremony she said simply that she had only done 'what any good Christian would do, a normal human reaction to any distress'. Following the ceremony Rosanne and I corresponded for a while and she added further details about those desperate times, always acknowledging Ura's fortitude and style. Ura's letter was presented by its finder, Mervin Bruck, to the Yad Vashem archives, where it was listed as item 8298 in the Entry Book.

I was unable to attend the ceremony in Marseille, but Eric and Lilian Mendoza travelled from Israel and Mervin Bruck, whose mother-in-law Ida was a sister of Ura, came from America. After the ceremony, I wrote again to Rosanne Romagnan, and she replied immediately. In a further letter she confirmed that the contact with Ura had been made through Elie Pardigon, whose office for the Family Allocations Fund was adjacent to their apartment. She wrote that she had taken the initiative, seeing how Ura was being pursued by French and German police, and brought her into her home. She underlined that 'Je suis seule responsable de cette démarche.' ('I was solely responsible for this step') but clearly, she could have not sheltered Ura without the constant practical help of her husband. Indeed, he had taken the initiative in sheltering her. Rosanne said that what she did was not exceptional but was a normal response to someone in distress.

In December 1993, now aged 80 and with nine children and nineteen grandchildren, Rosanne sent me another letter. She told me that Ura had described to her the cultured and comfortable life she had enjoyed in Paris and in turn she described Ura was a 'femme libre', a smart woman who had been much diminished by her suffering although still able to display tenderness and love.

Given that Louis Romagnon had already passed away in 1975, the Mayor of Marseille, and his colleagues, requested the honour of Righteous Gentile only in Rosanne's name. Yad Vashem were prepared to award her the medal on the basis that her testimony matched the story that was in the letter. The family were shocked at the omission of Louis, who had been active in the resistance and in supporting Jews in distress. After all, she had been sheltered in his office and resided and worked in his home. Their son François decided to take action and managed to flesh out the story considerably. He began a detailed search for his father's work in the French Resistance pointing out that his father and the City Council had been exonerated from any accusation of complicity with the Nazis. He wondered if the Mayor had deliberately avoided rewarding his father because of some remaining suspicion of his wartime activities despite all the evidence to the contrary.

François was filling in the gaps of how Ura had survived in Vichy France, identifying her residence in Argeles and the Hotel Bompard, and the story of the Argentinian fiancé and visa. Armed with all his new information he contacted Laurent Fabius, a former French Foreign Minister, and many others in his quest to provide the honour to his father that he felt was due. He contacted Yad Vashem and asked them to re-open the file. He was quickly rebuffed and the department at Yad Vashem that deals with rescuers of Jews suggested that he should get some help from Ura's family to see if they had any additional information.

François had lost contact with the family members who had been at the ceremony in Marseille, but he had copies of letters I had sent to his mother. We had left our Giffnock home for Israel by this time and letters there were lost. François then tried a different tack, writing this time to the Glasgow City Council who forwarded the letter to the office of the Glasgow Jewish Representative Council asking them to send on the message to me. He had supplied an email address and we were soon in touch. He asked me as a relative of Ura for my assistance and I agreed to his request. I contacted Irena Steinfeldt, Director, Righteous Among the Nations Department, at Yad Vashem, who explained that the special Autonomous Commission which decides these matters relies on first-hand testimonies of the persons that were rescued and on primary archival documents of the period of the Shoah. The Commission's rules stipulate that a case can be resubmitted only when there are testimonies of the helped person or archival documents that shed a new light on the case. She concluded that even though there was sympathy for the family arguments, they had to abide by the decisions of the Commission for the Designation of the Righteous. Yad Vashem considered the case was closed, and François's frustrations persisted. For him and the Romagnan family both Louis and Rosanne were *Benemeriti*, a term that Italians use when describing those who helped Jews during the war.

Report in local Marseille newspaper of the Righteous Gentile Award to Rosanne Romagnan, June 1991.

While his researches did not convince Yad Vashem to recognize his father as a Righteous Gentile, François received many positive comments. The Archbishop of Marseille, George Pontier, paid tribute to him and those involved with the Provencal Family for their testimony and their courage, making them the pride of the diocese and of the city. Moreover, Jean-Claude Gaudin, the Mayor of Marseille from 1995-2020, recognized that Rosanne's actions could not be dissociated from that of her husband, implying that both should have received the award. Gaudin served also in the French National Assembly and later the Senate and was a government Minister from 1995-1997.

Finally President Jacques Chirac and Madame Simone Veil paid tribute to Louis and his colleagues who 'embodied the honour of France, its values of justice, tolerance and humanity'. Without François' painstaking work, so many details of Ura's life in France would have been lost, and we would not know of his father's services for France during the war.

The post-war era was not a good time for a 'westerner' to arrive in Russia. It was the height of Stalinist paranoia and all those with links to the west were seen as subversive elements, even those like Ura who naively believed that the membership card of the French Communist Party would guarantee her safety. Further, Stalin's campaign against rootless cosmopolitans, a thinly-disguised attack on Russia's Jews, caught many thousands of people like Ura. Her arrival posed a dilemma for Anna, herself a returnee from the West, albeit some twenty years earlier. To live in Moscow required a residence permit which Ura found was not forthcoming. She was even unable to obtain a Soviet internal passport despite having been born in the Ukraine. Ura had arrived in an unwelcoming Moscow.

Anna would have wanted to help Ura more but not at the risk of her own security and that of her student son Julius. Indeed, this was a real danger. Anna herself was dismissed from her job at the Moscow State University during the antisemitic 'Cosmopolitan' campaign which ran from 1949 to 1952. Ura had not long arrived at Anna's when she was visited by the KGB, who described her as an 'unwelcome visitor' and undertook to relocate her to Tashkent in Central Asia. Trusted Soviet agents who had operated in the West faced two risks to their lives: being shot by the enemy or sent to the Gulag on return to Russia. Simple survival was an achievement. From Moscow Ura's trail goes cold. Anna received a communication in 1949 to say that Ura had died, aged only 54 years, although there was a feeling that she may have survived for a few more years.

There had been other avenues besides a return to Russia which were open to her. She could have made for Britain where the family was ready to welcome her. Palestine was also an option as boats of the clandestine *aliya bet,* which tried to get past the British Mandatory restrictions on Jewish immigration, were sailing from Marseille. It was the prospect of renewing her friendship with her cousin (and sister-in-law) Anna in Moscow which clinched the decision to head east.

What then are we to make of Ura's tragic life and her ability to make mistakes with major decisions in her life? She could have returned to Britain in 1939, or again in 1945. We have already commented on how Benno Schotz could see through her into the future when he titled his sculpture *Ura the Exile: a Russian Émigrée who had Lost her Roots.* But Ura was not the only one to have had such a trajectory: Her life-path was from Ukraine to France, Scotland, Palestine, France and finally the Soviet Union. The journey through Eastern Europe to Palestine and then France was not unusual. One startling example was laid out by Leopold Trepper in his *The Great Game: the Story of the Red Orchestra* (London, 1977). Trepper had been the leading figure in the Red Orchestra, a network of Communist agents, risking their lives every day to sabotage the Nazi war effort and send vital information to headquarters in Moscow. The story shows how the agents faced death daily. The majority were captured, tortured and executed by the Nazis, and the few survivors were cruelly betrayed by Stalin's Soviet Union, betrayed by the Communism they had believed in.

I am not suggesting that Ura spied for the Soviet Union during the Second World War. It is highly unlikely that she had access to the radio transmitters which were sending vital information about Nazi activity to Moscow. However, there were Red Orchestra agents in both Occupied and Vichy France who would have needed information from people on the ground. Could her experiences in Vichy France have given her the opportunity to be of use to the spy network? There are just two indications in support of this theory. First there was her arrival back at the Romagnans' at the end of the war in military uniform, suggesting an active role in the Resistance. Secondly, was the fact that she had not initially planned to travel back to Russia on her own but thought that she would be travelling in the company of a Russian government official. If she thought that would guarantee her safety on her return, she was very much mistaken.

Trepper himself had been born in 1904 in Galicia, a part of Poland then ruled by the Austro-Hungarian Empire. He had been attracted to the left-wing Zionism of the pioneering Hashomer HaTzair group and was in Palestine from April 1924 to the end of 1929. Besides his back-breaking agricultural work, he involved himself increasingly in the work of the Palestine Communist Party and spent some time in jail as a political agitator. Many other left-wing Jews had left Palestine at the same time. Ura had left in 1927. Like Trepper she had gone directly to France, while the others who identified ideologically with Communism returned to Russia, where suspicion of foreigners, especially those who had lived in the British protectorate, was already on the rise. Most of these idealists were 'purged', and even those who took the challenge of settling in Russia's attempt to create a Jewish utopia in Birobidzhan in Eastern Siberia fared no better. Trepper graphically described the fate of those who chose to come to Moscow for Communist indoctrination in Moscow:

> At night in our university, where militants from all countries were living, we used to stay awake till three in the morning. At exactly that hour, headlights would pierce the darkness and sweep over the facades of the building… Standing at the windows, stomachs knotted with insane terror, we would watch for the cars of the NKVD to stop.

Another young woman who had been active in Hashomer Hatzair in Poland was born into a comfortable family in Lódz in 1906. Zosha Poznanska had settled in Palestine in 1925, but ultimately left, disillusioned with life in what she saw as a British colony. She had been a member of the Palestine Communist Party and had been recruited by Trepper when she was in France. She was an active codifier sending classified information to Moscow, but she was captured in December 1941 and on 28 September 1942 she hanged herself in her cell, remaining silent to the end. The State of Israel awarded her a posthumous decoration as a fighter against the Nazis. Her story was told in Yehudit Kafri's book, published in Hebrew in Jerusalem in 2003, *Zosha: From the Jezreel Valley to the Red Orchestra*. These life journeys match that of Ura.

Ura had lived a comfortable life at home, then with Shimmel in Paris and with the Collins brothers in Glasgow. When she came to Palestine there was a family network with her father, two married sisters and a younger brother. She had not endured the privations experienced by Trepper and his friends trying to establish themselves in France, but she had aligned herself with the French Communist Party which could still command mass support with millions of voters until comparatively recent times. When Trepper finally returned to Moscow in early 1945 after the liberation of France he expected acknowledgement, at the very least, for all his dedicated work for the Soviet Union. We don't know what Ura's 'resettlement' in Russia involved. Was she deported to Central Asia or imprisoned in Moscow and sent to the gulag where she perished? We may never know.

Trepper was to be rewarded with years of imprisonment, both in Lubyanka and Lefortovo. It was not until 1954, after the death of Stalin, that the charges against him of treachery and espionage against the Soviet Union were held to be false. He was rehabilitated and allowed to join his family after almost a decade in jail and to return to Poland, where he had a leading role in the small post-war Jewish community. Trepper came to Israel in 1974 where he died in 1982. Ura did not live long enough to enjoy such freedom.

5

The Russians

The Russian Revolution of 1917 and the chaos of the Civil War did not spell the end of Kagarlitsky family life in Russia. Although Zev and three of his children, Ida, Motti and Clara, had left for Palestine and Zelman was soon to leave for London, there were many family members making their new way in the Soviet Union. They would be joined by Anna and Iosef who would return to spend their lives in Moscow, where a significant family presence was being established. The family tree contains the names of many other cousins and more distant relations who spent their lives in the Soviet Union, although many of them were to leave for Israel and America as conditions permitted from the 1970s. Many of these were the descendants of Zev's brother Asher, whose son Tevye, the manager of a chemical fertilizer plant, was regarded as the head of the family in Russia until his death in the 1980s. Tevye's sister Lily had migrated, as a teenager, to the United States in 1913 and for many years I carried on a correspondence with Lily's son Sam Altschuler who was a ready source of information about the family in Russia.

One of his cousins, Anya, had fallen foul of the Tsarist authorities for her left-wing views and had been exiled to Siberia. Freed after the Revolution she became a translator, famously working for Kliment Voroshilov, a prominent Soviet military officer and politician during the Stalin era who held the rank of Marshal, the highest of the Soviet Union. Another cousin, Alex, had been sent to the labour camp close to the port city of Magadan in the Soviet Far East. It had been founded in 1930 and was a major transit centre of a vast and brutal gold-mining and forced labour camp system. The town gradually developed a port for exporting gold and other metals mined in the Kolyma region and in the 2010 Census had a population of 95,000. Alex settled there after his release, as did many other former gulag prisoners. A third cousin, Arkady, had managed to leave Moscow for New York in 1979 with his wife Mira and son Alex. Arkady had been a dentist in Moscow but set up successfully as a dental technician in New York. During a visit back to Russia, after he had obtained American citizenship, Arkady had wanted to entertain relatives and friends with food and drinks. As the shops were bare, he contacted a former patient who was a well-known Party official, and a deal was made. Arkady would perform some free dental treatment, American style, while the Party official would organize the food.

Alex, who told us this story, was to visit us in Glasgow over a weekend in 1989 when my mother and two of my aunts were still alive. He was then a law student in Boston and was already a very impressive young man with what seemed like a very successful international law career ahead of him. He told us of his first years in Moscow and his time at the High School programme run for Russian immigrants by Yeshiva University. He charmed all the family members he met and it was a sense of total sadness and almost unbelief when we learned that he had been killed in a car crash on a visit back to Moscow just a year later. Arkady and Mira were devastated.

Sam Altschuler also recorded frequent marriages within the extended family network. Thus, there were three marriages between Kagarlitskys and Listvoibs and their descendants live today in Russia and America. Tevye's younger brother Moisei (Maurice) married Fanny Listvoib. He left Russia to study medicine in France, and when the Russians attempted to recall him to the army in 1916 he moved on to the United States and transferred to veterinary medicine, studying at Ohio State University. Returning to Russia after graduation he entered the veterinary service in Tbilisi, Georgia becoming head of its Veterinary Institute. During problems within the livestock industry, he was accused of sabotage in 1941 and had to confess to crimes he had not committed in order to save his wife and children. He died a victim of Stalin's purges but was posthumously rehabilitated under Khrushchev. His wife and children were left destitute and lived for many years under the cloud of the accusations. His descendants today still live in Moscow, leading, I believe, successful lives.

By the time of the Revolution in November 1917 my grandfather and his full brothers, Shimmel, Sam and Shuka, were in Glasgow, Winston-Salem and Buenos Aires. The one sister by Zev's first marriage, Reysie (Raisa), had a different story. She was born in Kovshevata in 1875 and married Moyshe Briskman in January 1895. Her story will be told in a later chapter. Iosef Kagarlitsky, my grandfather's half-brother, served in the Russian Army during the First World War. He took part in the February Revolution which brought Kerensky to power and seems to have been elected to the chair of a soldiers' revolutionary group. These were dangerous times and Iosef had to look out for the welfare of his group members. He was elected to the first Congress of Soviets in the spring of 1917 on the Menshevik list.

Before the November Revolution he left Russia, greatly concerned with the deteriorating conditions in the Russian Army. As the war with Germany was still waging, he moved east to China settling first in Harbin and subsequently in Shanghai. There he was employed by an English company and his thought was to marry Anna in London, where she was living after having left Glasgow. Anna had arrived to study in Glasgow in 1912 around the time that my grandparents settled there and her college certificates refer to her as Anna Collins. She remained in Glasgow for a while after the war ended before moving to London. Working there, Anna set up her own workshop copying the latest fashion items she had seen in the expensive West End stores. These were produced for a fraction of the price of the originals. The practice of companies producing cheap imitations of high fashion endures today. Anna and Iosef had been separated for ten years before Iosef travelled west and Anna came east to marry in Moscow.

Motti had pleaded with Anna not to return to Moscow. He had lived through the Revolution and the Civil War before reaching Palestine and he knew just how desperate the situation was in Russia. In a frank letter written from Jerusalem in November 1921, he told her that her 'reasons for the move are deeply upsetting' and that her possessions would be stolen, unless she could prove that these had been charitable donations for her to dispose of at her discretion. The warnings were clear and stark, but Anna was not interested.

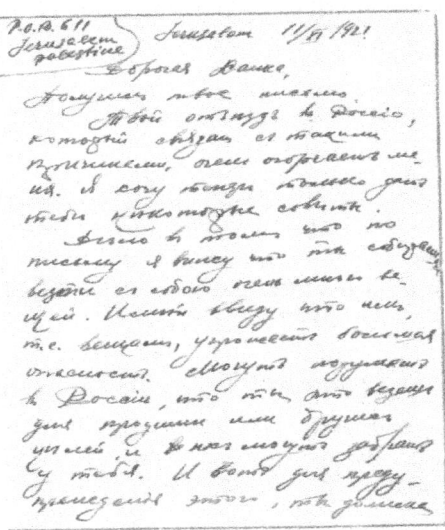

First page of Motti's letter to Anna sent from Jerusalem prior to her departure for Moscow.

Anna insisted on the move to Moscow, which she defended on ideological reasons although family members felt that there were other motives too. Her sister Evgenia had remained in Moscow and she wanted to be near her to tell of their experiences in China and Britain. This might have seemed quite exotic at the time, although later it would have added a touch of danger. Their lives and families abroad, and Iosef's activities with the Mensheviks, could have led them into serious trouble with the authorities but they never suffered the persecution that many others in similar circumstances endured. However, they did suffer from the petty antisemitism which pervaded Soviet life, involving university study, work prospects and social attitudes. Anna lost her job at the Moscow State University in 1949, during the years of Stalin's anti-Jewish paranoia, when many leading Jewish intellectuals were killed or imprisoned in the notorious gulag camps. Fortunately, she soon found new employment being especially skilled as an English-Russian translator.

In Glasgow Anna was friendly with Manya Taylor, known in her younger days as 'Red Manya'. They would have been regulars at the Workers' Circle, a social and political club for the Jewish immigrants situated above a small bakery. This was close to the family's first home in Glasgow in Oxford Street and here there were books and pamphlets written by socialists and anarchists. The pictures on the wall were of Kropotkin, Marx and Proudhon. When Anna made the decision to marry her cousin Iosef, then working for a British company in Shanghai, it may not have been too surprising that she would want to set up home in Moscow. Conditions in Russia seemed to be settling with the New Economic Policy, and a number of Jews with left-wing leanings were returning to share in the prospects that the brave new society was offering.

Anna was to fare much better than Flora Leipman, who endured many years in notorious prison camps after her mother and stepfather took the family back to Russia in 1932. Flora had been born in Glasgow in 1918 and was fourteen when she arrived in Leningrad. It took the intervention of the British Foreign Secretary Geoffrey Howe to negotiate her return to Britain in 1984, allowing to her to visit Glasgow to stand by her father's grave. A cemetery worker told her that her brother had visited recently, having reached America after escaping from the gulag, traipsing through Siberia and stowing away on a ship bound for California. She had no idea that he was still alive. They were to have a very emotional reunion. Ralph Glasser, in his *Growing up in the Gorbals* (1986), recalled the Varnett family who left the Gorbals in Glasgow with great fanfare to return to Russia in 1924 and despite letters and official enquiries were never heard of again.

Fortunately, despite Stalinist repression, suspicion of those who had returned from the West and institutional anti-Semitism, Anna survived in Moscow into advanced old age. She even managed to keep in regular postal communication with the family in Glasgow and kept abreast of family developments and maintained a collection of family photographs. Concerned about conditions in Moscow, Solomon managed a trip to Russia in 1934, ostensibly as part of a small Scottish textile trade delegation with a member of the Scottish Co-operative Wholesale Society. Anna's son Julius was eight years old at the time and during a visit to Glasgow 50 years later he recalled it, and the gifts from Glasgow, as one of the highlights of his childhood.

The family outside the Soviet Union were well aware of the dangers posed by Stalin to its Jews. Glasgow, like many other Jewish communities in Britain and North America, had welcomed the Director of the Moscow State Jewish Theatre, Solomon Mikhoels, and the poet, Itsik Fefer, in 1943 as they raised funds for the Soviet war effort. Their Jewish warmth impressed but the manner of their deaths left a permanent bitter taste and could never be forgiven. Mikhoels was killed in Minsk by security agents who staged the murder as a car accident and Fefer was executed on the infamous 'Night of the Murdered Poets' on 12 August 1952. My grandfather pondered the idea of visiting Moscow after the war but was warned that it was just too dangerous.

Julius Kagarlitsky

Their son Julius experienced more difficulty because of his background. As a Jew he failed to get into post-graduate studies in Moscow. The only work opening following his first degree he found was in Chita, in eastern Siberia. Later, he moved to Gorky (Nizhny Novgorod), and only finally re-joined his wife when he returned to Moscow, where his main research and teaching was carried out. By 1960 Julius and his wife, Raisa Pomerantseva, were well settled in Moscow and his son Boris remembered the decade as a good time for the Soviet state when the Kagarlitsky family in Moscow felt at ease in what he described as 'an intellectual family'. Raisa, later a well-known translator of English literature, was fortunate in obtaining a position as a post graduate student (аспирант or 'aspirant' in Russian) at Moscow

State University. Although her own family suffered from repression her Russian origin gave her certain advantages.

I became aware of Julius Kagarlitsky, not just an expert on H.G. Wells but someone who had published widely on science fiction, when a translation of his work on Wells was published in 1966. I immediately contacted the publisher who informed me that Julius was aware of his family in Glasgow and would welcome contact. I never heard any more and was later surprised to learn that he had visited Glasgow in the 1950s on an academic visit, staying with Peter Henry, the first holder of the Chair of Slavonic Language and Literature at the university. Henry lived in Glasgow's West End near the university and the two men discovered common links in their backgrounds of Jews living in a very non-Jewish milieu. Julius made no attempt to contact his aunts and uncles and cousins, perhaps worried about the consequences for himself and his family back in Moscow given that he had required a special exemption in his visa as a Soviet citizen travelling so far from London. He may even have been unsure about how to contact the family members he had long since lost touch with.

Julius made another visit to Glasgow, again staying with Peter Henry, in April 1987 following his visit to London at the invitation of the Wells Society. I arranged to collect him from Henry's home and bring him to us for a meal and to meet, as he said lapsing into Yiddish as he did frequently with us, with the *mishpucha*, family. Most of his cousins were there and we had an interesting evening as he told us that my grandfather's visit to Moscow in 1934 had been the highlight of his childhood. My grandfather had brought a selection of clothing from his factory, ostensibly making the trip a business affair. The clothes were left with Julius's parents and the Scottish boys' clothes clearly made a big impression.

However, the evening did not go so well. Perhaps Julius was tired. Perhaps the Glasgow family expected a more emotional response from such a long lost relative. Perhaps Julius expected the gifts that usually go with family reunions. However, the following evening we arranged a gathering of Russian Jewish émigrés which included Alec Nove, who was delighted to see that Julius had brought a bottle of the best Georgian brandy. Julius and Alec had attended the performance of a contemporary Russian play, in English translation, at the experimental Tron Theatre before arriving at our home, and the experience led to the two men, especially after imbibing some of the brandy, to reflect on the experiences of Jewish academics in Moscow and Glasgow. Nove was the son of Jacob Novakovsky, who had been a Menshevik like Julius' father and had, as we have seen, known members of the Kagarlitsky family in London where his father and Zelman had been in a similar line of business.

Alec Nove was born in St. Petersburg in 1914 but his family came to London when he was eight years old. His father, Jacob, had moved the family to London in 1922, working for a Dutch company importing goods from Russia just as Zelman was doing. Alec completed his education in London. He graduated with a BSc in Economics from the London School of Economics and worked in British military intelligence during the war. From 1947 to 1958 he was a civil servant, based in Glasgow, tasked with producing reports on the economic situation in the Soviet Union. He then returned to a university post in London for a few years before he was appointed Professor of Economics at the University of Glasgow and was Director of its Institute for Soviet and East European Studies. By the time I first met him, at an address he gave in 1966 to Jewish students about the situation of the Jews in the Soviet Union, he had already published two influential books, *The Soviet Economy* (1961) and *Was Stalin Really Necessary?* (1965).

During the day I had taken Julius to visit the recently-opened Scottish Jewish Archives Centre, of which I was joint founder and chairman. Parking was, as always, difficult around the Centre at the Garnethill Synagogue, situated at the top of a very steep hill. It was then that I realised that Julius had serious problems with angina as he popped one tablet after another under his tongue as we climbed the very steep Garnet Street to our destination. We met with the archivist Ben Braber and Julius expressed his amazement that a non-Jew could have such a devoted interest in Jewish studies.

Julius's problems with angina came back to me some months later when he wrote, from Moscow, that he was having prostate problems and that he needed surgery. However, he did not trust the hospital that he had access to, given his additional problem with angina, as the best hospital was only available to the *nomenklatura*. This group included leading bureaucrats and leading figures in the government, party, industry and education, but not college experts in science fiction. He asked if the operation could be done in Glasgow. I consulted with a urologist colleague who suggested that we should see an ECG before making a decision.

The ECG duly arrived from Moscow and it indicated a pattern of very severe ischaemic heart disease. The urologist indicated that prostatectomy would be risky and that it would be best if it was done only after cardiac surgery had been performed. He asked if there was anyone in Scotland who could provide post-operative care, especially if surgery provoked a heart attack or a stroke. I had to inform Julius that we had reached an impasse. However, Julius was soon able to sort out the problem for himself. He had been invited to a lecture tour of American universities and while in Washington he developed prolonged chest pain. It was clear that he was having a heart attack and was taken to George Washington Hospital and its prestigious cardiac surgery department. They quoted an astronomical figure for surgical treatment but on learning of the reason for Julius's visit to America they agreed to operate without charge in honour of *glasnost* and *perestroika*. Julius then asked if they could they do his prostate too? They could! He returned to Russia with a new lease of life, and actually remarried (his first wife Raisa had died in 1989). He contacted me about another visit to Glasgow, this time with his new wife but we were abroad at the projected time of his visit and we never met again. We were to meet Svetlana, now a widow, on our visit to Moscow in 2014.

Julius' literary career was centred around the academic study of science fiction, and in particular of the works of H.G. Wells, but I was intrigued to discover that he considered David Daiches to be his 'teacher' of English literature. Daiches was for many years Professor of English Literature at the University of Sussex but was also the son of the Edinburgh Rabbi, Salis Daiches. Daiches' work *Two Worlds: an Edinburgh Jewish Childhood* (1956) has been a constant favourite of mine. Daiches had shown that he lived in the two worlds of Scottishness and Jewishness simultaneously, completely at home in both. Julius had said that he would have been proud for Daiches to have known of the effect he had on him.

His choice of specialisation was to bring Julius international recognition and the ability to make a number of significant trips abroad. In a perceptive book review by Margaret Ferry in *Science Fiction Studies* of Julius' *What is Science Fiction?* (что такое научная фантастика?), published in Moscow in 1975, she addresses the author's concerns about the conflicts inherent in the genre, describing his approach as of 'popularizing intention... pleasingly fused with solid erudition'. She notes how Julius considers that science fiction is based on the 'dialectics of the investigative mind' and reveals the way in which Julius gives consideration to the social bases of, mainly, British and American writers of science fiction. Ferry saw in his writings that he considered that the pessimism of contemporary science fiction writers as a 'function of limiting themselves to progress only along the lines of bourgeois materialistic societies'. Julius was careful in the society of his time not to step outside Marxist norms. However, as Karen Rosenberg wrote for *Index on Censorship* in 1988:

Soviet science fiction of the post-Stalin era provided a great way of beating the censor as themes that wouldn't have been acceptable if set in the modern-day USSR passed scrutiny when the characters were aliens of the future. Soviet readers said this in private; critics in the West printed it; and you can be sure the censors, too, soon knew it perfectly well.

The censors would try to ensure that writers did not overstep the boundaries, but here was a field where writers could tackle controversial topics with a reasonable degree of confidence. The more relaxed era following *glasnost* meant that the subterfuge was no longer required, and the euphemisms employed by writers were no longer needed. Not that greater openness means the demise of euphemisms or of editorial gate-keeping, but it may make the circumlocutions and allusions of much Soviet science fiction seem timid and dated. Newspapers and journals suddenly became riveting in the Gorbachev era. 'Some two years ago, almost no one read them, but now they take so much time that it's hard to read outside of one's speciality', Julius told Rosenberg, on her visit to Russia in 1998, that:

> There was a period when science fiction was the leader in literary developments, but, at the moment, I don't know any serious people who are science-fiction addicts. It has dropped to the status of children's literature.

The demise of critical science fiction may have been premature as writers have continued to stretch the bounds of the possible in Putin's Russia.

Much of Julius' career in the field of literary science fiction studies has been covered by Patrick Parrinder of the University of Reading, in the journal *Science Fiction Studies*. He recalled that Moura Budberg's translation of Julius's *Herbert Wells* (Moscow, 1963) was greeted by one of its British reviewers as a 'sign of the times' reflecting the climate of de-Stalinization and short-lived ideological *rapprochement* in the Cold War. In her Foreword to the English translation, which appeared as *The Life and Thought of H.G. Wells*, she wrote:

> As I have gone through the always reverent, often critical, sometimes naïve pages, it has occurred to me how much H.G. would have approved of the author, with his determination, intelligence, and

courage. H.G. would have been delighted to read this painstaking, if controversial, study of his work.

The reviewer, Maurice Richardson, concluded that 'You can learn a lot from this book.' Parrinder described Julius, then a senior lecturer at the Moscow State Institute of Theatrical Art, as writing 'as an undoctrinaire Marxist'. Parrinder had been in correspondence with Julius since the 1970s but had not actually met him until 1987 when, as he clearly sensed, the Soviet experiment was almost at its end. As Parrinder noted, the importance of the book lay in the author's experience of living through the Stalin years.

Julius had enhanced the Russian original for the English edition and, in his Preface, he quoted a review from the Moscow periodical *Novi Mir* which had said that:

> Kagarlitsky's book on Wells reads like a tragedy where the stage is our century and the main character [is] Wells' conception of the world; we are the audience that anxiously watches the vicissitudes of this intellectual tragedy.

Wells had been incredibly popular in Russian and sales of his works reached a million copies. Julius had helped in the preparation of a two-volume edition of Wells' selected works in 1956. In 1964 he was the editor of a fifteen-volume edition and he remarked that Wells' popularity in Russia had not diminished. In 1972 Julius was the third recipient of the Pilgrim Award, which is presented annually by the Science Fiction Research Association for Lifetime Achievement in the field of science fiction scholarship. The award was created in 1970 and named after J.O. Bailey's pioneering book *Pilgrims Through Space and Time*. Fittingly, Bailey received the first award. Julius was able to attend the Science Fiction Conference *La Fantascienza e la Critica* which was held in Palermo, Italy, in October 1978.

On 2 November 1983, the Moscow correspondent of the London *Times* reported that Professor Julius Kagarlitsky had been 'arraigned' before a disciplinary panel at the Lunacharsky Theatrical Institute and removed from his post. Sources said the move was linked to 'dissident activities on the part of Professor Kagarlitsky's son, Boris', who was part of a 'new left' discussion group criticizing Soviet society from a Marxist standpoint. Since then, Julius had been unable to travel abroad. The *Times Literary Supplement* reported that his permission to attend the International H.G.

Wells Symposium in London in July 1986 had been withdrawn at the last moment. The threat to his position had been known to colleagues in the West for some time and they had found the story perplexing especially as Boris, who had been held by the KGB for several months, was released without trial in the spring of 1983.

Parrinder called on *Science Fiction Studies* readers to make known their feelings about this case, which he considered 'deals a devastating blow to Soviet scholarship and criticism in our field'. He noted that 'experience has shown that the Soviet authorities are swayed by international criticism of their actions' and hoped that 'the victimization of Professor Kagarlitsky will be lifted, and that he will be promptly reinstated in his post'. However, change was happening in the Soviet Union. Mikhail Gorbachev became General Secretary of the Communist Party in 1985. After the Chernobyl nuclear disaster in 1986 he committed the country to more openness (*glasnost*) and a restructuring of the economy (*perestroika*). The new atmosphere helped Julius to come to London for a visit in April 1987 at the invitation of the Wells Society (of which he was a Vice President) and with the assistance of the British Council and the Soviet Writers' Union. His concluding remarks in the conference book of proceedings was that Wells has always been admired and needed in Russia as 'a country with such strong social dynamics'. During this trip he took advantage of the opportunity to visit Glasgow.

At a well-attended meeting, he read the paper he had intended to give at the previous year's symposium, and it was reported that he held his listeners spellbound with an extempore account of Wells' reception in the USSR, ranging from pre-revolutionary times to the circumstances surrounding his collected edition of Wells in Russian and his critical book *The Life and Thought of H.G. Wells* which had been published in English in 1966. In 1988 he completed a fictionalized biography of Wells and a review of recent Wells studies scheduled to appear in *Voprosy Literatury*.

Galya Diment was the editor of *H.G. Wells and All Things Russian* (2019) which was published by Anthem Books, Cambridge, 2019. Parrinder contributed a chapter entitled 'Yuly (Julius) Kagarlitsky's Life of Wells' and a translation of Julius's article on 'Being a Soviet Biographer' appeared in the book's Appendix. Julius had an article which had been written in 1998, published in the translation of H.G. Wells' *Experiment in Autobiography*, but it only appeared in 2007, some seven years after his death. Julius related that he had been taught German in school but 'very much wanted to read a few [of] the English-language books that we had'. He had to persuade his mother to teach him the language, as at the time she was teaching at the College of Oil and Gas and later at the Moscow State University. At first she did not want to be busy in the same way at home but she soon gave in. Anna's home teaching proved successful and he began to read in English, encountering H.G. Wells in an abridged and adapted series suitable for young readers, but not yet finding his science fiction material.

Julius wrote that he had not been expressing an abstract and irrefutable 'Marxist point of view' but was writing as someone who is:

> ... a husband and a father, who has lived almost permanently in Moscow, the Moscow of 1948, '53, '56, '64 – in other words a real man, a citizen who, like millions of others, has happened to meditate on life, on men, on the times we live in... I have already mentioned that one of the people who have most helped my understanding of life was Wells. Alongside this, life's experience and my belief in the rightness of Marxism have helped me to form my own opinion... But the years went by and science confirmed again and again that Wells' direction had been the right one. Some of his characters' thoughts seemed to have been artificially planted in their heads by the author. But after a lapse of time writers began to credit their characters more and more often with the very same thoughts, this time taken from life.

Boris Kagarlitsky

Manya (Zam) Taylor, Anna's Marxist friend from her Glasgow days, spent her last years in the Jewish Old Age Home in Pollokshields in the late 1980s. She still remembered Anna well and knew that she had returned to Russia to marry her fiancé. She was intrigued to learn that Anna's grandson, Boris, was visiting Glasgow and that he was keen to meet with her. This would have been in 1988, when Boris was in London to collect the Isaac Deutscher Memorial Prize for his early writings on the changes in the Soviet State created by *glasnost* and the new leadership in the country. After the conversation, in Russian, was concluded I asked Boris what he and Manya had talked about. He said that Manya had asked him why his grandmother had left Glasgow for Moscow; he had just answered that 'it was a mistake'.

Boris came to Glasgow on the night sleeper from London accompanied by his wife Irena and their young son Goscha. Travel out of Russia was still strictly controlled and it was unusual for someone who had expressed dissident views and spent some time in Lefortovo Prison to be allowed to leave the country with his family. Perhaps the authorities were hoping that they might not return! On the Saturday evening before their arrival, I had just returned to our street from the end of Shabbat services in the synagogue when I noticed someone lingering outside. When I entered the house, Irene expressed her concerns about the man who was wandering in the street, explaining that he had been there for some time and she was worried that the KGB had caught up with our expected guests.

A few minutes later the doorbell rang, and our visitor introduced himself as a member of the local Fabian Society and they were desperate to hear from Boris, who was becoming well known as a Marxist writer and journalist, about the evolving situation in the Soviet Union. He knew that Boris had been in London to collect the award and Boris's English publishers told him that Boris was taking some time out with family in Glasgow before returning to Moscow. This caused some puzzlement to the Glasgow Fabians, as a visit to Glasgow by such a proponent of democratic socialism could only be to people of like minds, such as their

The author with Boris and Goscha Kagarlitsky at Newark Lodge (the Jewish Old Age Home for Scotland), Glasgow, 1988.

Society or perhaps an academic department at the University of Glasgow. There, our visitor had a major stroke of luck. He had contacted Alec Nove, who had been a guest in our home at the time of Julius' visit a couple of years before. Nove said that if Boris was visiting family he would be with us in Giffnock and he explained how to be in touch. The mystery was solved.

One of the highlights of their visit was a family wedding. The bride's mother, Gloria, and I were both second cousins of Boris and the local family was thrilled and enchanted by their visitors from Russia. Boris said that he hadn't realized just how many relatives he had. Rabbi Fletcher had offered to perform a Jewish wedding for Boris and Irena at the Queen's Park Synagogue immediately after guests were leaving for the celebratory function at Carmichael Hall in Eastwood Park. We had to point out that while Irena's mother was Jewish, that of Boris was not, so that by halachic standards he could not have an Orthodox synagogue wedding. Besides visiting Manya, we showed Boris the areas of Glasgow that his grandmother would have known although most of the key buildings in the Gorbals had long been demolished.

During these years Boris became well known in Britain, becoming a favourite commentator on BBC radio and television as the Gorbachev era progressed, then ended, to be followed by the Yeltsin years. His early experiences as a dissident earned him eighteen months in the Lefortovo Prison in 1982 and 1983, having been arrested three times, twice under Brezhnev and once under Yeltsin. When he visited Scotland we took him to see Edinburgh Castle. When we entered the eighteenth-century dungeons, he commented that it reminded him of Lefortovo. However, conditions in Lefortovo were not so bad. Boris acknowledged, in an interview for an on-line Jewish magazine, that the conditions were 'quite humane' and that the food was 'pretty tolerable'.

As political prisoners could meet with imprisoned business people, Boris learned much about the Soviet economy and developed his own views on what he felt had to change. With the rise of *perestroika*, he was able to return to his studies at the State Institute of Theatrical Art in 1988 and two years later, just after his visit to Glasgow, he was elected to the Moscow City Soviet and then to the Executive of the Socialist Party of Russia. His arrest during the constitutional crisis during Yeltsin's leadership led to international protests and he was released the next day. Boris was again detained by the authorities in Moscow on 15 July 2020 after participating in a protest concerning the official, and disputed, results of Putin's constitutional plebiscite.

Boris's wife Irena also comes from a cultural family. Her uncle, Leonid Genrikhovich Zorin (1924-2020), was a Russian Jewish playwright. He was born in Baku and studied at the Azerbaijan University and at the Maxim Gorky Literature Institute in Moscow. He was author of numerous plays and screenplays and is best known for his most performed work, *A Warsaw Melody* (1967). Her cousin Andrey Zorin is Professor of Russian and Fellow of New College, Oxford University, researching Russian Literature and Culture of the eighteenth and early nineteenth centuries. His Ph.D is from Moscow State University and he has an MA from Oxford.

Boris has an impressive literary output. I had bought a copy of his *The Thinking Reed: Intellectuals and the Soviet State from 1917 to the Present* when it was published in 1988 and he was delighted to see it on my bookshelves when he visited. He didn't take long to figure out an appropriate message in writing 'from Kagarlitsky to Collins' – very apt and quite symbolic. Many other titles followed charting the course of Russia's grappling with new economic and political realities. Titles included *The Dialectic of Change* (1989), *Square Wheels: How Russian Democracy Got Derailed* (1995) and *Back in the USSR* (2009), where he notes that the leadership, in twenty post-Communism years had not created a new national ideology.

Boris has considered that the West is wrong to see President Putin and his entourage as the enemies, seeing them as economically liberal and pro-Western. An article in the *Sunday Times* in October 2016 mentioned Boris in an article about Jeremy Corbyn's links to the hard-left group Stop the War, named by a Kremlin-funded organization as its UK partner. Stop the War was said to have close links with the Institute of Globalisation and Social Movements of which Boris is the Director. Boris was angered by the article but reckoned it would be futile to take action against the newspaper. Indeed, Boris has spoken at rallies in the presence of Corbyn, widely criticised for presiding over an atmosphere of antisemitism in the British Labour Party, which he led to its biggest general election defeat in over 80 years in December 2019. Boris felt that Corbyn was not antisemitic himself but was too weak to deal with the conflict over it raging within the party. However, a report for the Labour Party on antisemitism in the party carried out by the Equalities and Human Rights Commission (EHRC) didn't quite agree. Corbyn dismissed the report on the day it appeared on 29 October 2020, calling the allegations of antisemitism 'dramatically over-stated' and was immediately suspended by the Party. Boris remains a highly informed and controversial political commentator.

On a family level, divorced from his traditional politics, Boris and I have even managed to participate in a literary creation – that is, in 2010 Daniel Harbour's volume of his great-grandfather's articles and letters. Boris reflected that Zelman's views can 'easily make you nostalgic for lost historic opportunities. But lost opportunities are also lessons for the future.'

We have met up with Boris and Irena in Moscow a couple of times, most recently in 2014 when they were accompanied by their teenage daughter, born after their Glasgow visit. We met in the comfortable lobby of the Marco Polo Hotel in Central Moscow, a location we had chosen because of its proximity to the Chabad Synagogue on Bolshaya Bronnaya. The synagogue had been built as a private synagogue by the pre-Revolutionary millionaire Lazar Polyakov and was confiscated in 1926. (The pre-war rabbi was executed by the Soviet government in 1937.) The building had then been occupied by the local trade unions as a meetings hall. When the building was returned to the Jewish community in 1991 Boris had been part of the group negotiating the process, permitting folk dancing classes to continue upstairs while religious services were being held on the lower level. Boris described it to me as his 'favourite synagogue'.

In 2014 we were impressed by the huge transformation of the building from our previous visit ten years earlier. The renovation provided many new facilities including classrooms, a bookstore, a lecture hall, mikvah and a roof-top kosher restaurant. We met with Svetlana, Boris' stepmother, and Rebecca Mendoza, who was visiting Moscow at the same time as us, for dinner at the restaurant. Rebecca had hoped to see some of the family archives during her visit but frustratingly this never happened, despite her visit to Svetlana's apartment. All she learned was about the state of plumbing in Soviet era buildings. In 2004 we had been struck by the security around the synagogue building. There had been a failed bomb attack in 1999 and in January 2006 the synagogue was attacked by a neo-Nazi skinhead who stabbed nine people. We could not fail to be impressed by the rabbi, Yitzchok Kogan, who had overseen all the changes. We enjoyed the lavish kiddush as we schmoozed with Rabbi Kogan, who told us his remarkable story. He came from a religious Zionist family and had been a refusenik during the Soviet era when he had worked as a naval engineer. In the 1980s he was known as the 'Tzaddik [righteous one] of Leningrad' and he and his wife, a dentist, were only allowed to leave the Soviet Union in 1986 before returning from Israel a few years later to be the synagogue rabbi.

Alla and Dimitri Linsky

One branch of the extended Kagarlitsky we came to know well was that of Anna's sister's (Evgenia) children, Dima (Dmitri) and Alla, grandchildren of Zev's brother Motya (Matthew). Motya was still in Kovshevata in 1913, listed in the business directory as a pharmacist. Dmitri and Alla were scientists but Alla had time to be close to close to her aunt Anna in her last years. I had met Alla for the first time at a family gathering in Tel Aviv just after she had arrived in the country in the early 1990s. Her husband, Joseph Andrushkin, had left Moscow more than a decade earlier, but she chose not to join him while their son Sergei was uncertain about his future. As Sergei was still unsure about his future ten years later, Alla decided it was time to leave. Joseph was not to have much time to enjoy life outside Russia, dying in America from cancer. Sergei finally arrived in Israel around the time of our visit to Haifa in 2017, some 40 years after his father. Joseph had been a refusenik and had been allowed to leave in 1978, the decade which saw more than a quarter of a million Jews come to Israel and to the United States. Joseph Andrushkin was a Kagarlitsky relation himself even before he married Alla – another family-cousins relationship! His mother was Sonia Kagarlitsky, the sister of Anya, who had translated for Voroshilov and his grandfather, yet another Iosef, was another of Ilya's very many sons.

We visited Alla in Haifa in 1997 just after we had a second set of celebrations for our son David's *barmitzvah* in Jerusalem. She produced many photographs that Anna had shared with her, including some from the time she had spent in Glasgow. Here were pictures of my grandparents as young people in their thirties and my father and his siblings as children. It was a very emotional experience. She also had many family pictures, typical of Soviet families with Komsomol children and men with rows of medals covering their chests. At a later visit she produced an album we had not seen before and again we froze. We knew that my father's older brother Alf had been given a 21st birthday present in 1928 of a trip to Egypt and Palestine, and that he had spent a few days in Tel Aviv with his grandfather, Zev. Alla had a photograph of the two together. I had tears in my eyes. My father had never known his grandparents who had all lived and died outside Britain. Here was the only encounter between Zev and a Collins grandchild, recorded on a very grainy photograph.

Alla's photograph of Alf and Zev, Tel Aviv, 1928.

Alf also managed to be photographed for a Rosh Hashanah card from Tel Aviv, in the same style as the one my grandparents had received from Clara, addressed to Shama and Zlata. The card was the only indication that my grandmother Golda had been known as Zlata to the family in Russia. My cousin Lynda who had grown up in our grandparents' home had never heard my grandfather refer to her as Zlata, the Russian equivalent of Golda. Most, if not all, of the correspondence between Zev's children had been in

Russian rather than, as we had previously presumed, in Yiddish. While my grandparents were very much at home in Yiddish, they were part of a very bi-lingual family which needed Russian as its members moved out of the *shtetl*.

Alf Collins poses for a New Year card, Tel Aviv, September 1928.

Like Joseph Andrushkin, Dmitri had also managed to leave Russia in the 1970s early enough to establish a career in Israel. He had taken a research fellowship in Washington after his arrival in Israel but soon returned to spend the rest of his life in the country. An expert in low temperature physics, he worked for many years at Tel Aviv University continuing his research after retirement at the Weizmann Institute in Rehovot. Eric Mendoza was also in the same field of physics as Dmitri and frustratingly Eric had been present at a conference in Moscow which Dmitri had also attended but had been afraid to approach a British delegate. Dmitri quickly established contact with Eric and Lilian on arrival in Israel and even had a visit to Glasgow to meet with my father and my aunts and uncles. Dmitri had married an American, Dorrit, in Israel and they had a son, David. We were to see Dmitri and Dorrit again over the years, both in Tel Aviv and Glasgow. Dmitri had become a Russophobe in Israel, trying hard to avoid speaking the language and enjoying instead the new life he had created for himself.

6
The Siblings

I have spent some time on the stories of Zelman, Motti, Ura, Anna/Yosif and Solomon as these carry the most documented records, but Zev had fifteen children and most survived into adult life. Their lives represent Jewish experiences around the world. Solomon's siblings lived in different countries – Argentina, the United States and Russia – but he managed to keep in touch with all of them and even, as we have seen, visited family members in Russia in 1934 and hoped that another visit later might have been possible.

Although Jewish life in most countries today is more secure, the past recent years have seen a recurrence of antisemitism in Europe with the murder of Jews in France and Germany. The Jewish community in Britain felt threatened by Jeremy Corbyn's leadership of the Labour Party. The British general election of December 2019 saw Corbyn's Labour Party decisively defeated but many of the concerns remain. There has also been an upsurge of antisemitism, some of it violent, with loss of life, in the United States.

When we met Jacov Portnoy, part of the Argentinian family, in Beersheva many years ago he told us that he had been desperate to leave Argentina as soon as he left school, feeling the stifling atmosphere of antisemitism all around him. Argentina has had a troubled past and the Jewish community was not immune to national events. Between 1976 and 1983, Argentina was ruled by an oppressive military junta that made many opponents 'disappear'. During this period, Jews were a prime target of the government, partially due to the prevailing antisemitic ideology. Laura Schenquer has described, in an article on religion, politics and Jewish youth during the rule of the junta, aspects of the problems in Argentina during the military dictatorship of 1976-1983 as it affected Lomas de Zamora, the area that Shuka (Salomon) had settled in. Community leaders were wary of the anti-government actions of their younger members and were under pressure to suppress dissent.

Shuka (Salomon)

My grandfather had kept in touch with his brother Shuka in Argentina from his earliest days in the country. Shuka had arrived in Argentina in 1906, married to Liuba Poznick from Moscow. The family story was that Shuka had been a teacher and Liuba was from a rich family. They fell in love and made their way to one of the furthest parts of the globe from Russia. Shuka came from a family which was prospering based on the Ukrainian and Russian grain and timber trade, but still the Poznick family did not consider him to be a good match for their daughter. Between 1880 and the First World War millions of Jews were on the move westwards. Western Europe and especially the United States were the main destinations, but Argentina was also becoming a welcoming place for Jews fleeing from Russia.

They brought a samovar with them to Argentina, just as my grandparents had their own grand Russian samovar in Glasgow. Liuba's samovar was filled with her jewellery, some of which was sold to buy their home in Lomas de Zamora, where their five children were born. This was a growing area some twelve miles south of Buenos Aires, but is now well within the city's greater metropolitan area. Shuka wrote a brief account the history of the Jews in Lomas de Zamora in folksy Yiddish in a book of memories, *Zichroinos*. This was published in Buenos Aires and outlines the story, in a couple of pages.

Shuka had taken the lead in founding the first Jewish cemetery in the area, which still functions to this day. The group bought their first *Sefer Torah*, but it took some time to form a synagogue. The first attempts proved unsuccessful and prayers were held in members' homes. Eventually the *Sefer Torah* was presented to the Dr. Herzl Society on condition that they build a shul. The community, now affiliated to the Masorti movement, still functions as Comunidad Hebrea Dr. Herzl Lomas de Zamora, in a fine building. Shuka commented in the article that he and his community in Lomas de Zamora had 'come to America to make a life [and a] living'. Argentina may not have been the United States, but it was still 'America' and the immigrants were prepared to succeed in the New World.

Shuka was known as Salomon Cagarlitsky in Argentina. As we have seen my grandfather had been known as Shama within the family but took the name of Solomon at some stage after arriving in London. It would seem strange that brothers should have such similar names, but this was not the only name duplication in the family. My great-uncle in Glasgow was only ever called Shimmel but he chose the name Samuel when setting up in business. This was also strange as I doubt that Uncle Sam, presumably really Samuel, had any connection to Shimmel's business. Even more strange was the fact that Shimmel's Jewish (Hebrew) name was Simon after Zev's grandfather, but he hadn't chosen to use the name for his business. We always thought that Zev had named *all* the sons from his first wife after his grandfather as Shuka, Shama, Shimmel, Sam and even Zelman had something of a similarity. The family joke was that the brothers all had the same first name, but they or their children had different surnames!

In the middle of the nineteenth century many immigrants from Britain arrived as employees for the Buenos Aires Great Southern Railway. As a railway maintenance engineer this was a suitable place for Shuka to live and work. Railway engineering was considered important work in Russia, indicated in the Soviet-era novelist Anatoly Rybakov's novel *Heavy Sand* (English edition, 1981) about a Jewish family in the Ukraine through the troubled twentieth century: 'Even before the Revolution, a job with the railway was considered an honour and very desirable, and since the Revolution... a job there [in the depot] was regarded as one of the best...'

He was one of the first Jews in Lomas de Zamora, but the area soon became popular with other Jews from Poland and Russia. Shuka and Liuba brought up their five children, Sara, Berta, Rebecca, Moisés and Elias to have a passion for the education which would enable them to succeed in their professional lives as teachers. The sons left Buenos Aires with Elías in General Roca, Rio Negro, in the south of Argentina, and Moisés in Misiones in the north-east of Argentina. The daughters, Rebecca, Sara and Berta, all taught in Lomas de Zamora. The area boasts the Universidad de Lomas de Zamora (UNLZ), which today is one of the most important in the Greater Buenos Aires area with over 30,000 students. Despite the family connection to the locality, generations of Salomon and Liuba's family studied at the University of Buenos Aires.

Shuka never made the long journey to visit Solomon in Scotland, supposedly worried that he might die abroad and possibly not be buried in the cemetery he had founded, and as far as I know Solomon never visited Argentina. However, Solomon sent a regular supply of clothes from his factory so that the children would always have something nice to wear. Solomon was alarmed when he received a message that he should send Shuka a tallit (prayer shawl) to be buried in. Thinking that the demise was imminent he sent the tallit by air freight.

Just as Kagarlitskys from Russia and America get in touch electronically, I found it happened too with Argentina. Seeing a suggested connection on

LinkedIn from Agustin Carliski, an industrial engineer, I did wonder if this was a modification of Kagarlitsky that I had been unaware of. This was soon confirmed. Agustin's grandfather was Moisés, Shuka's son, and Cagarlitski in Argentina had been shortened to Carliski. I made contact with Agustin; Isaac and Sara Schujmajer's granddaughter Mariela and Shuka's grandson Gustavo (Chocrón) were soon in touch and have brought me up to date with their part of Shuka's family.

We did have visitors to Scotland from Argentina. I particularly remember the visit of Isaac (Ufo) and Sara Schujmajer to Glasgow in, I think, 1961. My father was delighted to meet his cousin Sara, and Isaac's professional interests meshed well with my parents. Isaac had been born into a poor immigrant family but managed to enter the University of Buenos Aires to study medicine, marrying Shuka's daughter Sara, whom he had met through contacts with her brothers Elias and Moisés in Lomas de Zamora. Gustavo described his grandfather as 'an affable character, outgoing but also tenacious and possessor of an outstanding intelligence' who had a strong belief in science and considered religion to be outdated. Some of his opinions were kept to himself as he was, in later years, regarded as the patriarch of the family in Argentina. Isaac was very keen to leave a gift for me before returning home and he gave me his leather-covered and pocket-sized notepad, which had a small metal strip with his initials on it. I prized this possession and was to use it for many years.

Their eldest daughter Norma studied at a British school in the hills of Zamora and became a teacher. After her marriage to Alberto Elias Chocrón they lived first in Puerto Madryn, a small port town with historic Welsh connections and now a major tourist centre in Patagonia. In 1967 they returned to the Buenos Aires area, living in Monte Grande, now a growing urban centre just outside of Lomas de Zamora. Norma's son Gustavo also attended a British primary school but had more problems with antisemitic elements at the military high school he attended. Nevertheless, he completed his schooling and graduated in medicine, becoming a specialist in lung diseases and spending time between Argentina and Spain, now also with an interest in yoga and Ayurvedic medicine which was a favourite interest of Zelman's son Emmanuel. Norma suffered from asthma all her life and, back in Europe, she spent her last years working in tourism in a small town in the mountains in the south of Spain, in the same town where her son Gerardo still lives. It is a matter of pride to Gustavo that one of his twin daughters, who still lives in Monte Grande, is a paediatrician working in the same hospital in Lomas de Zamora where his grandfather founded the ophthalmology service.

Lilian had told us of a visit of her cousin Susie Portnoy, the daughter of Shuka's daughter Rebecca, to Israel in 1991 for the *brit milah* (circumcision) of her new grandson. Their son, known as Jacov in Israel, had become strictly observant and had been living on a West Bank settlement for some time. Lilian had learned that Susie was a retired dentist pursuing academic studies in Jewish history while her husband Mario (Pepe) was a psychiatrist. We were to make contact many years later with Jacov in a strange way. He had left the settlement and began studies at Ben Gurion University of the Negev in Beersheva, eventually joining the university staff. His mother made a *barmitzvah* visit to Israel in 2004 and decided to visit her grandfather's grave in Tel Aviv. She was put in touch with our daughter Rachel who was then living in Tel Aviv, and she explained the locale of the cemetery and where Zev's grave was situated.

We discovered that Jacov was now living in Beersheva and was a staff member at the university. We were totally amazed as I had just returned to Scotland after a short sabbatical at Ben Gurion University, and as it turned out had been living very near Jacov and his family. Moreover, he was well known to many of our closest friends in Beersheva as a regular worshipper in a small synagogue we had visited occasionally. We exchanged emails and arranged to meet on our next trip to Israel at the mall in the town centre. On the following trip we visited him at home. He explained how he had been desperate to leave Argentina and its endemic anti-Semitism as a teenager, and came to Israel without any higher education and had only come to it many years later.

It was a pity that in our two visits to Buenos Aires over the next few years we were unable to meet up with family, especially when I discovered that one of my close medical history colleagues, Jaime Bortz, a native of Buenos Aires, whom I have met many times, most recently in Mexico and Spain, had been a contemporary of Gustavo's at university. Bortz' father had treated Gustavo for allergies when he was a child.

Sam

Of all the siblings of my grandfather who lived outside Britain, Uncle Sam was the best known to the family in Glasgow. He had frequent, and often very extended, trips to Glasgow and on at least two occasions, in 1949 and 1955, he made attempts to establish himself in Glasgow and obtain British nationality. However, he always left Glasgow before there was any progress on either front. I don't remember him as much of a conversationalist and he didn't reach out at all to Solomon and Golda's grandchildren. We just knew the basics: that he had changed his name to Kagar, settled in Winston-Salem in North Carolina, had been married to Ray Braverman and had a daughter Sylvia, born in 1918, who was a left-wing activist. There is no recollection of Ray ever coming to Glasgow.

Sam and Ray Braverman were possibly married in Kovshevata as he was one of the last of the family to leave the village, doing so just before the First World War. In her US Naturalisation Certificate, Ray indicated that she had been married in Glasgow on 10 June 1914. There are no documented records of this, although if a couple already with a civil marriage in Russia wanted to have a Jewish ceremony in Glasgow before moving on to America, this would not have been too difficult to arrange. There were Bravermans in my grandmother's family and as both Golda and Ray had been born in Boyarke it is likely that they were related. There would be another Kagarlitsky-Braverman marriage in Glasgow in the next generation: my aunt Mona to Syd (Braverman) Barrie.

Sam was the only one of his siblings who affected a middle name. The brothers would all have used the patronymic Wolfovitch while in Russia but generally dropped it when they left. Sam is often listed as Samuel Wolfe Kagar on American documents, the Wolfe being an abbreviated form of the traditional patronymic.

Ray's naturalisation certificate was issued on 2 November 1923 and is interesting as it gives their date of arrival in New York, on 29 November 1916, sailing on the *SS California*, with an address at 236 West 112th Street. They had sailed from Glasgow to New York, indicating that they had spent more than two years in Glasgow before crossing the Atlantic. Ray's mother was already in New York having reached America from Southampton in 1903. This address may have been very temporary as they were soon on their way to Winston-Salem, although Sam, Ray and their daughter Sylvia, born in 1918, were listed at the New York address in the 1920 Census.

In 1920 Winston-Salem was still a small town with a population of around 48,000, but it was growing rapidly. There was a small Jewish community never numbering more than a thousand. In 1919 Sam bought the Southern Hotel and Café in Winston-Salem and a few months later bought the Matthews Lunch and Bakery. The hotel purchase was not a wise move as just a year later he was in court and fined $250 for running a 'disorderly house', a euphemism for permitting prostitutes and their clients to use the hotel rooms. The night manager seems to have shared some, or maybe even all, of the blame for allowing to the women to bring men back with them when they had been removed by the police on previous occasions.

Sam's naturalization was dated 1923 at which time he declared living again at 236 W. 112th Street, but Ray and Sylvia were living at this time at 943 Avenue Saint Joan in the Bronx. Sam and Ray were living apart and at a divorce hearing in New York in 1925 Ray alleged cruelty, a charge Sam denied. He countered that she was not happy with the humdrum life of small-town Winston-Salem and had a wanderlust which took her frequently away from home. Sam, now described as a prosperous shoe merchant, had followed her to New York but Ray was not yet ready for a reconciliation.

Documents show many different addresses for Sam, even in the space of two years. In 1923 he was, as noted, at 236 W 112th Street but at the time of the divorce case he gave his address as 2787 West 36th Street, Coney Island. The newspaper account of the divorce case concluded by saying that judgement was reserved, and they must have got together again as the 1930 Census shows Sam, Ray and Sylvia living at Olinville Avenue in the Bronx. Despite the New York address Sam maintained his business connections in Winston-Salem, now as a clothing salesman, perhaps importing goods from Solomon in Glasgow. At this time Ray was working as a nurse, involved in programmes to help Native Americans and poor children. Another move, perhaps just temporarily during the Second World War, saw Sam as Captain of a National Guard unit in Altoona, Pennsylvania in 1943.

There was a story that Ray chained herself to the White House railings during a protest against the war in Vietnam. My aunts did not approve of such behaviour, as they believed that Jews should always keep a low profile. They described this action as *meshugas* (craziness). However, contemporary photographs show that she was merely parading beside the railings, sometimes wearing placards carrying detailed reasons why she felt the war to be immoral. Ray's political views, and her vehement opposition to the Vietnam War, came out of deep conviction. She was aware that communism as a system was not workable and identified as a socialist.

Their daughter, Sylvia, married Martin Fine in New York in 1943 while he was in the US Navy, but she had several marriages and shared some of her mother's political beliefs. She had spent time as a student in London attending the Clapton County Secondary School for Girls in Laura Place. The school was progressive in its ethos, encouraging its girls to develop resilience, self-belief and an eagerness for learning. Its graduates were empowered to achieve at the highest levels and to overcome individual barriers to success. Spending time at a secondary school outside America must have been unusual in the 1930s. Given the uneasy home situation,

Collins family get-together around 1950 to welcome Sam Kagar and daughter Sylvia from America. Solomon is near the front on the left with daughter Mona's hands on his shoulder; Shimmel is near the centre while Sam is in the back row (seventh from right) with his daughter Sylvia (fourth from right).

learning away from home would have been a good option and the presence of Kagarlitsky family members, in the form of the late Zelman's wife Chassia and children, Emanuel, Victor and Lilian, a distinct advantage. Shipping records show her travelling with her mother back from London in 1932 so the length of her stay in London is not clear, as she was described as a graduate of the school at the time of her wedding. This suggests that she could have been there until she was eighteen. She identified as a communist, so her family were wary of her in the 1950s as McCarthyist fears of subversion swept across American life.

Sam died more than two decades before his wife Ray passed away, in March 1986. She had been living in Washington DC for many years but in Sam's last years they were again living apart, so that by the time of his visit to Glasgow in 1955, which I remember, he had probably retired from business and was free to come and go as he pleased. However, he always returned to America and he died in Winston-Salem in 1960 at the age of 77.

Some of Sam's businesses were in partnership with Louis Roush (original name Choroszcz). Louis' mother, Peshie Leah Roush, was a sister of Zev's first wife Sarah Milevski, so Louis and Sam would have been first cousins. They set up some businesses together. Some, like the shoes and lunch-time diner, were successful but others less so. My grandfather was in regular touch with members of the Roush family and there were meetings on his various trips to New York and to Winston-Salem. I have email correspondence going back to 2003 detailing this connection from Louis' niece, Polly Liss, and these have helped to fill in missing details of the extended family.

Raisa (Reysie)

Reysie, who was born in December 1874, was the only daughter of Zev's first wife and thus my grandfather's only 'full' sister. If the birth date is correct, she would have been Zev's oldest child, born when he was just nineteen years old. She and her family remained in Russia all the years of the Soviet Union before grandchildren and great-grandchildren settled in Israel or the United States from 1991 onwards. Reysie had married Moisei (Moyshe) Briskman from Germanovka in January 1895 and they had two sons, Iosef, Zev's first grandchild, born at the end of 1895, and Ilya who was born ten years later. There was also a daughter Channa who was born in 1900 but no other records for her exist.

The Briskman family had lived for many generations in the larger community of Vasilkov (Vasylkiv) whose 4,400 Jews made up 40 per cent of the population in 1897, but part of the family had settled in Germanovka (now Hermanivka) and it was there that the wedding took place. Jews returned to Vasilkov after the Second World War and a Jewish community still exists there today.

Around 1905, they left Ukraine and moved to work in Azerbaijan, which was part of the Russian Empire. They settled in the city of Lankaran, on the Caspian Sea, near Azerbaijan's southern border with Iran which boasted a significant fishing industry. Its humid subtropical climate with the availability of good arable land and water stimulated a large agricultural industry. Iosef, my father's cousin, graduated from high school in Lankaran with a gold medal in 1917. This was the year of the Russian Revolution and the turmoil did not pass Azerbaijan by. There was a short-lived British-controlled anti-Communist regime, the 'Provisional Military Dictatorship of Mughan' founded in the Lankaran region on 1 August 1918. The insurrection was led by the White Russian Colonel T.P. Sukhorukov, who acted under the protection of the British occupation of Baku and declared Mughan to be an autonomous part of 'single and indivisible Russia'. British troops had been in Baku in November 1918 to supervise the withdrawal of the Turks, but they left by the end of 1919 and the short-lived Republic of Azerbaijan ended in April 1920, when the Red Army arrived and established the Azerbaijan Soviet Socialist Republic.

By 1918 Iosef was already in the Red Army near Tsaritsin (later called Stalingrad but now Volgograd). Moyshe and Reysie later settled in a small town nearby and both passed away before the Second World War, in around 1937. Iosef soon moved to Leningrad, where he graduated from the Leningrad State Institute of Technology (Technical University), married in 1922 and lived there until the war. After the war Iosef settled in Moscow, where the family remained until leaving for Israel in 1991. Iosef had married Rita (Riva Gitl) Geller and they died in Moscow in 1977/8.

Their second son Ilya lived all his life in Leningrad (once again St. Peterburg). Ilya married Alexandra Speranskaya and their older son was named Vladimir, possibly after Zev, which is how he was often addressed in Russia. I had no knowledge of this part of the family even though Iosef and Ilya were my father's first cousins, and while I saw Reysie's name on lists of family members, and even had a photograph of her with Moyshe and Iosef, taken around 1906, we had no contact with her. However, my grandfather must have been in touch and would have known that she had died at the age of just 48 in 1922. Reysie's husband Moyshe, who died in 1937, was still alive when he visited Russia in 1934 so maybe he had come from Leningrad to Moscow to see him at the home of Iosef and Anna at Lefortovo Soldatsky pereulok 8, the address I have for them in 1930. At any rate, he was in contact with her enough to know that by 1950 she had passed away and to persuade my parents that my sister, Irene, should carry also the Jewish Yiddish name of Reysie.

Yosif's son Michael, who had been born in Volgograd in 1926 made *aliyah* to Israel in 1993, with his wife Valentina Brodskaya, following their son Simeon and daughter-in-law Polina Kemelman who had arrived in Israel two years earlier. Simeon's sister Maria and her family live in New York. It was with a sense of great excitement when Simeon's email, sent through contact with JewishGen – the Jewish genealogy website – arrived. My sister was especially thrilled that contact had been made with a descendant of the great-aunt she had been named after. Simeon was able to point out that we had been recording the family name incorrectly. I had only ever seen it written as Brickman but of course the letter C in Russian is pronounced like the S in English. I was also intrigued to see that Simeon's son is called Ilya, the name of Zev's father, while Simeon is, of course, the name of Zev's grandfather.

We did have a copy of a photograph of Reysie with her husband and older son, although the Briskman surname had, as just noted, been misspelt and Yosif had been mis-named as John. While his sister and family are in New York, Simeon and his physician wife, Polina Kemelman, live in Kfar Saba, a town adjacent to Hod Hasharon where our youngest daughter Rachel lives, and consequently it was easy to meet and catch up on more than a century of family news. Simeon had a great collection of family photographs and had already completed some interesting research on Clara but lamented that his parents, Michael (Yechiel) and Valentina Brodskaya, had left so much memorabilia behind in Moscow and they are no longer with us to recall their family stories. His research through Ukrainian archives is ongoing and continually produces new information.

Simeon observed that he knew from childhood that the family was Jewish and different from others. At the same time, though all his friends in school and at the university were Jews, they observed little of any tradition or religion. Simeon's mother graduated from a university with specialisation in film industry economics, but it was around 1952, at the end of Stalin's era, and she had to settle for factory work for a few years. Although the family did not suffer much from specific acts of antisemitism, they all lived in the shadow of these events, with their behaviour following their perception of the surrounding reality and their attitude to it.

With a combination of luck and setting reasonable goals and expectations from the environment, they were able to survive the Communist era and make their way successfully to Israel after the break-up of the Soviet Union.

Clara

We presume that Clara, the youngest of Zev's fifteen children, born in 1902, managed to leave with her father Zev soon after Ida, Jacob and Motti arrived in Palestine on the *SS Ruslan* in December 1919. There had been a considerable migration from Russia immediately following the Russian Revolution in November 1917, but by the time that Clara and Zev left the doors were closing. The Yevsektzia managed to exile a large group of Zionists, including the Hebrew poet Chaim Nachman Bialik and others involved in Hebrew life and culture, through Odessa in 1921. This marked, for the most part, the close of emigration to Palestine and we have to assume that this is also when Zev and Clara arrived in Jaffa.

My parents met up with Clara in Israel in 1973 purely by chance. Those were the days when, if you wanted Israeli currency you took traveller's cheques into the bank, stood in line for the counter clerk to get a note for the cashier, for whom you would have to queue again to receive your money. It was a time-consuming procedure but there was little alternative. My father made his way slowly to the counter clerk at a bank near the hotel in Herzliya. The clerk was originally from Glasgow, and my father knew some of his relatives very well. My father heard that the clerk had recently met an older customer in the bank who had recognized his accent and asked him if he knew any members of the Collins family.

He quickly managed to put my father in touch with his aunt who remembered a visit to Glasgow some 40 or more years earlier when my father was about ten years old. She had spent some time in America but was now back permanently in Israel. My parents spent some time with her, and she was in touch afterwards with Lilian and Eric. Clara had been married to Joseph Amzalem, who was born in Jaffa of a Moroccan family, and had been working in the Palestine Police Force, set up by the Mandatory authorities. For most, if not all, of Zev's years in Tel Aviv he was living with Clara, Joseph and their daughter Ruth, born in 1924. Thanks to some documentary research by Simeon Briskman, it would appear that Clara, and Joseph left Palestine for France with their children in 1931, spending six years there.

This was probably not so much of a surprise. The year since the death of Motti and then the passing of Zev on 24 March 1931 must have been exceptionally difficult. Clara had remained with her father in Odessa in 1919 awaiting the next available boat to join Motti, Ida and Jacob and had been with her father after Ida and her husband and Ura had left Palestine. Clara was pregnant at the time of Zev's death and she was delivered of a son just nine days after his passing. The baby was named Ze'ev, after his grandfather. Zev had outlived seven of his children: Gudis (suicide), Zelman (suspicious sudden death), Motti (work accident), Reysie plus three others, Mosiei, Alek and Meir, who had died young. The emotional turmoil of the year since the death of Motti and the departure of her sisters Ura and Ida must have prompted the need for a major change in her life.

As the son of parents from French Morocco it was easy for Joseph to obtain entry to France and gain citizenship. In fact, Joseph and Clara did not get Palestinian citizenship until 1940 and the French passport may have been their first. Ura was the only family member then in France and it may be that they joined her in Paris. They returned to Palestine in 1937 and Joseph took up work as a clerk for the Tel Aviv municipality. The situation for Jews in Germany was becoming increasingly dangerous and antisemitism was also on the rise in Eastern Europe. Jewish migration to Palestine had been at an all-time high in the past three years and it must have seemed a good time to return to Tel Aviv.

There was also a story of a divorce by the time that my parents met Clara, then aged 71. She had lived for a time in America before returning to Israel to live in Herzliya until her death in 1978. Simeon had discovered that she had already possessed an Israeli Identity Card and thus was still in Israel in 1948. We have some records of correspondence with her over the years and family members, such as my father's brother Alf and sister-in-law Ethel, met her son Ze'ev on visits to Israel in the 1950s and 1960s. Ze'ev had served in the Israeli Army for two years during and after Israel's War of Independence. He left Israel in 1954 travelling first to Brazil on a journey, as he said, 'to check out the world'. After living in Brazil, Mexico and the Caribbean he settled in the United States making his name as an artist and art-dealer with exhibitions in Florida, Texas and California. After studying the art of Rembrandt, Cezanne, Van Gogh and Turner he developed his own unusual technique using chopsticks as tools in a variety of different media – 'hide, mix, grab, slap, draw'. His view is that a work of art should reciprocate the viewer's admiration and be proud of its creator.

Ze'ev Amzalem with one of his artworks.

In recent years there has been no contact with Clara's daughter Ruth Amzalem (now Harris) who had settled, we believe, in the Philadelphia area.

Ida (Hinda)

Ida and Jacob's Russian marriage certificate from May 1918 has survived describing the marriage of Hinda-Mirel, daughter of Wolf Kagarlitsky, and Jacob son of Bentsion Rashal. In addition to the details of the bride and groom the document is duly stamped and signed by the so-called 'Crown Rabbi' appointed by the state to record events in the Jewish community. The ceremony took place in the groom's community of Zlatopol, barely a mile from Ida's home in Novo Mirgorod. By this stage the two were getting ready to leave. Jacob had spent two years in Palestine from 1912 completing his education, most likely at the new Hebrew Gymnasium which was the pride of Tel Aviv. He would have learned Hebrew as a modern language there which would stand him in good stead as they prepared to leave Russia via Odessa in 1919. As Turkey had entered the First World War on the side of Germany and Austria-Hungary, we have noted that Jacob, as a Russian, became an enemy alien. He managed to leave Palestine on an American ship bound for Egypt from where he returned to Russia.

Jacob took an important role in the organizing of the *Ruslan*. He knew the urgency of the need to leave and he was a genuine Hebrew-speaking refugee from Palestine. He was able to convince the British Consul in Odessa that although the group were not all refugees like himself, in fact only a quarter of their number were, they had a need to leave before the Bolsheviks captured the city. There was clearly sympathy for this approach and Motti, and the others, were able to get his permission to immigrate too.

After arriving on the *SS Ruslan* on 19 December 1919, Jacob and Ida (Hinde) settled in Tel Aviv. Some of Tel Aviv's growth in the early years of the British Mandate came from the incorporation of contiguous Jewish neighbourhoods from Jaffa. They could have settled in Neve Tzedek or in one of the newer neighbourhoods of Tel Aviv where Jacob set up a chemicals business, eventually developing an extensive portfolio of goods. There was ink, vegetable fat, soap powder, vinegar and the popular tahini-based dessert halvah – Israeli halvah does not contain wheat flour or semolina and does not have any dairy products, so differs in taste and texture from halvah products in other markets. Rashal's vegetable fat carried the approval of the Jerusalem rabbinate as a kosher product and its labelling was in Hebrew, Yiddish and English. Other products also carried the *hechsher*, kashrut certificate, of the rabbinate such as their soaps. Some products were aimed at the Arab as well as Jewish market and were manufactured in Jaffa, while other products, such as custard powder, would have been more to the taste of the British employees of the mandate authorities. Rashal's vinegar was advertised as ideal for salads as well as for preserving marinated fruits.

This was a very comprehensive collection of products and the company should have been able to expand rapidly as the Palestine population, and its Jewish community, the Yishuv, grew during the 1920s. However, change was on its way. The Palestine economy suffered a severe downturn at the end of the 1920s and for a couple of years there were more Jews leaving than arriving. Ida and Jacob, with their daughter Rita, were among those leaving choosing to settle in New York. Their grandson Gary Martel has furnished me with a comprehensive set of product packaging, most of which belongs to the 1920s in Tel Aviv. However, there were a couple of items which belong to the American period.

Collage of Rashal products from Palestine and the United States of America.

One was Rashal's Steel Wool, which was advertised as an ideal companion to Rashal's soap. Another was a Chocolate Dessert sold under the label of Ver-E-Gud.

Rita married Mervin Bruck and they had two sons, Michael and David. Rita died in 1979 and it was after her death that Mervin found the letter from Ura, which he began to share with family around the world. Lilian's receipt of the letter started the chain of events which led to Rosanne Romagnan being recognized as a Righteous Gentile by Yad Vashem for sheltering Ura. Mervin travelled to Marseille for the ceremony and was most moved by the occasion.

Jacob and Ida had a second daughter, June, born after relocating from Tel Aviv to New York in March 1929, arriving on the *SS Sinaia*. Jacob had only received Palestinian citizenship, and a British-style passport, during 1928. This was probably part of the preparation for the move to the United States as a British colonial citizenship would have been more acceptable than old Tsarist Russian ones given the existence of new national quotas. In 1942 they became naturalized American citizens. June Rashal married Julius Martel, a native of Brooklyn. He had proposed to her in the Catskill Mountains, a favoured holiday location for New York's Jews, where he had been working in the summer as a waiter.

Julius studied medicine in California where June's sister Rita and her husband Mervin Bruck were living, in Oakland. The Martels settled in small-town El Sobrante, just 12 miles from Oakland, where Julius was a country doctor visiting patients at home and delivering their babies. June had a life-long interest in fashion design, but after Julius set up his medical practice she ran its business side. Their son Gary has been active in volunteering since retiring from dentistry, supporting not-for-profit organizations which find solutions for the homeless, strengthen their financial well-being and helping migrant and seasonal farm workers, or their children, to obtain the equivalent of a high school diploma. Gary and his wife Sheryl maintain a vegan diet due to their ethical concerns for our environment and respect for animals.

Gudis

I would not have been aware of the fate of my grandfather's young half-sister Gudis but for the two weeks I spent with my Uncle Alf at his home in West Kilbride in the summer of 1964 during the long weeks before starting university. By day we played golf or had walks in the local countryside or just enjoyed the ambience of his beachfront home. In the evenings he told me some of his memories of family history, and he had much to tell. Alf was my father's older brother and had been born in London in 1907. He knew no English until he started primary school in Glasgow when the family arrived in the city in 1912. His Yiddish was fluent and when starting out in the textile business with my grandfather he would travel round Scotland buying cloth and selling goods to independent clothes shops and the correspondence would be in Yiddish.

One of his earliest memories of business concerned Gudis. It was April 1921, when he was barely 14 years old, and my grandfather was getting concerned that Gudis had not been seen for a few days. She was also working in the business, as a drapery traveller, and although the relationship with her half-brother had recently been tense, with some questions about sales and income unresolved, there had been no suggestion that there were any major problems. If anything, problems were more on my grandfather's side as the business was on the brink of bankruptcy. Gudis lived at 166 Main Street, now called Gorbals Street, just a couple of streets away from the family's Gorbals workshop. So, Alf was sent to look for his aunt. The door was locked, and I don't remember if he had a key or if he had to call the services of some locals to break down the door. Gudis was dead. There was no suspicion of foul play and the police surgeon confirmed death by suicide with self-administration of a corrosive acid.

This was a terrifying experience for a young teenager and the memory had haunted Alf for more than four decades. My grandfather, as next-of-kin, signed the death certificate using his original surname of Kagarlitsky. Unlike my grandfather, Gudis had not changed her name so the two surnames matched. My grandfather gave his address as that of the workshop at 57 Oxford Street and the family details were noted as showing her father as Wolf Kagarlitsky, described as a timber dealer. As this was more than three years after the Russian Revolution and was around the time that Wolf was settling in Tel Aviv, he would not have been dealing in timber for some time. However, it was his last occupation. The death certificate stated that Gudis had been born in 1894 and was therefore 27 years old. No date was entered for her day and month of her birth. However, in the 1897 Russian Census she was listed as the oldest of Zev's children from his second marriage when she was nine years old. A suicide would have been difficult for the family as it carried a stigma in those days. Proscribed by religious law the railed-off grave was probably the norm for burial of a suicide in a Jewish cemetery. Today, there is a greater understanding of the pressures which leads to such acts and indeed, one medieval authority had already stated that traditional burial should not be denied to someone who commits suicide due to a multiplicity of troubles, worries, pain or utter poverty.

A rare surviving picture of Gudis (1888-1921).

Gudis disappeared from the family story and these lines, and a railed-off but otherwise unmarked grave (no.438) at the Sandymount Cemetery of the Glasgow Hebrew Burial Society, are the only evidence of her life and its tragic ending.

Motti with Ida and Alik (in military uniform), 1917.

Alik, Meir and Moisei

Alik, Meir and Moisei all died young. Alik was born in 1900 – one of the youngest of Zev's fifteen children and one of the seven that predeceased him. Meir died at the age of twelve, possibly in a drowning accident, while the only reference to Moisei that I have found suggests that he died in 1914 at the age of twenty. We have one striking picture of Alik in the uniform of a Russian soldier, probably taken during the last months of Russia's involvement in the war. Sadly, it seems that he was a casualty and did not survive to join his father and siblings when they sailed from Odessa to start their new life in British Palestine.

7

Solomon the Businessman

There is a lack of clarity in Solomon's birth year. In his naturalization papers he gave the date as 1878, while later he maintained that he had been born in 1882. However, he arrived in London no later than 1898 as an older teenager so a year earlier, that is 1881, seems much more likely. The whole story of birthdates is somewhat fraught. Records of births in Kovshevata do not always match with when Solomon and his brothers thought they were born. We also know that Solomon sometimes took weeks or months to register the births of his own children.

The story of his departure from Ukraine began with a trip to Vienna for a hernia operation. Possibly, he was accompanied to Vienna but there he made a decision which would shape the direction of his life and many of his family members. He decided not to return home, whether to his father or brother Zelman, but to strike out on his own and head for London. His mother had died some years before and his father had remarried. Zev and his second wife Rebecca had already produced the first six of their nine children. Solomon remained on good and close terms with all his siblings, but I sensed some tension when he spoke about the changes in the family back in Russia and the birth of a new set of half-siblings. When he left in 1897 or 1898 there were already six half-siblings aged from three to nine years old in the family home. He simply acknowledged it was time to move on.

Despite his arrival in London in 1898 he does not appear in the 1901 Census. Census returns are often quite unreliable especially where enumerators have to cope with immigrant areas where little English is spoken, and surnames are hard to spell. If he had been a lodger with a large family his presence might just have been missed. I have also found no evidence for members of the Kagarlitsky family in London at the time but there were plenty of Jews from Ukraine and possibly some members of his mother's family living there. His first couple of years in London, in the teeming East End, were of unremitting poverty, and he earned money by peddling trinkets. He must have come close to regretting his decision to come to Britain. Gradually, things improved. He started working in a textile workshop near where he lived in Tenter Street, named for the frames (tenters) used for drying washed woven cloth which would be attached to the frames with tenterhooks. He then graduated to a workshop where he owned his own sewing-machine and was therefore technically self-employed. From there it was a short step until he was able to start his own workshop, with the help of some financial support from his brother Zelman.

On 3 March 1904 he married Golda Packer (née Packerovsky, although many variant spellings exist – Pockeropsky appears on her marriage certificate and there is also a mention of Pogorovsky) at the East London Synagogue in Stepney Green. Golda was born in the Ukrainian *shtetl* of Boyarke and therefore shared some of the same background as he did. Boyarke was just eleven miles from Kovshevata and migrants to New York had set up one the largest *landsmanschaft* groups in the city. These groups of people from the same community acted as friendly societies, encouraging social cohesion and providing benefits in times of need. Golda had family members in London, the Braverman and Harris families, and Solomon was now part of a new extended family network. With some financial stability the family moved to Rectory Road in more genteel Stoke Newington, certainly by 1910, and he was now able to consider the next stage of extending his textile business.

Just as he was becoming frustrated with attempts to launch a larger scale textile business in London and was contemplating the possibility of a move to New York, help came from Glasgow. His cousin Rose (Reysie), daughter of Zev's brother Yankel, and her husband Wolf Antonowski had been living in Glasgow for more than a decade and Wolf had been following the local manufacturing scene. Wolf, now known as Wolf Anton, was involved in wholesale and retail textile sales, and confirmed to Solomon that with the recent closure of some big companies the time was opportune for him to move to Glasgow.

Wolf Antonowski was already in Glasgow in 1895 and was later joined by his wife who had still been in Kovshevata with the children at the time of the Russian Census of 1897, so they had been separated for at least three years. The 1901 Census shows Wolf and Rose living in Graeme Street in the Gallowgate area, with their two children Fanny and Solomon, some distance from the centre of Jewish community life in the Gorbals. The 1911 Census has only Wolf and his 18-year-old son Solomon living in a heavily Jewish tenement in Warwick Street in the heart of the Gorbals. They are registered as lodgers in the home of Harris and Leah Katz, and their three young children. Rose was by this time in Boston with Fanny, and her son joined her later, but she did pay a return visit to Glasgow with her 18-month-old grandson Jack (Shuman) just about the time that Solomon and Golda arrived. When Wolf died in 1928 the death certificate mentions a second wife, Lizzie Gorsky, and details were supplied by the son-in-law of Wolf's brother Jacob. Wolf had died while out for a walk and there was an (unproved) suspicion that Lizzie had poisoned him.

Solomon visited Glasgow, liked what he saw and in April 1912, now with three young children, Sarah aged 6, Alf aged 5 and David just a few weeks old the move was made. There had also been twins born in London in March 1910. Jacob had died just after birth and Rebecca lived only until December. This was a family trauma that was scarcely mentioned in the years ahead. The babies' names were unknown to us and only retrieved recently by a search of London deaths.

Glasgow may have been the city of promise but at first it must have seemed far from being the Promised Land. The family's first home could not match the genteel prosperity of Stoke Newington and they found themselves in Oxford Street in Glasgow's teeming Gorbals. Solomon needed funds for the move to Glasgow and to establish his business, and a loan of 500 roubles from Zelman made this possible. However, he had to compromise on the housing and so he and Golda settled for a flat in Oxford

The first Glasgow Collins workshop, Gorbals, 1912.

Street in the heart of the Gorbals, with a workshop nearby. The first pictures of Solomon's workshop have survived and show him, standing at the back, presiding as workers look up from their diligent toil at their sewing machines. The photograph shows a spacious area unlike the traditional image of the ghetto sweatshop.

Situated just south of the River Clyde the Gorbals had been a smart district in the early and middle parts of the nineteenth century, but by 1912 the remorseless waves of immigration had reduced most of the area to slum conditions. Jews from Eastern Europe joined Scottish Highlanders, Italians and Irish in creating the most cosmopolitan area in Victorian and Edwardian Scotland. Parts of the southern Gorbals, around Abbotsford Place, where my mother spent her first ten years, maintained some semblance of elegance for another generation, and was home to the community's rabbis and doctors. The legendary kosher Geneen's Hotel was also situated in Abbotsford Place, much beloved for its fusion of Jewish and Scottish fare. Oxford Street was in the heart of Jewish Glasgow, a district not different in character although smaller in scale than the Whitechapel and Aldgate in London's East End that Solomon had first entered in 1898. Chaim Bermant said, in *Coming Home* (1976) it reminded him of Dvinsk in his native Latvia:

> There were Yiddish posters on the hoardings, Hebrew lettering on the shops, Jewish names, Jewish faces, Jewish butchers, Jewish bakers with Jewish bread, and Jewish grocers with barrels of herring in the doorway... One heard Yiddish in the streets – more so, in fact, than English and one encountered figures who would not have been out of place in Barovke.

I have written extensively on the Jewish experience in Scotland, usually focussing for the most part on Glasgow. The story of Solomon and Golda and their children are part of a dynamic process which eased the path for themselves, but especially their children, into Scottish society. The growing Jewish community in Glasgow, already numbering around 10,000 in 1912, produced a considerable array of institutions which served the social, religious, educational, cultural and political needs of its members.

The classic Scottish writer Lewis Grassic Gibbon and poet Hugh Macdiarmid described the Gorbals some twenty years later as hardly being Scottish, describing the 'stout men in beards and ringlets and unseemly attire' and 'Ruth and Naomi go by with downcast Eastern faces', indicating that 'there really were and actually are other races on the earth apart from the Scots'. The poetry of A.C. Jacobs, the anarchic musings of Ivor Cutler and the novels and journalistic writings of Chaim Bermant catch the mood of the city's Jews. Evelyn Cowan's nostalgic memoir *Spring Remembered: A Scottish Jewish Childhood* (1974) showed the Gorbals as a warm, nourishing and traditional Jewish community. A far grittier picture of the immigrant generation was provided by Ralph Glasser in *Growing up in the Gorbals* (1986) with its pictures of family disruption and unremitting poverty.

My father David had been born on 18 February 1912 but either through Solomon's distrust of authority, which was common in Russia, or just a lapse through the upheaval of the move to Glasgow, there was a delay in registering the birth. The upshot was that David's birth, on 18 February was not registered until 20 April, and rather than admit that the birth had not been registered during the permitted 21 days Solomon simply told the Registrar of Births that his son had been born the day the birth was registered. The error was not discovered until David sought to claim his National Health Service and Old Age Pensions in 1977. As the family name changed soon after arrival in Glasgow David never took possession of his birth certification using his change of surname document instead. He had to wait nine unexpected extra weeks for his pension.

At the same time Solomon had a further change of surname. The Londoners had great difficulty in pronouncing Kagarlitsky and he had 'simplified' it to Kalinsky and this was the surname on the first children's birth certificates. When he came to Glasgow, he was told that his choice was illogical – it was neither his real name nor an English one and he should think again. The story was that he heard the Irish surname Collins in connection with an Irish republican politician called Michael Collins and decided that the name would suit. Joe was the last Kalinsky, born on 12 September 1915.

For politics there was the Socialist Workers' Circle, situated over a kosher bakery in Gorbals Street. During her time in Glasgow it was visited by my grandfather's cousin Anna before her move to London and eventual return to Russia. However, the major Jewish political movement over most of the twentieth century in Glasgow was Zionism. Here Solomon was at an advantage. There were few community members who had a parent and siblings in Palestine, and he attended meetings and commented on the way his brother and sisters were contributing to the economy there. He was also a synagogue supporter, if not an active attendee. While not strictly observant he and Golda maintained a traditional Jewish lifestyle at home, especially as Golda became increasingly crippled by rheumatoid arthritis. Successful businessmen were expected to support the religious life of the community and Solomon was a council member of what began life as the *Beis Medresh HaGodol*, a breakaway group of another Gorbals synagogue, and on moving to Hospital Street was known as the (New) Central Synagogue. The *Beis Medresh HaGodol*, literally the Great Study House, was close to the premises of the Glasgow Jewish Board of Guardians and to Fogell's Bakery, whose barrel of herring stood guard at its doorway. I still have the ceremonial key which was presented to him by the synagogue at a ceremony to renew the building in 1934.

Two years after arrival in Glasgow Britain was at war. There was a need for the substantial production of military uniforms and Solomon took the plunge and opened a large factory in the small town of Barrhead just a few miles to the south of Glasgow. It was then convenient for the family to move out of the Gorbals and Solomon chose a modest Victorian stone villa in the Kennishead area which had an orchard behind. Although living in Kennishead it was still necessary to visit the Gorbals. There were the kosher shops to buy groceries and meat, bread and herring. There were the *chadarim,* the Hebrew classes for the children, the kosher restaurant to meet and *shmooz* with friends. It was, however, a two-way street. Gorbals folk liked their visit to the 'country' and many of the Jewish social groups liked to stage their events at Kennishead. Joseph (Joe) was the only one of the children to attend the local primary school. The older children attended schools in Glasgow, but Joe had to go to Thornliebank Primary School, where many families were extremely poor and children attended school without shoes. Joe removed his before being seen by his schoolmates.

The three brothers were only given first names, but Joe had Hyman (Chaim) added during a serious childhood illness. It is a Jewish custom that when illnesses become life-threatening the name can be changed to confuse the Angel of Death. Anne, who was born in 1918, married Arthur Kaplan who also given an extra name as a baby. His mother had experienced some neo-natal deaths and although his parents had chosen the name Moshe for him, they were advised to give him the Yiddish name 'alter' meaning old. So, Alter Moshe became known as Arthur. Solomon and Golda's last child, Mona was born in 1921. Alf added the middle name Alexander during his school years and my father had a short-lived attempt at the middle name of Samuel while at school but dropped it before starting university.

Solomon was still of military age when Russian-born Jews became liable for conscription in 1917, but his work as an army contractor presumably enabled him to avoid the military draft. In addition, he served locally as a special constable during the war years. With his business south of the city he also invested in a motorcar. In those days there were no driving tests. One bought a car and just drove off on roads which were without traffic lights but which had plenty of horse-drawn carriages. Family legend has it that while cars were available the supply of motor fuel was in its infancy and Solomon's first car – an Argyll, Scotland's first significant production car manufactured in Alexandria, near Glasgow – returned home with Solomon still at the wheel, but out of petrol, and the car was pulled by a large Clydesdale horse.

The house at Kennishead was to attain almost mythic status in family memory and like successive family homes in Pollokshields and Whitecraigs it was known as Goldina House. The row of villas at Kennishead was demolished around 1960 to make space for the construction of a series of multi-story apartment blocks. There was a family outing to visit the house before it was swept away along with its neighbours. It was thus a surprise to the grandchildren just how small it all seemed. Even the aunts and uncles, visiting it for the first time in 40 years, felt that the whole empty building seemed to have shrunk. The garden though was a delight. We could see where the family pictures had been posed: where Sarah had been photographed looking like 'Rebecca at the well'; where a young David had posed with his bicycle and many of the family group pictures were staged. Kennishead provided a comfortable home for the younger children as they

Solomon, Golda and children with Ura, Kennishead, Glasgow 1922.

were growing up and it remained the family home until the mid-1920s when they moved to Nithsdale Lodge in Pollokshields.

There were two regular family visitors at Kennishead. One was Ura who had arrived from Paris soon after the family were settled there and it was not long before she met Benno Schotz and divided her time between Kennishead and Glasgow's West End. The other was Solomon's cousin Anna, who lived with the family for some time while she was studying in Glasgow before leaving for London and eventually returning to Russia. They both adopted the Collins surname while in Glasgow. Motti appeared from Palestine to visit his brothers Solomon and Shimmel, sisters Gudis and Ura and cousin Anna. Glasgow was now a major centre for the Kagarlitsky family. In April 1921 Zelman had visited briefly during his plans to take up employment with the All-Russian Co-Operative Society (Arcos) in London the following year. Ida and Clara also paid visits around the same time. There are many collections of photographs of these visits all over the world. There is one of Motti and Anna taken in a photographer's studio both dressed elegantly for the occasion with smart hats and leaning on canes. Other pictures show Solomon, Golda and family with Ura, while another popular one was of Sarah with her aunt Ura and cousin Anna.

Anna had arrived in Glasgow not long after the family, but Ura and Shimmel (Simon) both came to Glasgow from Paris in 1916. Jerome told me that his grandfather Shimmel had been in Paris to study at the Sorbonne and although his studies had gone well he had also decided to go into cap manufacture as his brother Solomon had done. Maybe Ura had been studying there too acquiring the perfect French accent which served her well during the Second World War. In Glasgow, Shimmel set up his own business opening a clothing factory in Glasgow's London Road, under the name Samuel Collins. It never attained the size and scale of his brother's enterprise but it was successful enough for his son Gerald, a talented ice-hockey player, to be able to sell out to the Scottish textile giant Dawson for a substantial sum in the 1980s.

This was the age when every man in Glasgow would wear a cloth cap, so the market was substantial, and many of the larger Jewish-owned textile businesses began in this way. Some, in the simplest of materials, were those of the working man, others were more stylish. Family legend has it that Louis Blériot wore one of Shimmel's caps when he made the first flight across the English Channel in 1909. Blériot won £1,000 in prize money from the *Daily Mail* for the historic flight. However, the name of the cap manufacturer is not recorded and contemporary photographs show Blériot wearing standard aviator headgear. In any case, I am not sure that Shimmel was making any kind of cap as early as 1909.

Around 1921 Solomon's new and rapidly expanding business, known as the Globe Hat and Cap Manufacturers, faltered and crashed. The company went bankrupt with debts of over £30,000, a colossal sum for those days and equivalent to more than a million pounds at today's rates. Nothing daunted, Solomon was quickly back in business in the same premises with a new company headed by his young son Alf, just out of school at the age of fourteen. Alf paid his father a salary until the new business was able to pay off obligations and Solomon could resume full control once again. By the end of the decade Solomon had moved out of cap and hat manufacture into women's clothing forming the Scottish Costume and Mantle Manufacturers Company with a factory again in the Gorbals, firstly in Buchan Street and then in Oxford Street.

At the same time Solomon realized that he would need a British passport to be able to travel to Belgium and Germany to buy the cloth his business needed. He had been using his old Tsarist passport until it was no longer acceptable as an international travel document and in any case he required a full British passport to enter Germany. He stated that he had no wish to obtain a 'Bolshevik' passport. His application for British nationality should have gone smoothly and Solomon could point to voluntary work as a special constable besides his factory's manufacture of military wear during the First World War.

However, the application was complicated by a complaint against him from former business associates. The details became clear on receiving the Naturalization Papers from the National Records at Kew in London. Shimmel's papers covered just one page, Solomon's file had more than 50. As British citizenship had only been granted in 1929 and there had been issues in the process, I discovered that there was a 100-year embargo on the papers. Not keen to wait for more than a decade I found that I was able to make an application to gain access under the Freedom of Information Act, and that for a small fee someone would photocopy the paperwork and send it to me. Solomon had gone to a Jewish lawyer in Glasgow, Franklin Karno, in early 1926, who had tried to guide him through the various forms and declarations required.

On reviewing the details, a number of errors jump out. His year of birth is given as 1878 and not 1881 or 1882. His wedding date is given as 1903 instead of 1904. In the list of family, he mentions his father in Palestine, a brother in Buenos Aires and another in the United States and three sisters in Palestine, but omits the brother in Palestine and the sister still in Russia.

The Application Form notes that he adopted the surname Kalinsky on arrival in Britain, but the accompanying narrative says that the surname only dated from 1909, yet Kalinsky appears on the birth certificates of David, Joe and the twins. The financial declaration makes no mention of the bankruptcy while an accompanying narrative has full details of the business crash of 1921 with its £30,000 of debts.

However, none of this was the cause for the delay. As part of the process, adverts had appeared in the *Evening Times* and *Evening News*, both Glasgow newspapers, indicating that Solomon Collins had applied for naturalization and that anyone who had any information about his character that would make him ineligible for British citizenship should come forward. Two men made complaints. These were Edwin McLaughlan, a woollen agent in St. Enoch Square, in Glasgow's city centre and John Goldberg, an immigrant from Russia living in Aspley Place in the Gorbals. McLaughlan said that he had loaned Solomon £100, but Solomon claimed that he had supplied McLaughlan with £1,500 worth of goods, which had not been repaid. The story with Goldberg was much more complex. The two men had known each other in Stoke Newington in London, where both had been cap-makers. Goldberg had run into financial trouble in London and he had followed Solomon to Glasgow. Solomon had taken him into his business at the then substantial wage of £5 a week, allowed him to lodge with the family and even brought Goldberg's daughter to Glasgow to work as his clerkess. Things started to go wrong when Goldberg, who had received help from Solomon to establish his own business, again ran into financial trouble. Solomon was not inclined to bail him out and, as he had paid for Goldberg's shop, he sold the premises. Goldberg then alleged fraud and also cited Solomon's bankruptcy. Despite affidavits from four referees who had testified as to Solomon's good character, including former Provost Weir of Barrhead and the local doctor James Strang, his good war record and the feeling that McLaughlan and Goldberg represented petty business squabbles, the complaints persuaded the Crown Agent to delay decisions for some years. This was despite his checking with the local police in Glasgow, who confirmed that Solomon was 'a most respectable person'.

It was not till the end of 1928, some 30 years after arriving in London that he was now a British citizen. Solomon had made a financial arrangement with McLaughlan although the situation with Goldberg was unresolved. It was revealed that Goldberg had carried out a fraudulent transaction using Solomon's name, which ended with Goldberg in serious financial debt, and that Solomon had given the family some support. The

Crown Agent in Edinburgh now recommended accepting the Application, rather than the year by year delay of the past. A fee of £9 was paid and the saga was over.

The family remained closely in touch during the 1920s but were soon to be divided by the political ideologies of the twentieth century. Solomon and Shimmel and family had comfortable lives in Glasgow while the dramas of the new life in Palestine and the deteriorating situation for Jews in Europe were part of the life of the immediate family. Zev was alive during this decade, but Solomon never made the journey to Palestine to see him. However, Alf was given a trip to Egypt and Palestine in 1928 as a 21st birthday present. This was both an exciting but quite exhausting journey. Train to London and then on to Dover, ferry to France and the long train trip to Marseille before the Mediterranean crossings. He spent about four or five days in Egypt and Palestine, visiting the Pyramids at Giza before sailing to Jaffa for a meeting with his grandfather, aunt Clara, uncle Joseph and cousin Ruth. Alf had good Yiddish, so conversation with his relatives was quite easy although I am not sure just how much of Alf's world Zev would have understood. Alf had told me of this visit, but as noted, it was only recently that I found a photograph of the encounter in a visit to Alla in Haifa. Alla had said, 'Take it with you' but we were satisfied with a good photographic copy which we could easily store on a computer file.

After the First World War it was decided that the family should move to nearer the heart of the Jewish community and Nithsdale Lodge, 204 Nithsdale Drive in Pollokshields was purchased. The villa at Kennishead, while lying within the Glasgow city boundary, was just one building in a row of four homes surrounded by farmlands. Pollokshields was just three miles from the Gorbals and by the 1920s had become popular with Jewish families. It is now a conservation area with the western part composed of large villas with gardens along tree-lined streets while the eastern part has mainly three-storey sandstone tenements arranged in a grid pattern. Nithsdale Road is at the core of the western area and was an ideal base for Solomon and Golda's children as they were growing up. Within ten years there was a small synagogue, in a converted villa further along Nithsdale Road, and a kosher delicatessen a few streets away. When my parents married in 1946, they too chose this area buying, with parental help, a substantial stone villa in Newark Drive, just a few hundred yards from Nithsdale Lodge.

During these years the first signs of serious deterioration in Golda's rheumatoid arthritis were becoming apparent. In one of Chassia's letters to

Nithsdale Lodge, 204 Nithsdale Road, Pollokshields, Glasgow.

Zelman in 1911 she had referred to Golda's health commenting that she should travel abroad for a 'cure' rather than running up large bills with doctors. Her arthritis became quite deforming, but I still remember her walking in the early 1950s, using a home-constructed kind of walking frame. In earlier years she was more mobile, but her activity was now becoming more restricted and the centre of family life was her home. I could only ever remember her once leaving her home, for the dinner party for my cousin Jeffrey's *barmitzvah* in 1956.

Solomon paid close attention to medical developments and when American reports in the early 1950s that steroids were being considered to be a miracle cure he immediately crossed the Atlantic and returned with numerous treatment vials and a very neat system for injections, which my parents used in their practice for many years before disposable syringes and needles became widely available. Steroids turned out to be a major hazard producing a huge list of potential side-effects. In fact, the fear of steroid medication was such that when the next generation of anti-inflammatory drugs were produced, they were described as non-steroidals. Fortunately, Golda did not experience the side-effects and did benefit from a short-term remission but it was soon clear that the disease was progressing remorselessly with continuing joint deformity and kidney complications, which were to end her life in 1958 when she was only 72 years old.

It was during the late 1920s that the first two of Solomon and Golda's children were married. Sarah, the oldest child, married Hymie (Nissenbaum) Ness. Hymie had come to England from Brest Litovsk in Poland to join an uncle in Leeds after the death of his father in 1912, when he was just 12 years old. He volunteered for army service towards the end of the First World War which he knew was a straightforward path to British naturalization. He said that he was a jeep driver but given his poor eyesight that always seemed improbable. Perhaps his sight was better then. With some hard work after the war he had put enough money by to bring his mother and four sisters to Leeds. I never forgot the Polish names of the four sisters: Manya, Tonya, Genya and Batya. The three oldest sisters settled in Leeds but Batya, now known as Betty, came with Hymie to Glasgow and she married, opening a hairdressing salon on Fenwick Road in Giffnock. She retired to Bournemouth but decades later the shop is still there and is still called Bettina.

Hymie worked as an agent for a number of different furniture manufacturers travelling the length and breadth of Scotland. Some of these companies came from contacts he had made in Leeds, but he picked up other agencies through his ability to sell. One of his recognizable features was the red carnation in his buttonhole which he had all year round. He worked out an arrangement with a florist to sell him a new bloom every week at an average price for the year, so he wouldn't need to pay more in the winter although he could have paid less in the summer. The flower was watered by a small chrome water-holder which fitted neatly behind his lapel just behind the buttonhole. Sometimes people remembered the carnation before they remembered Hymie.

There were Jewish furniture stores in many different parts of Scotland such as my in-laws in Falkirk and Bernstein's in Dunfermline, places where there were small Jewish communities, now no more. He always talked about his visits to Irene's grandfather in Falkirk and how Louis Taylor was always careful not to buy what he could not afford. Taylor's was not the only Jewish furniture business in Falkirk, the 'competition' being Cembler and Marks, and Rifkinds. Hymie used his sales time to keep his Jewish customers informed about what was going on in the community in Glasgow and in later years he expected donations for the furniture sale conducted annually for the Bazaar of the Jewish Old Age Home for Scotland. One year, Mr Bernstein told him that he couldn't manage a donation, but nothing daunted Hymie just picked up a coffee table on the way out and sent him a receipt for the donation after the sale. 'I couldn't let him miss the opportunity of a mitzvah (doing a good deed)', he said. Their daughter Anita Zelma, named after Zelman, was born in 1931. They always wished for a son, but it never happened.

Alf married Doreen Brown at about the same time, and they had a son Dennis. There had been something of a sense of shock that he should have chosen a wife who was not Jewish, but pragmatism governed the reaction and Doreen agreed to convert. Things were much less formal in the pre-war days and I think that arrangements were made in Manchester for the conversion and they were able to have a Jewish wedding. Some of these conversions, both in Manchester and Glasgow, were not recognized in later times by the London Beth Din and the Office of the Chief Rabbi but as Dennis' wife Adrienne Reubens was impeccably Jewish there were no later repercussions.

In 1938 and 1939 the situation for German Jews deteriorated, especially following Kristallnacht, the Night of the Broken Glass, when hundreds of synagogues and Jewish businesses were looted and burned. Many Jews were beaten up and others arrested. The British government agreed to admit 10,000 unaccompanied children in what became known as the Kindertransport from Germany and Czechoslovakia without the need for visas and Jewish organization began the struggle to find accommodation for them all. Some were accommodated in hostels around the country. One was not far from Glasgow at Whittinghame House, the home of the Earl of Balfour. However, it was agreed that good foster homes would be best and both Hymie and Sarah and Alf and Doreen agreed to take a child. Shimmel and Becky also agreed and fostered an older child while Sarah and Alf took much younger children.

There had been a story that Alf and Hymie went to Edinburgh to collect 'their' children. Hymie had been promised a boy and Alf a girl. By the time they reached Edinburgh they had decided that if they switched round each would then have a boy and a girl. This was, of course, just a story. Gertrude (Tula) Marcus had decided that she wanted to find foster parents for her daughter Eva and had already made contact with Doreen and Alf through an agency in Berlin where Kaete a sister of Gertude's best friend worked. It was only when Eva reached Glasgow in February 1939 that Sarah and Hymie indicated that they would foster a little boy. Kaete then made arrangements for Michael, the son of Arnold and Else Wolff, to join them in Glasgow. He arrived in Glasgow in June 1939 having been collected by Hymie from Liverpool Street Station in London.

Eva never saw her parents again and she has remained a close part of the Collins family in Glasgow ever since. Eva was a partner for many years in a kosher deli in Giffnock near our home and it was always a pleasant place to shop. She was one of the youngest of all the *kinder*, the Kindertransport children, and has no memories from before she arrived in Glasgow. Eva does however have relatives in London and has maintained contact with them over the years. Michael's parents managed to get visas for Bolivia after their son's arrival in Glasgow. His mother left Germany during wartime, on 10 January 1940, and made her way directly to Bolivia stopping only in Panama and Chile on the way. This was a brave move for a woman on her own with no knowledge of Spanish. She arrived in La Paz on 1 March with just her luggage and $4 in cash.

Michael's father decided to use the Bolivian visa for a transit stop through Glasgow but the journey in Britain proved to be far from simple. Arnold Wolff arrived in Britain on 23 August 1939 and was almost immediately interned at a camp at Richborough. Five months later, in January 1940, he was able to come to Glasgow to visit Hymie and Sarah. Michael, still not four years old, was obviously confused as to the identity of the visitor and it did not help that Arnold was soon interned again, this time on the Isle of Man. At the outset of the war Britain had become paranoid about the threat from German spies and Jewish refugees were being interned along with Nazis who just happened to have been in Britain when war began.

Hymie took Michael to Liverpool in July 1940 to meet up with his father who now had a passage booked for Argentina, and onward travel to Bolivia. However, his papers were not found to be in order, and he was arrested again. They tried again in December and this time Michael was reunited with his father and they said goodbye to Hymie and Sarah. There was some nervousness as there had been a bombing raid over Liverpool the night before departure and they had to face the risk of U-boats while crossing the Atlantic. It was not until 11 March 1941 that Michael, Else and Arnold were reunited.Michael Wolff eventually told his story in *Full Circle: A Young Boy's Escape from Nazi Germany and his Reunion with Family* (2016)

Sarah took some time to recover from the departure of Michael. Anita, aged nine, missed her little foster brother. Sarah corresponded with Else for a while but unknown to Sarah and Anita, Hymie continued to write to the Wolffs until his death in January 1974. Contact was then lost for nearly twenty years until a friend from Glasgow who had been in California for a family *barmitzvah* had met Michael and brought back his contact details. In January 1994 Anita, who really did not like to fly, and Eva visited

California and met Michael and his mother. It was an emotional reunion, not just for Anita but also for Eva as Else was probably the only person still alive who had known her birth mother.

Solomon's younger sons were active sportsmen. My father, David, was a member of the High School of Glasgow's most successful rugby team ever. They had scored over 300 points conceded less than 30 and not lost a single game through the whole 1929-1930 season. A photograph of the team, with the details of their record season was on the wall of his consulting room in his medical practice, and when he retired it adorned my wall too. Today it has a place on a wall of our daughter Tamar in her home in Israel. For most of the 1930s my father was a medical student at the University of Glasgow. His brothers gravitated to Solomon's business on leaving school, but David was utterly devoted to his career choice of medicine. Solomon gave him every encouragement. It was a matter of great pride for the children of Jewish immigrants to enter higher education and medicine was usually the preferred subject. Many of Solomon's closest friends had sons who became doctors. Unfortunately, David found that the end of the year examinations often stood in the way of his ambitions and Hymie said that David got a new suit every time he failed an examination to console him and spur him on to passing at the next opportunity. It seemed to work as he qualified in 1939.

He came across the last stumbling block with the university final examinations but was able to pass those of the Triple Qualification of the three Scottish Royal Medical Colleges, which was an alternative route to medical registration. The Triple Qualification enabled him to put the letters LRCP LRCS (Edin) and LRCPS (Glas) after his name and I used the flamboyant certificate he received on graduation as the endpapers of *Go and Learn,* the book about Jews and medicine in Scotland. This was based on my Ph.D thesis, and on which I had started work just before he died in 1982.

Joe, the youngest brother, was a real sportsman. He played competitive ice-hockey in Glasgow and was much in demand for his skills on the ice. He also played at the highest levels and was one of the leading Scottish players of his generation. He was in the British team at the World Championships in Switzerland in 1939. Local newspaper reports were full of comments about his prowess in every game he played. In the summer of 1975, more than twenty years after Joe had retired from the sport, I went into Lizar's in Glasgow's Buchanan Street who sold a full range of photographic equipment. The salesman kept looking at me quizzically in between searches for the item I requested for my father's antiquated ciné projector. Eventually he said to me, 'Is your name Collins?' I asked him how he knew, and he replied that he was a keen follower of the Scottish ice-hockey scene and that my Uncle Joe had been one of his favourite players. He was sure he had spotted a family resemblance and I was proud to acknowledge the relationship.

8

Glasgow – Wartime and After

After the the Second World War many in the Glasgow family moved home. My grandparents sold Nithsdale Lodge and bought a large villa in Elphinstone Road in Whitecraigs, one of the leafiest of the southern neighbourhoods surrounding Glasgow. The Glasgow Jewish community had been moving southwards and the family followed the trend. Alf and Doreen had been living in Giffnock but soon moved nearer my grandparents with a house at the corner of Kenmure and Roddinghead Roads. Joe and Ethel lived close to my grandparents where Elphinstone Road joins Erskine Road. It was a large house with an enormous garden and often on Sunday afternoons, which was the time that the extended Collins family got together, the grandchildren would go to their home, Cairnmohr. Here there was a flat grassy area that seemed to us children the size of a football pitch, much better for play than the steeply sloping terraced garden of the grandparents.

Goldina

The great evenings at Goldina, as the family home was known, were of course the formal Yom Tov, Festival, meals. The table swept from one end of the extensive living room to the other, accommodating grandparents, their six children and spouses, the nine grandchildren and a couple of great-grandchildren. Then there were close family members like the Bravermans, cousins of my grandmother, and some close friends too. The atmosphere was warm and the noise level high. Syd Barrie always conducted the Pesach, Passover, Seder. Syd had grown up in Poplar, in the East End of London and had a good Jewish education which enabled him to lead synagogue services, so as we always had a *minyan* at these meals, we would sometimes have the festival prayers services there first. The seder always ended very late but Syd kept everyone attuned through the recitations, food and songs. Unlike at my other grandparents, potatoes were substituted for the green vegetables at the beginning of the Seder ritual, as that was what had been done back in Kovshevata, where winters were long and hard.

On other occasions, with the family and friends, perhaps almost 40 people, round the large table the evening ended with speeches as well as the familiar Yiddish songs. Every Collins family member was expected to say a few words. The stars were of course Joe, who was an exceptionally witty raconteur, and Sarah, who could always be trusted for some accidental verbal *faux pas* and she always took the responses in good humour. I can remember that even as a ten-year-old I was expected to make my contribution to the evening, making references to the importance of family, and especially this family, and usually managing a sentence or two on the Festival and its significance.

Food was very important to my grandparents. They retained a liking for the foods of home and some of these were passed down to the children and grandchildren. Items included *borscht* (beetroot soup), *blintzes* (fried filled pancakes), *holishkes* (cabbage leaves stuffed with mince), *kasha* (buckwheat fried with egg, mushrooms and onion), *kasha knishes* (kasha wrapped in pastry dough), *cholent* (a beef stew left simmering overnight for Shabbat lunch), *tzimmes* (a sweet stew with prunes, carrots and dumplings) and *p'tcha* (calf's foot jelly). Chicken soup wasn't chicken soup without *kreplach* (pasta pockets with mince accompanying soup), *mandlen* (homemade baked soup 'almonds'), *lochshin* (thin pasta strings) and *kneidlach* (matzah meal balls). These and many other items distinguished our diet from the local Scots, although many Scottish recipes found their way into Jewish homes These sometimes had to be specially adapted for the kosher kitchen. Fusion cooking is said to have included Scotch Broth with kreplach. A great staple was *gefilte* fish. In its Eastern European version, it was stuffed carp but in Scotland it took two forms. Minced haddock and whiting were mixed with matzah meal and egg, formed into balls and boiled. Alternatively, the fish balls were fried and usually eaten cold.

In these last years of Solomon's life there were regular visits from family members from around the world. Nathan and Gussie Carl's visit from Portland, Oregon in 1958 was particularly memorable. Nathan's father Shneur was a first cousin of Solomon's and his grandfather Yaakov (Feter Yankel) was a brother of Zev. Nathan confirmed my grandfather's tales of the countryside around Kovshevata with its greenery, its fertile soil, forested hills, valleys and cool streams and lakes. This had always met a degree of scepticism from listeners but at last there were Kagarlitsky visitors prepared to confirm the stories. A year or two later the Schujmajers from Argentina added an exotic touch to these family visitors, but as the only common language for the adults was Yiddish the younger generations missed much of their stories.

My grandfather died while the business was still riding high. He had taken a back-seat in his last years as management gradually devolved to Joe, but he continued to attend the factory every day until the last weeks of his life. My grandfather, as I remember, had few hobbies. He read Yiddish novels. This was interesting as his siblings tended to correspond in Russian while he much preferred the Yiddish medium and had no reading material in Russian. He liked a flutter on the horses, especially backing the rank outsiders. It wasn't a very profitable approach although very occasionally one would win and he recovered some of his losses. His great pride and joy was the garden and the extensive row of greenhouses at the foot of a very long back garden which had a fairly steep incline. Even here he aimed beyond the standard hothouse fare of tomatoes, corn cobs, peppers, courgettes and cucumbers. Passing through the greenhouses the temperature got hotter and hotter until reaching the last area, where the temperature and humidity were tropical. His greatest achievement was cultivating watermelons. Someone unkindly commented that it would have been cheaper to fly to Spain or Italy and bring them back one by one.

Solomon, one of the last of all the siblings, survived only by Clara the youngest of all Zev's children, passed away on 13 July 1964. This corresponded to the 4th of Av in the Jewish calendar which meant that the *shiva*, the week of family mourning, fell during the first nine days of the Hebrew month of Av. These days recall the destruction of the Temples in Jerusalem leading up to the fast day on the ninth of the month, Tisha B'Av. Besides the thrice daily prayers at my grandfather's home, we spent Tisha B'Av at the synagogue observing its special mourning practices.

Alfred (Alf) and Doreen

When the Second World War began Alf and Doreen were living in Park Road, Giffnock with their two children, Dennis and Eva. Alf was, at the beginning of hostilities, an Air Raid Warden making sure that homes complied with the blackout regulations. Nazi warplanes were making sorties to bomb shipbuilding and port facilities on the River Clyde a few miles to the north. Homes also had makeshift shelters in their back gardens and a bomb obliterated a home in Hathaway Drive, just a couple of streets away, during one of these raids. During the war he was called up for service in the Royal Air Force and following this he was seconded to the Board of Trade, a British Governmental body concerned with commerce and industry which had a key economic role in the post-war era. At the same time, he became involved in Red Cross work.

Alf took a leading role in the sales side of the business after the war. He began to identify export markets and in 1948 he undertook a month-long visit to the United States trying to identify importers for the company, now known as Collins (Juveniles) Ltd. He was based at the Hotel New Yorker but also planned visits to Chicago, Philadelphia and San Francisco. Solomon and Alf, and now joined by Joe, aimed big. They visited London regularly and established a base at the Dorchester Hotel. After taking Solomon on holiday with us to Torquay after Golda's death he treated us to a couple of nights in London at the Dorchester. We had never then, and hardly ever now, seen such an opulent hotel. Their buyers were well entertained in London and in Glasgow.

These years saw great times for British textile manufacturers. The tartan children's clothes being turned out in a beautifully appointed factory in Glasgow's Alexandra Parade, near the Wills' cigarette factories, provided good company profits. Alf bought a Rolls Royce and for a few years lived at Todhill at the edge of Newton Mearns, a mansion house set in extensive grounds. At the same time Alf was a deeply caring individual busy with charitable activities within and beyond the Jewish community. In his younger days had supported charities linked to the Glasgow Jewish Board of Guardians and by 1949 he was the founding chairman of the Jewish Old Age Home for Scotland and was its leading influence for 25 years.

Alf was not just a consummate fundraiser. He went out to poorhouses and institutions around Scotland seeking out Jewish patients and inmates who would welcome transferring to a Jewish home. It was charitable work at its best. The Home began with the gift of a substantial Victorian villa in Newark Drive, just across the road from our home. The Home soon outgrew its original premises and Alf, with his brothers, bought the villa next door as its first expansion in 1950. He also persuaded my father to become the Home's Honorary Medical Superintendent in 1962 and I took over from him after my father's stroke in 1978.

Alf was also involved with the Scottish Veterans Gardens City Association, which provides homes for ex-service personnel, again taking a leading role for many years. His work for the Veterans earned him an OBE (Officer of the Order of the British Empire). He had presided over a one-time fundraising effort for the Notre Dame Child Guidance Clinic, which functioned under Catholic auspices. He also took part in funding for Israeli causes. In the early 1950s he became interested in the Bikkur Cholim Hospital in Jerusalem. This hospital began in the Old City in 1826 and in 1898, during his visit to Jerusalem, the German Emperor Wilhelm II donated a large enough sum for purchasing the plot of land on which the present hospital was built on Nathan Straus Street. Alf needed to see what his efforts were producing, and he visited the hospital in 1955, bringing with him Rev. Dr. I.K. Cosgrove, the minister of the Garnethill Synagogue. He was instrumental in setting up the Child and Youth Aliya group in Glasgow, supporting youngsters needing support in Israel and was chairman both of the Blue and White Committee which raised funds for the Jewish National Fund (*Keren Kayemet L'Yisrael*) and of the Glasgow Friends of the Anti-TB League for Israel, which attracted many doctors, including my parents.

In 1957 with the introduction of independent television to Scotland which, unlike the established British Broadcasting Corporation (BBC), carried advertisements Colwer used the new medium to solidify its customer base. The factory operated on many different levels. Colwer was the name of the children's clothing under the parent company Collins Juveniles. Other companies, added by the acquisition of a number of smaller local manufacturers, dealt with women's clothing, especially coats.

The Three Sisters

In the late 1950s my grandfather thought he had the ideal business for his three daughters. He opened shops under the name 'The Three Sisters' to sell factory produce but some other lines as well. It was a simple business model, but the experiment lasted only a few years. Sarah looked after a shop in Great Western Road near the university. The others were on the south side (of the River Clyde). Mona was in Victoria Road and Anne in Kilmarnock Road near Shawlands Cross. I remember visiting Sarah with my father in her shop and even at the age of eight I could see that she was the most unlikely shop manager. She would just disappear to the hairdressers, take some money out of the till for the taxi and the hairdo, and never manage to recall which purse the money had come from. She was the loveliest and kindest person, full of memorable remarks, like the time on her first flight she asked the stewardess to open the window as she thought the plane was a bit stuffy. She just wasn't cut out for retail.

Mona probably was the most business-like of the three. She eventually partnered her husband Syd Barrie in his fashion agency and learned to drive when he lost his licence. They had one son, Gregory, who was born in 1948. Anne and her husband, Arthur Kaplan, with their children Lynda and Jeffrey lived with my grandparents. Arthur was a commercial traveller, visiting shops around Scotland and taking the products of the Coutt's warehouse. He had a ready, and quite unusual, sense of humour which resonated with his young nephews and nieces. It is hard to recall his memory without a smile.

My grandmother's rheumatoid arthritis had meant that by the time the shops opened Anne was more concerned in running the family home rather than running a business. She made sure that the house operated efficiently and that there was food for whoever might turn up to see Golda at any time of the day. Life centred round Goldina, as the house was known, and was open to the extended family but also many of their closest friends, and anybody that their closest friends brought along. One of Jeffrey's friends described it as somewhere he would go with a girlfriend after the pictures. It was always busy.

In the early 1960s, not too long after Golda had passed away, Anne had a trip to New York accompanied by her sister-in-law Ethel, to visit relations. After this trip we heard more about Golda's relations. Her sister Ida, and brother-in-law (Frank Madow) had visited Glasgow in about 1952 and contacts had been maintained. A highlight of the trip was a visit to the *Boyerke Landsmanschaft*, the organization formed by immigrants from Golda's *shtetl* and which provided social and welfare benefits for its members, similar to the Jewish Friendly Societies which proliferated in Glasgow at the time. Some saw in the cohesiveness of these *landsmanschaft* groups a lack of ability to enter the American mainstream fully, but for Anne the women's group *Boyerke Heimishe Ugent* (Boyerke Ladies' Auxiliary) provided more than just nostalgia. The stories she heard gave her insight into the early life of her mother as there were people there who remembered the Pogorovsky (Packer) family and even if they didn't remember Golda, they knew members of her closest family. The visit was just in time. The Jewish Friendly Societies in Glasgow had closed with the advent of the National Health Service and better approaches to communal philanthropy. In America, the *landsmanschaften* had catered to the immigrant generation and to a certain extent included their children too. Their assimilated grandchildren looked askance at the presence of the Yiddish-speaking *Der Heim*, the Old Country, in America.

Sarah and Hymie

Hymie was a shul (synagogue) man. He was traditionally religious, prayed with his tefillin at home every weekday of his life and was a leading figure in the Central Synagogue in Hospital Street in the Gorbals. Membership of the synagogue was declining as Jews were moving out of the Gorbals mostly to the southern suburbs, and it was agreed to close the shul in 1956 and amalgamate with the Great Synagogue in South Portland Street. The Great Synagogue was large and impressive. It dated back to 1901 and housed the core religious study groups of the community. It did not have the architectural grace of the Garnethill Synagogue in the north-west corner of the city centre just up the very steep Garnet Street from Sauchiehall Street. But then Garnethill cost £14,000 to build in 1879 – the Great just half of that just over two decades later.

The Great Central Synagogue was looked on as the heart of the Gorbals community and Hymie was its Parnas (senior warden) from 1956 until his death in January 1974. There was a committee and office bearers, but Hymie was very much the man in charge. My first years were spent in Pollokshields. Its small homely synagogue was a very short walk from our home in Newark Drive and I was allowed, from quite a young age to walk there on my own for Shabbat morning services. However, when my grandmother died in June 1958 my father and his brothers agreed that they would attend services in 'Hymie's shul' and say *kaddish*, the prayers for the dead, there for the eleven months of the year of mourning.

Sarah and Hymie's home was also a place for family gatherings, every week for Kiddush, after the Saturday morning synagogue service. The word Kiddush means 'sanctification' and refers to the prayer over wine, or grape juice, recited on Sabbaths and other Holy Days. It also includes the repast, which precedes the formal festive meal, usually biscuits and cakes, though often with the addition of other favourites including herring, smoked salmon and cold fried fish balls. While wine was customary for the blessing, whisky was the preferred drink for my uncles, and indeed today Scotch whisky, sometimes in its rarest and most expensive malt whisky products, has become an essential part of the Kiddush experience around the Jewish world.

The Gorbals may have been physically close to Pollokshields but it was also a world away. It represented the Yiddish-speaking past of the immigrants of my grandfather's generation. The rabbi was Naphtoli Herz Shapiro, who had been a graduate of the prestigious Radun Yeshiva in Poland, headed by the saintly rabbi known as the Hofetz Haim, from the title of one of his works. Rabbi Shapiro was living in Leeds until he came to Glasgow in 1936 to lead the Glasgow Yeshiva. This was mostly an after-school learning centre at a higher level than the general cheder system for younger children and unlike the Glasgow Hebrew College which also taught modern Jewish history and literature. At some stage, according to Hymie, the rabbi just walked into the shul and occupied the vacant rabbi's seat, which he held until the shul closed in June 1974 just a few months after Hymie died.

I learned a lot from both the rabbi and Hymie. The rabbi engendered a love of traditional Jewish learning. For all that he was a traditional Eastern European rabbi he identified with the religious Zionist Mizrachi movement and had even completed an MA degree at Glasgow University through attendance at night classes. His English was very heavily accented, but he had trained a generation of rabbis and educated layman and had run the Yeshiva with full-time learning for a number of religious refugee students.

Before leaving the synagogue, I should mention at least some of the characters who inhabited this special space. The *shammos*, or beadle, was Chaim Jarvis who had arrived in Glasgow with the soldiers of the Polish Army. He had spent the war years in Scotland, married a local woman and stayed. His Yiddishized English was delightfully laced with malapropisms and even as a young teenager I was always *di kleine doktorel*, the little doctor. It was, therefore, fitting that in his last months I really was his doctor in the Jewish Old Age Home. Benjamin Louis reminded me of the ultra-pious Karlkammer from Israel Zangwill's *Children of the Ghetto*. Like the fictional character he leaned so far forward in his devotions that he needed to pay for the seat in the row in front. Louis also had the custom to remain in the synagogue all night after the Kol Nidrei service constantly reciting *Tehillim*, the Book of Psalms.

One of the strangest figures in the shul was called 'Murphy'. His real surname was Bloch, and someone once said that he was related to the great whisky magnate and leading philanthropist of the Glasgow Jewish community Sir Maurice Bloch although I never heard that story substantiated. Murphy was a 'rag and bone' man, still plying his trade in the late 1950s. This meant a very precarious hand to mouth existence picking up discarded goods, mainly worn-out clothing, that could be sold on to dealers. He would spend his day pushing his handcart around the streets in the Gorbals area and along the Clyde wharves and would sell, each day, what he could to dealers. He would never be sure to have enough money for his basic needs of accommodation and food. A *Manchester Guardian* reporter followed a rag and bone man in 1958 as he collected rags, scrap metal, old shoes and furniture for a day earning the sum of £2 (about £20 in 2020 values).

When Hymie encountered him and realized that he was Jewish he offered him a position as a 'minyan man'. Sometimes the shul struggled to have ten men, the basic prayer quorum, present at early morning services during the week, and Murphy and one or two other unfortunates were paid to be present. Murphy was even allowed to store his unsold goods in the synagogue basement where the *mikva*, ritual bath, was situated. The extra pound or two made a difference to him. Murphy was one of the last paid Glasgow minyan men and one of its last rag and bone men. One afternoon, my mother collected me from school in the city centre, and at the traffic lights and level with our car was Murphy complete with handcart piled high with rags. I waved and got an immediate smile in return. I had to explain the Murphy story to my mother.

After my *barmitzvah* Hymie insisted that I recite the Haftara regularly. These readings from the Prophets complemented the Torah reading. I always had the worst voice in the shul, but they tolerated me and over the years I got to recite almost all of them. A couple of final memories. Regular Shabbat and Festival services were never very busy, so on one occasion, possibly the last day of Pesach, Passover, I noticed the shul filling up dramatically just before the Yizkor, Memorial, prayer. South Portland Street was just south of the City centre and people who worked in the offices and workshops there were particular in attending this prayer of memorial for departed relatives. Suddenly, the shul was almost full, and imperceptibly after the Yizkor prayers people started to leave. Suddenly, only the regular worshippers were left. Hymie explained to me, 'People may not be religious, but they know how to respect their ancestors.'

Simchat Torah was also celebrated in traditional style. This festival celebrates the end of the year-long cycle of Torah readings, and the beginning of the next cycle. As the men readied themselves to make the circuits round the shul, we children followed carrying flags, where the banners were situated far enough down the stick to allow an apple to inserted on top. Above the apple was a candle. I don't remember the candles being lit although they would have been in the past despite the risk of fire. The apples of course were consumed with relish and were a healthier treat than the bags of sweets that children expect today. I must have been ten years old, so around 1958, when I became aware that, during the circuits, the very back rows of the shul downstairs had filled up with women and children. These were not regular shul attendees – I didn't recognize any of them. They were simply Jewish Gorbals residents who had come as a form of identification with the shul and perhaps to partake of the modest repast which followed the service. I remember being concerned that no attempt appeared to be made to find out who the visitors were and how they could be included in the synagogue's regular activities.

My grandfather, who had been a member of the Central Synagogue of course transferred his membership to the Great Central. There were ten very prominent seats towards the front of the synagogue and my grandfather had one of them, next to Sammy (Rosenblum) Campbell, who was a whisky magnate and kept the shul stocked with White Heather Whisky, and Sam Lipsey a prominent figure in the Glasgow Jewish community. Many of these ten did not attend regularly but their donations at the festivals meant that membership fees could be kept to a minimum. Hymie also operated the synagogue's burial grounds at Riddrie in a similar way only charging people what they could afford.

It was a great surprise, later, to discover that my wife's family, the Taylors from Falkirk, were members of the same shul and consequently we were married there in July 1972. By this stage I recalled that I had been in the synagogue on the morning of her brother Raymond's *barmitzvah* in 1965, and I did remember seeing him in shul over the months before that. Given Hymie's family connection with me – I was looked on almost as a son by him – and his business connection with Irene's father, and grandfather before that, our wedding, in his shul was a special highlight for him. We had been worried about whether he would be able to attend as the cancer which affected him was becoming apparent to all. He was there but ironically his wife Sarah missed out, having taken a heart attack a few days earlier.

Joseph (Joe) and Ethel

Joe was born in 1915, just three years after my father. He was a colourful and charismatic figure and succeeded in many different walks of life. We have already noted his international abilities in ice-hockey, and he continued to play the sport after the war. His cousin Gerald (Gerry), Shimmel's son, was also an ice-hockey player and one of the stars of the Glasgow Mohawks team. He was a bit jealous of Joe's successes on the rink, once telling me that he was the better player but 'everyone just loved Joe'. Joe also had a very distinguished wartime service. He had already joined the Territorial Army in 1938 and was called up to the Royal Artillery as soon as the war began. He quickly rose through the ranks becoming a Lieutenant-Colonel and ending the war as an acting Brigadier. He served in East Africa training native troops for active army service in the Far East. In 1942 Churchill decided that Britain should capture Madagascar in an invasion known as Operation Ironclad. Joe was a senior Royal Artillery officer and was an important figure in the Madagascar action.

The very large island of Madagascar, slightly bigger than France, was a Vichy French colony and hostile to the British war effort. There were concerns that the Japanese might capture the island, with its large natural harbour at Diego Suarez (Antsiranana). This would make shipping round the Cape of Good Hope very risky at a time when crossing the Mediterranean to the Suez Canal was extremely dangerous. Germany also had designs for the island with plans to deport three million Jews there, an unlikely logistical exercise. With the British capture of the island the 'Final Solution' took place on European soil.

The invasion began on 5 May 1942. The Vichy French resisted strongly, and Petain declared that resistance had to continue 'by every means and to the last cartridge'. He called for assistance in repelling the British invasion from the Japanese; they sent three submarines in reconnaissance on 29 May. A few days later the 22nd (East Africa) Brigade Group arrived on Madagascar with native troops from Kenya, under British leadership, removing the roadblocks and other obstructions left by the French. In this they were assisted by supportive islanders,

John Grehan's book *Churchill's Secret Invasion: Britain's First Large Scale Combine Operations Offensive 1942* (2013) gives a comprehensive account of the Madagascar campaign. Grehan notes that Joe (Lieutenant Colonel Joseph Collins) was commander of No.3 Fighting Group, which was heavily armed, and included troops from several units of the King's African Rifles as well as some Seaforth Highlanders. After being involved in the capture of the capital Tananarive (now Antananarivo) Joe was the leading officer at the capture of Behanjy, a battle that lasted just a few hours and he remained in charge of the action until the British Army reached the resort town of Antsirabe. Doubts were subsequently expressed as to the benefits of the operation but in the dark wartime days of 1942 the successful invasion was a needed boost to British morale. In 1946, Joe was awarded an OBE by King George VI for his wartime service. Being stationed in Kenya he quickly learned to speak Swahili, the *lingua franca* of much of Africa, which I remember he once used on a Kenyan Airways flight much to the surprise of the cabin staff.

A chat-line on the Glasgow Guide Discussion Boards website in 2007 gives an insight into the size and complexity of the Collins factory. Workers remembered it as a pleasant place to work and after Solomon's death Joe was very much in charge as Alf began to take on a smaller work commitment. Joe was a very likeable boss and factory conditions were described as excellent. Workers from several departments explained the content of their work, mostly relating to the 1960s and 1970s. There was a Print Office churning our forms and flyers on a Gestetner machine. The Time and Motion Office assessed the work schedules and provided staff and management with an assessment of costs. The Sample Room employed sketchers and designers who would work on developing new lines. Even the factory floor was carefully regulated. As one worker explained:

> The girls who worked in the factory cut off numbers that related to the job they did on the garment, and each number had a price, and they put the tickets in a book, to be handed into the office. I took the books back up to the girls who worked in the factory and if I was a penny out on their earnings, they would give me a bawling out. They always knew to a penny what they had earned.

Around 1970 the factory moved to premises just around the corner from Alexandra Parade in Milnbank Street. I never quite understood the need for the move, but it must have been part of a cost-cutting exercise as by this time British textile manufacturing was in serious decline. Alf's son Dennis left Glasgow to be the firm's representative in London, but further retrenchment followed. Britain's textile industry had all but disappeared by the 1980s and the Collins factory was one of the early casualties. Solomon's brother's factory survived longer under the management of Shimmel's son Gerald, who managed to sell the business in good time to the large Dawson International enterprise. The demand from retailers for cheaper clothing led to outsourcing from Asian manufactures whose prices British producers could not match.

Joe was irrepressible. He called me one day to say that he had some tight central chest pain. I was there immediately, and the electrocardiograph indicated mild changes of a heart attack. Blood tests results received the following day confirmed the findings. I explained the situation to Joe. His condition was stable, and he agreed to bedrest at home, and I said would visit as often as I could. Within 24 hours he felt fine and was ready to go to Paris for a pre-arranged business meeting two days later. I told him 'No!' He then proposed to postpone the meeting for a few days and by that stage I had to let him go. He coped well with the end of the factory, creating a new career for himself in sourcing imports when others might have just decided to retire. On a business trip to Bucharest during the Ceausescu years he wanted to find the times of Shabbat services at the Choral Synagogue. No-one in the hotel could help so he called the first Goldberg in the telephone directory which led to a phone conversation with a security agent who wanted to know why a foreigner was phoning private Romanian citizens.

Joe had married Ethel Blin in 1941, and when he was sent abroad the following year she joined a mechanized transport group tasked with driving senior figures to planning meetings. She had been Vice-Admiral Harold Hickling's personal driver and meetings included the planning in Largs for the D-Day Landings. Having overheard an antisemitic remark by a couple of Canadian soldiers blaming the Jews for the war she resolved to work for Israel after the defeat of Germany. She became a leading figure not just in Glasgow WIZO, the Women's International Zionist Organisation, raising large sums of money for projects benefitting women and children in Israel, but was involved at a national level in British WIZO frequently visiting centres established in Israel through her fundraising. She was a businesswoman too. Her company, Granton Commercial Accessories, specialized in making belts and enjoyed considerable success and still functions many years after the deaths of Ethel and her son Charles, her business partner for many years. Being a businesswoman in the early days took courage and self-confidence as well as skill and judgement and Ethel passed the test for all of these.

Joe was also involved in fundraising for Israel through the Blue and White Balls and Bazaars which raised funds for the Jewish National Fund, which planted trees and helped reclaimed desert lands for agriculture. These were glamorous events and again substantial sums were involved. At a visit to Israel by parliamentarians of the Scottish National Party in 2016 they visited a grove named for William MacRae, a founder of the party and a great friend of the Jewish community and of Israel, which had been planted in the 1950s with funds raised by Joe and his colleagues. After their deaths, a Joseph and Ethel Collins Charitable Foundation has perpetuated their legacy and their daughter Sharman comes regularly from London to continue Ethel's WIZO work.

David and Hetty

My parents, David and Hetty Ockrim, had married in November 1946. Hetty had been a registrar in obstetrics and gynaecology but was ready to join her new husband in setting up a general practice. Hetty's consultant Albert Sharman was friendly with Stevan George, who had arrived in Glasgow as a First World War refugee from Serbia. He qualified at Glasgow University in 1923 and set up a practice, firstly in Kinning Park and then in 1929 he moved it to Ibrox. He was planning to leave Britain before the start of the National Health Service and told Sharman that he was ready to sell his practice. Sharman arranged for them to meet with Dr. George who agreed to sell them his practice, as had to be done in pre-NHS days. David started work in the Cessnock Street surgery in February 1946 and Hetty joined him a few months later.

My father's first medical job was at the Blawarthill Hospital in Clydebank. It was a small district hospital with few staff members and should have provided an easy entry into medicine. With the Battle of Britain and the German bombing raids on key shipping targets around the country Clydebank was a target, and the hospital had to serve the needs of injured civilians. It was hard and constant work, and he had an easier time the next year working in the Recruitment Offices in Rouken Glen Park doing medical assessments. He then entered the Royal Army Medical Corps (RAMC) where he worked as a general practitioner in the 9th Army, firstly in Algeria and subsequently in Italy. In Algeria he had been stationed near Bône (now Annaba) where a sculptor offered to make him a silver-covered metal silhouette. He modelled for the silhouette and a solid silver pen was melted down to make the coating. The likeness is impressive, and it is now in the possession of his grandson, David, born two years after his death and named after him.

David had already suffered his stroke when he had an unexpected visitor. Andrew Robb, the fashion writer and illustrator for the *Daily Express,* was writing his memoirs and recalled the Scottish doctor he had spent time with, in Rome and Florence after the liberation of Italy. He knew that David had shared his friendship with Count Buonacorsi, a scion of a noble Tuscan family, and hoped that David might have some photographs. He got the contact details from British Army records and came to Glasgow. David shared the photograph of the Count with Robb and himself and this appeared in Robb's book *Lifestyle* (1979) along with a short account of David's role as an army doctor. Returning to Glasgow after the war he was ready to start work and for general practice he needed no further training. Hetty was ready to take her hospital obstetrics into a medical system where few deliveries took place in hospital.

We moved from Pollokshields to a new area in Newton Mearns in 1961, where the builder offered purchasers the ability to 'design their own home'. Mona and Syd and Hymie and Sarah were near each other in Newlands just a few miles to the north on the way to the city centre. While our home was being completed we stayed with Hymie and Sarah for what was planned to be a few weeks but ended up being nine months. They were great hosts and it worked very well.

As almost everyone at family gatherings were patients of my father, he had to bring a prescription pad with him. There were even evenings where he had to bring his ear syringe to clear out the blocked ear canals of those present. Naughty children were threatened with 'good boy' or 'good girl' injections, but it was soon realized that this was just a joke. It was a kind of cabaret act between loud discussions and the singing of Yiddish songs. Everyone loved it.

I entered the practice in 1976 and had the privilege of working with both parents until David had a stroke in March 1978 and was never able to return to work. My mother remained in the practice until she retired in 1989. They made a great team. He was calm, approachable and understanding and the patients loved him. She was sharp, innovative and able to size up difficult situations and find solutions. She did not tolerate malingerers. Patients respected her and were fiercely loyal. Her parents, my Ockrim grandparents, were initially opposed to their daughter studying medicine, insisting she take an alternative science course. However, she persisted, switched to the Medical Faculty after a year and graduated in 1943. They became very proud of her.

She had a try at tutoring Jeffrey, Anne's son, for some of his schoolwork. It was an uphill and fruitless task. However, Jeffrey proved to be a good businessman, first in my grandfather's factory and subsequently as a jeweller in his father-in-law's business which he successfully developed and expanded. His death in his early sixties was a shock to us all. Jeffrey was five years older than me, just a bit too old to be part of the group of younger cousins which besides myself and my sister Irene, included Jeffrey's sister Lynda, Joe's children Sharman and Charles and Mona's son Gregory. Solomon's first great-grandchild Leonie, Anita's daughter, was also close in age to us. While all of Solomon's grandchildren grew up in Glasgow the next generation gradually moved away. Dennis was the first to leave, followed by Lynda, Sharman and Gregory. With us leaving in 2009, the passing of Anita and the untimely deaths of Charles and Jeffrey my sister and Eva are the only cousins who remain in Glasgow.

Family illness concerned me greatly. In the early days of building their practice my father enrolled all the family, my mother's as well as his, as patients. I was to deal with them all after qualifying as they all began, in older age, to suffer the effects of their heavy cigarette smoking. Most of them passed through the local Southern General Hospital during the 1970s and 1980s leading the nursing staff to think that I must have the most enormous family. Alf, Joe and Mona all died of lung cancer, my father and Sarah had smoking-related heart disease and Anne had vascular dementia. Alf was the heaviest smoker, getting through up to 80 a day, sometimes lighting one and finding he had nowhere to put it as he already one between his lips. A family gathering was always covered in smoke. My father was promised £100 when he was eighteen if he agreed not to smoke until he was 21. He agreed but started smoking when my grandfather paid up.

Shimmel and Rebecca (Becky)

Shimmel, my great uncle, did not marry until he came to Glasgow. So unlike all his siblings who had left Russia he had a wife from a local family, Becky Winston. Shimmel's business also prospered in the post-war years, but it never possessed the glamour of Solomon's. The factory in London Road seemed outdated but it was well-run and very efficient. Their children were Sylvia, who married Isidore Gerber, a member of a well-established Jewish business family in Glasgow and Gerald who married Delia Max from Liverpool. These were our closest Collins family. Sylvia's son Jerome was in the same class as me at my first primary school. He wasn't cut out for academic studies but proved to be remarkably skilful with his hands building models of aeroplanes for wind tunnel testing during a few years in Israel and on return to Glasgow teaching at a technical college. His ex-wife Obba is Icelandic and one daughter, Svana, lives in Iceland while Nicola is in Israel.

Jerome's sister Gloria worked for a time as a receptionist in my parents' practice and later ran a newsagents in Giffnock with her husband Henry Freer. Gerald's daughters Dawn and Suzie moved to England, while Stephen remained in Glasgow running a successful burglar alarm business. Their older son Adam (Shimon) now lives in the ultra-Orthodox Israeli town of Kiryat Yearim (Telz Stone), where, after many years of religious studies he works as a *sofer*, religious scribe. My mother commissioned three Purim scrolls, the *Book of Esther*, one each for her grandsons and one for me just before she died. His scribal skills show an artistic talent and we all much enjoy reading them. He wrote the *mezuzot* (the parchment containing scriptural verses affixed to the doorposts of a Jewish home) for our home in Jerusalem. Adam is the nearest Collins relation to us in Israel and we have been at some of his family celebrations, weddings and *barmitzvahs*.

9

The Doctor and Medical Historian

Growing up I was aware that our family was just a little different from the other Jewish families in Glasgow. Many of my contemporaries also had grandparents who had been born in Poland or Russia, but in general either the whole family had settled in Scotland or moved on to the United States. No-one had relatives remaining in Russia and few were even aware of where their extended family had settled. Solomon and Golda had fairly soft Russian accents but spoke good grammatical English unlike Uncle Shimmel who could be difficult to understand. The family had remained traditional, keeping their homes kosher in a time when the vast array of foodstuffs now available for the Jewish home did not exist and meals and snacks had to be prepared from scratch. Both of my parents' families were very close. Saturday afternoons were spent with the Ockrims and Sunday afternoons with the Collinses and it was rare for a family member to be absent. As Jewish festivals outside Israel are observed for two days, rather than one, it meant that, for example, we could spend one Pesach seder with the Ockrims and one with the Collins family.

The foods might have been similar, but the Collins family was much more boisterous and with the very charismatic Joe we knew that any evening together would be lively, entertaining and above all enjoyable. My Ockrim cousins were also a few years younger while there were Collins cousins of the same age who could put on shows, which I had usually scripted and produced for the adults. I was one of a group of cousins with my father's family but with the Ockrims I was the oldest and could enjoy the fuss which first-born status provided.

My mother took a break from work before I was born leaving my father to look after her general practice patients and her obstetric list. My father could cope with all of the routine work but a difficult delivery in a small, poorly-equipped tenement flat led him to call her in. When the midwife saw the doctor herself almost ready to deliver, she sent my mother home and had to send the patient to the hospital. From that moment it seemed to be accepted that David and Hetty's son would be a doctor like his parents. Mealtimes often involved my parents swapping incidents that occurred that day in the practice. The talk fascinated me but must have bored my sister.

At the age of eight it was decided that I should sit for one of Glasgow's private schools, which all admitted a significant number of pupils for Primary Five. I had been a pupil at St. Ronan's, a small preparatory school near our home in Pollokshields which only went up to Primary Four, so all the pupils had then to leave for other schools. My mother had attended the Hutchesons Grammar School for Girls and recommended the Boy's School. These schools were maintained by the Hutchesons Trust which subsidized the private schooling so that it was provided at a nominal cost. The Boy's School was still situated in the Gorbals in 1956 and had long been popular with the Jewish community. My father had attended the High School of Glasgow, founded in the long-distant past, but was now based in Elmbank Street near Sauchiehall Street and thus in the city centre. The school was something of an anomaly, being a council school that charged modest fees, no more than about £7 for a term when I was at the secondary level, worth around £160 at 2020 prices.

I was accepted quickly by Hutchesons Grammar and my parents sent confirmation of the offer which had a deadline before the High School informed candidates about whether they had a place. When the positive letter came from Glasgow High my father was so pleased that I had the opportunity to attend his old school that he was prepared to go back to Hutchesons and cancel the place. It was an awkward start. Before I left St. Ronan's it was announced that I was to be Proxime Accessit, the title for the runner-up to the Dux. My mother was most unhappy as I had generally outperformed the Dux in class assessments. She felt that antisemitism was involved and insisted that my father speak to the head teacher Kathleen Kemmet. The school had a high proportion of Jewish pupils and the day-to-day atmosphere was comfortable enough. My father did not like to make a fuss and understood that such a complaint could poison the atmosphere at a time when I was just days before leaving the school for good, but my sister would be there for another two years. So, nothing was done, but we had all learned a lesson.

There were many examples of petty antisemitism around in the 1950s and 1960s. Many Jews by this stage were moving to Newton Mearns, a rapidly developing southern suburb of Glasgow yet there were house-builders who would not sell to Jews. Most golf clubs in the Glasgow area would not accept Jewish members and until a Jewish golf club opened at Bonnyton Moor near Eaglesham, Jewish golfers had to go further afield. The Jewish club was instantly highly popular. My father had been a member of the Hamilton Golf Club but switched immediately to Bonnyton.

The male family members were all keen golfers and their addiction to the game led to the institution of the Collins Cup, a solid silver trophy competed for on an annual basis by family and friends at Bonnyton. The event took place during a late summer Sunday and players and friends gathered at Goldina to share results and discover whose name would be engraved on the trophy. By a strange stroke of fate, I was to be the last holder of the cup, the trophy being awarded to me in 1962. My cousin Gregory and I were the youngest players and deemed too insignificant to play with the adults. We were monitored the Sunday before the main event, a gloriously sunny day, and were given the highest handicap levels. When this number was deducted from our score, we achieved a very good result, with me just ahead of Gregory. The weather was much less favourable the following Sunday and no-one could match the target set by my round of the previous week.

The Jewish community was, by its nature, somewhat insular. My parents' circle of friends was exclusively Jewish and when they were not interacting with their families the only visitors to our home were Jewish. The pattern hardly changed over our generation. At the same time, the Jewish community integrated into Scottish society and its civil, cultural and professional life, faster and more effectively than any other minority. There was a Jewish city councillor before there was one from the much larger Catholic community and the children of the immigrants entered the universities of Scotland in substantial numbers. Not only was there no quota limiting Jewish numbers for medical studies, but the Scottish medical schools accepted hundreds of Jewish students from America who could not get places in many medical schools in the States due to the existence of a *numerus clausus*. As the leading Scottish historian, Sir Thomas Devine, wrote in his Foreword for *Two Hundred Years of Scottish Jewry* (2018), of which I was the Chief Editor:

> The weakness of antisemitism and the resources of human and social capital among the Jews of Scotland enabled them to make a positive impact on Scottish society at an earlier stage than most other immigrants.

Devine noted that the range of work of the immigrant generations, the tailors, carpenters, hawkers and traders did not impact adversely on the work market and the Jewish self-help networks meant that Jews were not seen as a drain on the communal purse. As Zevi Golombok, Editor of the Glasgow *Jewish Echo* put it in November 1930: 'The difference between antisemitism in an intolerant country and antisemitism in Britain is that one spills blood and the other spills dignity.'

I was very happy at the High School of Glasgow and remained there until entering the University of Glasgow. The school had over a thousand pupils and the Jewish contingent numbered around a hundred, making up fully 10 per cent of the school roll. There were Jewish prayers every morning, held when the other pupils were at Assembly in the main hall. From Monday to Thursday one of the science teachers, James Low, known to all as 'Doc', was in charge and our Assembly always concluded with us singing *Adon Olam*, which ends the Shabbat morning service while he accompanied us on the piano. On Fridays, the minister of the Garnethill Synagogue, the Rev. Dr. Isaac Kenneth Cosgrove, visited, and he always had something interesting to tell us of the Jewish world and its place in wider society. His sons, Malcolm and John, had attended the school and he felt very much at home with us. At the end of each year he organized an essay competition, the prize for which would be presented at the main School Prize-giving. I felt able to enter the competition when I reached Secondary 4 and was delighted to receive the prize and attend Prize-giving. I tried again the following year when Rev. Cosgrove announced that he was ready to accept entries. I subsequently discovered that I had been the only entrant and Rev. Cosgrove decided that he felt obliged to reward the Jewish head boy and would not be awarding an essay prize that year.

With my school in the city centre and my sister's in the West End either parent would bring us to school in the morning before heading for the surgery, just south of the Clyde. When we moved to Newton Mearns the arrangements changed. My grandfather had stopped driving and the business employed someone who would drive him about and be available for whatever was required at the factory. Ernie, the chauffeur, collected us along with cousins Charles and Gregory who were at Kelvinside Academy. It was a convenient start to the day and early morning traffic in Glasgow was much lighter in the early 1960s than it is today.

The Rector, as the head teacher was known during my years at the school was David Lees. He continued the policy of offering pupils a broad-based curriculum with room for individual choices within the sciences and languages. I got to know Lees well after I graduated when medical complications brought him to the Southern General Hospital when I was working there. He had an outstanding career, and his achievements were recognized by the award of a CBE and an honorary Doctor of Laws at the

University. He always took a positive interest in the progress of all the boys in the school and I was aware that he knew just how well each pupil was performing. He took a special pride in the presence of the Jewish boys in the school, part of a Scottish Presbyterian tradition which understood the contribution of the Hebrew Bible to his faith. He once told me that he believed that our Jewish religion was received by Moses 'from a higher authority'.

As an academic school with frequent pupil assessments we always knew where we stood relative to our classmates. It was only when we reached the end of our school years and many pupils sat the Glasgow University Bursary examinations which offered pupils, from all over Scotland, financial support from a variety of trusts that the university administered, that we knew how well the school shaped up with regard to the competition of other schools. In my year no less than ten pupils finished in the first hundred, I was only 139th, but the first three places went to classmates. This was an unequalled school performance. These were the days when the tawse, the leather belt, was used by teachers to keep classroom order. It was used through the school and Lees was known to wield it for serious miscreants and for pupils who did not meet his exacting standards in the Latin class. I managed to avoid this now discredited punishment. Brian Lockhart's *The Town School: A History of the High School of Glasgow* (2010) covers the school history from its shadowy origins in the twelfth or thirteenth centuries, although occasionally whitewashing the deficiencies of the weaker teachers.

I entered the University of Glasgow for the basic sciences year in 1964. I found the emphasis in these first years on rote learning, especially in the anatomy studies, somewhat tedious. I had always been interested in why things were the way they were rather than being able to quote verbatim pathways of nerves or biochemical reactions. At one stage I had toyed with the idea of switching to a history degree, but I decided, with family encouragement, to continue with the medical course, realizing that the aim of the undergraduate studies was, as I wanted, to produce a fully-trained medical practitioner who would be sensitive to the needs of their patients. The last clinical years of the course went by much more easily.

The Six-Day War in June 1967 took place towards the end of the academic year as university examinations loomed. There was a general groundswell of sympathy for Israel as the neighbouring countries threatened to eliminate the Jewish state. As not everyone saw things this way, I sought to publicize Israel's plight on campus, in the agonising weeks before hostilities. To my great surprise the Jewish student leadership in Glasgow decided that as British citizens they could not take sides in a foreign debate. With a few friends, and the support of Morris Linden, Editor of the weekly (Glasgow) *Jewish Times*, we produced flyers and pamphlets which explained Israel's case and managed to distribute them all before the war ended. The Six-Day War has now been recognized as a catalyst which energized the Jewish world, producing an increased Jewish awareness amongst my contemporaries. The Glasgow Jewish community raised previously unheard-of sums of money and there were many who answered the call for volunteers.

Two years later, I attended the Hadassah Hospital summer programme for overseas medical students. It gave me my first insight into Israeli medicine, and I became aware that their students didn't just take learning from lectures and textbooks, as we did, but used the literature to keep up to date with medical advances. One day that sticks out in my memory is our visit to the Hansen Leprosy Hospital and its Director, Professor Yaakov Sheskin. In 1969 there were still more than 30 inpatients at the hospital, but the numbers were declining as modern treatments meant that most new patients could be treated as outpatients. There had been leprosy in Europe in the Middle Ages and a leprosarium had existed in Glasgow until around 1730 but visiting a contemporary functioning leprosy hospital was a rare event. Sheskin had made the serendipitous discovery that the sedative thalidomide could treat the fulminating form of leprosy and he was to receive many awards. The discovery was, of course, troubling as thalidomide had already been banned in most countries because of the severe birth deformities it caused, but judiciously used it proved of benefit in leprosy until newer products came on the market. When we purchased our apartment in Jerusalem, 35 years later, we found that the Hansen Hospital was just across the road from our building.

Towards the end of my studies, I was with a group of medical students accompanying a consultant on a ward round. The patient, whom I had not seen before, recognized me, and addressed me by name and told the group that she was a patient with my parents and had known of me since my birth. Such events were not unusual. After graduating in the summer of 1972, I began working at the Southern General Hospital in the Govan area of Glasgow which was the local hospital for my parent's practice. Consequently, I saw a few of their patients who turned up at the hospital. Once I told a young patient that she could not have a routine test during the night, and she replied that she would report me to my mother! The four post-graduation hospital years were mostly focussed on general, or internal, medicine and included a short period in psychiatry. I learned a lot during these years. The consultants were skilled diagnosticians whose powers of observation made up for the lack of the sophisticated medical equipment which became available in later years. The saying was that you should have a good idea of what was wrong with the patient by the time he or she took their seat. Observation was all. Without it, even today, something valuable is lost.

In July 1972 Irene (Taylor) and I were married. We set up home in Giffnock's Mains Estate which proved to be the perfect place for us. We had room for the growing family and it was well situated for transport links and within easy walking distance of the Giffnock Synagogue. By the time that I entered my parents' practice our first two children had been born: Eve in October 1974 and Tamar in July 1976. Rachel arrived in April 1979 and David in December 1984. We also had a baby daughter, Judith, who had been born in November 1983 profoundly handicapped and survived only until David was ten days old.

Irene worked through the years while the children were growing up, usually either part-time or on short-term cover for teachers who were off work through sickness or were on maternity leave. Through her work in home economics she also got to know the lives of pupils from backgrounds similar to that of my patients. She usually had to negotiate Friday afternoon leave in the winter when Shabbat begins around 3.40pm and almost always found the school staff understanding and helpful. Having four lively and articulate children meant that the house was always welcoming and full of noise, and when they left home they all achieved success in their chosen fields. We were proud of them all, and as they married, and each gave us three grandchildren, we were happy to count our blessings. We had a steady stream of visitors at home on Shabbat, often Jewish travellers from Israel and America, and the children could always be relied on to enliven the occasion. These visitors gave us fascinating insights into the Jewish world abroad and we once, but only once, received hospitality from a couple who had visited us, the Katzensteins from Englewood, New Jersey.

In November 1976, I began working in my parent's practice becoming the fourth doctor. Besides my mother and father there was a third partner, Dr. Ian Russell, a very congenial person who had joined my parents when I was just a year old. I had the privilege of working with both parents, just a year with my father before his stroke, but twelve years with my mother. When she retired in 1989 I devised an oral history project for her, interviewing former patients, which she took up with her usual enthusiasm generating thousands of pages of transcript the study of which I am only now completing. Before she retired she wrote a series of letters reflecting on her medical work and wondering about what the future would bring.

She put them in an envelope, wrote the words 'Letters to No-one' on the outside and we only discovered them eighteen years later after her death. My account of the letters and her oral history study won the Rose Prize for the History of Medicine, awarded biennially by the Royal College of General Practitioners and the Worshipful Society of Apothecaries in 2019. It was a great tribute to her, almost exactly one hundred years since her birth.

In all, I spent over 30 years in the practice, marking more than 60 years since my father started working there. There were many memorable incidents over the years. It was continually-pressured hard work, but for the most part the most rewarding aspects were the continuity of seeing families through their life cycles, providing comfort when it was required and making sure that patients got the treatment they needed. Many younger doctors passed through the practice, but it was with Dr. Barry Adams-Strump that I spent the longest time in partnership. We saw eye to eye on all the developments that were needed as the years went by and together we welcomed a succession of younger doctors to the practice, including Ken O'Neill when Dr. Russell retired and then Dr. Alison Thomson, when my mother retired in 1989.

In 1983 I had the first of two short sabbatical breaks from the practice, both at the Ben Gurion University of the Negev in Beersheva. The introduction was made by David Stone, a Glaswegian then working in epidemiology at the Medical School and later Professor of Paediatric Epidemiology at the University of Glasgow. I undertook to act as a mentor to some young doctors working in family medicine clinics in the northern Negev, travelling beyond Beersheva to clinics in Dimona and Yerucham. It was in Beersheva that I first heard about AIDS, which was exploding into world consciousness. Besides the medical aspects, we learned some Hebrew and our older daughters attended primary school and our youngest daughter was at a *gan*, kindergarten. My father had passed away, aged just 70, just a month before we were due to leave Glasgow but my mother insisted that we go. His health had been declining after a stroke a few years earlier and his hoped-for return to work never happened.

It was not a great time for Israeli medicine. The sophistication of the Israeli medical scene lay sometime in the future. Academics were having pay cheques deferred and just before we left the doctors were on strike. Nevertheless, it was a very worthwhile experience and our exposure to Israeli life and religious practice served us well. We returned to Glasgow to resume our old activities, and I soon found that new community avenues were opening.

Irene and I returned to Beersheva in 2003, this time with a more formal arrangement with the university. This was an anxious time in Israel. The Second Intifada and a murderous wave of terrorist attacks which claimed the lives of more than a thousand lives was raging as we made the arrangements for our visit. I had been invited during an international Medical Ethics Conference in Beersheva in November 2001 by Professor Shifra Shvarts, a leading figure in the history of medicine in Israel, to take up a Dozor Visiting Professorship. Harry Dozor, from Philadelphia, was a prominent philanthropist and a great supporter of the Ben Gurion University and he was a member of its Board of Governors. Although the Intifada was coming to an end there were few Dozor applicants for 2003. As my stay required agreement by the National Health Service to take the time away from the practice for an approved purpose, the invitation also came from the Department of Family Medicine. Beside clinic attendances, I studied the local family medicine provision for terminal care, known as the 'home hospice programme'. There was time for medical history too and I completed a study of the eye disease trachoma during the British Mandate, which was endemic in Palestine in the first decades of the twentieth century. It was eventually published as part of a supplement in *Korot: the Journal of the Israel Society for the History of Medicine and Science*, on infectious diseases in the Holy Land, of which I was a Guest Editor.

The Conference in 2001 was also affected by the Intifada as most of the projected attendees cancelled and the organizers thought long and hard before deciding that the event should go forward even with greatly reduced numbers. The Conference still proved to be successful. All the lectures were held as plenary presentations and my paper on living wills was well received. Dr. Fred Rosner, probably the leading figure in the field of Jewish medical ethics at the time, was present and he not only gave me some ideas for further study but agreed to come to our synagogue in Glasgow as scholar-in-residence. His visit proved to be truly outstanding. He spoke twice to members of the shul, met with the Scottish Health Minister to give the Jewish point of view about transplantation and addressed students at both Glasgow and Edinburgh universities. He and his wife stayed in our home for the week of his visit and we were able to collaborate on a number of books in the years ahead.

It was therefore a great pleasure to share in editing a festschrift, *In the Pathways of Maimonides* (2015), to mark Fred's 80th birthday, along with Professor Eddie Reichman from New York and Rabbi Professor Avraham Steinberg of Jerusalem, both leading figures in the field of Jewish medical law and ethics. I was able to include a brief mention of Fred's reunion, at our home in Glasgow, with the woman who, as a young helper, had looked after him for the first months after he arrived in England with the *Kindertransport*.

The Second Gulf War had just begun as we arrived in Beersheva and within a few weeks the Americans invaded Iraq. There were concerns about a chemical attack on Israel and we were issued with gas masks, which we were delighted to be able to return unused at the end of our visit. The British Embassy in Tel Aviv also made contact telling us that they were advising their nationals to leave and if we remained we did so at our own risk. We decided to stay. Our time in Israel had a dimension that was different from the previous sabbatical in 1983. Our youngest daughter, Rachel, had decided to remain in Israel after a gap year spent partly at Kibbutz Lavi but mainly at the Bnei Akiva Seminary *Midreshet haRova* in the Old City of Jerusalem. Her course in optics had not worked out, but she was already working in Tel Aviv on her way to a career in commercial real estate by the time that we arrived. Our son, David, who was born the year after we returned from the first sabbatical had left school and was at a Bnei Akiva programme at the Hesder Yeshiva in the desert town of Yerucham, not too far from Beersheva. We were near enough to be helpful but far enough away for him to assert some independence.

My mother and sister joined us for Pesach (Passover) and in retrospect the very first signs of the Alzheimer's Disease which affected the last four years of my mother's life were already present. By the next year I was aware that she was dementing but she was still able to convince the psychogeriatrician that all was well, and it took a brain scan to confirm the diagnosis. Our younger daughter Tamar, husband Daniel and children Adi and Matan, were also with us for Pesach and just four years later they made *aliya* and immigrated to Israel, now with a third child, Keshet. Our oldest daughter also had a visit along with her husband Josh and Irene's mother came too.

It was on return from the first sabbatical in Israel in 1983 that my involvement in Jewish community matters really began, when I was elected the Honorary Secretary of the Glasgow Jewish Representative Council. I served two terms as President and was the first Chairman of the Scottish Council of Jewish Communities when it was set up in 1999 after the inauguration of the Scottish Parliament. I was also for a time the Chairman of the Glasgow Board of Jewish Education and the Giffnock Synagogue, although it was my time as the *parnas*, responsible, along with the rabbi for the conduct of the services and maintain the customs and traditions of the shul, that I most enjoyed. However, it was the Scottish Jewish Archives

Centre which has been my longest and most meaningful period of chairmanship. The Centre was opened in 1987 as a partnership with the historic Victorian Garnethill Synagogue, where it is situated. Drs. Jack E. Miller and Sidney Naftalin joined with Harvey Kaplan and myself as founders and Jack and I were joint chairs until his death in 2008 when I became the sole chair. Harvey soon became the Archives Director, and together we watched the Centre develop, build up an enviable collection of documents and artefacts and sponsor academic research and publications. As I write this during the Covid-19 virus pandemic, plans to create a Scottish Jewish Heritage Centre are coming to fruition, and even from Israel I am able to participate in regular meetings with those in Glasgow through ZOOM.

The Scottish Jewish Archives Centre (SJAC) acted as the publisher for many of my books on the Jewish community, and in Israel, the Medical Library of the Hebrew University and the Maimonides Research Institute both published two books. There was one exciting week at the end of 2015 when three books were published at the same time. My Ph.D was published by Aberdeen University Press as *Go and Learn: the International Story of the Jews and Medicine in Scotland 1739-1945* (1988). Our work in SJAC has brought the presence of the Jews of Scotland into the mainstream of Scottish historical and archival accounts. Harvey has claimed an important place within the world of Scottish, as well as Jewish archival research and recording while I have been gratified to see how modern accounts of Scottish medicine include references to Jews in the profession.

The Jewish place in Scottish society was also emphasized by an article in the *Dictionary of Scottish Church History and Theology* (1993) where I was able to describe the Jews of Scotland in the context of their encounter with Christianity, whether as welcoming friends or less commonly as confrontational missionaries. I also contributed two articles, on the Jews in Scotland firstly as a religion but also as an ethnic group, as a part of the fourteen-volume *Scottish Life and Society* in Volume 9 on *The Individual and Community Life* (2005) and Volume 12 on *Religion* (2006).

Undertaking a full-time Ph.D in the Social Sciences Faculty while working as a full-time GP was not easy. When my studies began, in the pre-internet era, research visits to archival sources had to be carefully organized and I relied on my mother's help in the practice and Irene's at home to see the degree through to graduation in 1987. Our oldest daughter attended the graduation and my supervisor, Anne Crowther, warned her that being a plumber might be an easier career than the one her father had chosen. Having written about Jewish doctors in Scotland I had the idea of writing about how the immigrant Jews coped with health and welfare issues in Glasgow. With time constraints for research and writing the book was written at the rate of a chapter a year over a decade. Tuckwell Press, of East Linton near Edinburgh, published it as *Be Well! Jewish Immigrant Health and Welfare in Glasgow: 1860-1920* (2001).

I was not finished with academic studies. In 1989 I enrolled in the first Masters' course on medical law and ethics at the University of Glasgow. Led by Professor Sheila MacLean we spent Thursday evenings over two years gaining an understanding of the basics of the subject and then had a year to complete a dissertation. The course included doctors and lawyers from a variety of backgrounds and it was only when we had an evening on forensic medicine and the law that we realized that many of the participants were just as well versed on the subject as some of the more junior lecturers. There was one evening when a case was presented which had affected the understanding of mental health on criminal behaviour. My classmates included the lawyers for defence and prosecution and the psychiatrist had assessed the accused. The course was one of the best educational experiences I have taken part in, both for the quality of the teaching and the personalities of the participants.

The M.Phil from the Law Faculty meant that I had the unusual distinction of three degrees from the same university awarded by three different faculties. My mother was very proud and excited as one of her role models was Lord Boyd Orr, the Glasgow physician and nutritionist who had received the Nobel Peace Prize in 1949 and had graduated from the Arts, Science and Medical Faculties. Three degrees from three faculties was something she highly approved of.

On retiring from the medical practice in August 2007 I carried on with some sessional medical work for the out-of-hours general practice service, usually working on Tuesday evenings until midnight and on Sunday mornings. The work was interesting and had proper back-up in the form of office, nursing and security staff with an ambulance driver to bring in patients who had no transport of their own. At the same time, I spent most days at the Centre for the History of Medicine of the University of Glasgow as a Senior Research Fellow. In September 2008 at a Congress of the International Society of the History of Medicine, I was appointed as English language Editor of their bilingual journal *Vesalius*, named after the famous Belgian anatomist and published in French as well as English.

I was to become the longest-serving Editor of the journal, and as English became the predominant language of the publication I was appointed Chief Editor. I had been attending Congresses and Meetings of the International Society since Antwerp in 1992 and managed almost all subsequent events. These took us to Mexico, Argentina, Georgia, Italy, Cyprus, Hungary, Turkey, Spain and Greece. It also enabled us to have two visits to Arab countries, Tunisia and Egypt, and brought additional invitations to Moscow and the Island of Zakynthos, marking the quincentenary of Vesalius' birth. I have described our visit to Moscow with the opportunity to meet there with Boris, Irena and their teenage daughter. Of course, we had time to visit the Kremlin, see an exhibition of Faberge Eggs and visit the Tretchikov Gallery with its collection of Russian art. For the Zakynthos trip I produced a special edition of *Vesalius* as Andreas Vesalius had died on the island in 1564.

Zakynthos, known also as Zante to the holiday makers who crowd its beaches and taverns in the summer, had an interesting Holocaust story. The Nazis arrived on the island when Italy surrendered to the allies in 1943 and they were seeking to deport its 300 Jews to Auschwitz-Birkenau. The Nazi Commander called in the Mayor and the Bishop and asked them to compile a list of the island's Jews. They asked for a couple of days to complete the list and when they returned they handed the Commander a sheet of paper with just two names on it, that of the Mayor and the Bishop. During these two days the Jews had gone into hiding and all survived until Germany's defeat. The community re-established itself in the island's main town after the war but a devastating earthquake in the old town in 1953 caused the Jews to move to Athens or Israel.

The visit to Tunisia in 1998 was especially interesting. I presented a paper on the great Jewish physician and philosopher Isaac Israeli (c. 850-950 CE) who had lived in the Tunisian city of Kairouan. He was still recognized as an exponent of Arabic medicine and his figure appeared on a postage stamp issued specially for the Congress, along with images of the Muslim physician ibn-Al Jazzar and the Christian Constantine. In the original medieval illustration of three physicians Israeli had appeared in the centre but for the stamp the Muslim representative, now changed to al-Majusi, was in the middle. Medical historians from Libya were very interested in the presentation and we exchanged letters after returning home.

On the day that Congress members left the hotel in Carthage for the Museum in Tunis we took a day trip to the island of Djerba to visit the historic al-Ghriba synagogue in Hara Kabira near the island's main town of Houmt Tsouk. The small Jewish neighbourhood was still busy, with local shops, small prayer-rooms and the sounds of children of the Talmud Torah chanting their learning to the beat of a metronome. Wandering through

Houmt Tsouk we entered a jewellery shop that had a mezuza on the doorpost and spoke to the owners who advised us that the town had a kosher restaurant. It proved to be closed, or at least we discovered that it had no food to serve us, but we had our own supplies with us and were not bothered. We also discovered that the hotel shop was run by Jews from Djerba and as a wedding was planned for the day we were leaving, the hotel filled up with Jewish visitors from Italy.

The Congress was in Egypt in 2008 and took place at the Al Shams Medical University. We had never seen driving like it – even in Israel, Italy or Turkey. Traffic lights did not stop anyone and crossing a road was a life-threatening move. We managed to visit the famous Ben Ezra Synagogue in the old Coptic area of Fostat where Maimonides had prayed, and the Cairo Geniza had been located. The building was in beautiful condition, well maintained and guarded by a group of very friendly Egyptian soldiers. Our Congress organizer, Professor Nasser Kotby, hosted some of us one evening. He showed me his library which contained an eclectic mix of books in English and Arabic and included standard works on the Holocaust such as those of Martin Gilbert, as well as a book on the art of the Israel Museum. Sometime later we read that Kotby had gone to Berlin in 2013 to receive the Yad Vashem Righteous Gentile award from the Israeli Ambassador, the first awarded to an Arab recipient, in honour of his uncle, Dr. Mohammed Helmy who had sheltered Jews in Berlin at great risk to himself.

The Congress in Italy in 2012 was very special. Although most of the events were held in the spa town of Abano Terme it was the day spent in the historic buildings of the nearby University of Padua that was the most memorable. I chaired a session in the lecture theatre of Galileo and visited the dissection room with its steeply tiered gallery, of the great Renaissance anatomist Andreas Vesalius. The proximity of the Congress to Rosh Hashanah did not allow us time to return home and we spent the New Year holiday in the new kosher hotel in the former Casa di Reposa, the Jewish home for the elderly in the historic Venetian ghetto. Synagogue services followed the Italian rite. On the afternoon of the first day services were held in the Canton Synagogue, now part of the Jewish Museum. After *mincha*, the afternoon service, the windows behind us were opened and we recited the *Tashlich* prayer, recited over a body of water, facing the moving life of the Venetian canals.

It was at our second Congress in Granada in 1994 that I first met Professor Samuel Kottek, Strasbourg-born and holder of the Harry Friedenwald Chair of the History of Medicine at the Hebrew University of Jerusalem. This was the beginning of a professional relationship and a deep friendship which led to my retirement position as Visiting Professor in the History of Medicine at the Hebrew University. We met frequently. He invited me to speak at the opening study session for an exhibition on the history of Jews in medicine at the Diaspora Museum in Tel Aviv in 1995 and many of my researches in the history of medicine were published in *Korot*. Since arriving in Israel we have met almost weekly and have collaborated in the publication of books on the medicine of Moses Maimonides and Isaac Israeli. A third work on Tuviya HaCohen, author of the first Hebrew medical encyclopaedia, published in Venice in 1708, was delayed because of the Coronavirus but should be published soon.

Along with (now Emeritus) Professor Kottek I have been working with Helena Paaviliainen, who is originally from Finland and who completed her Ph.D under Professor Kottek's supervision at the Hebrew University. A gifted researcher and a serious student of medieval medicine in Hebrew and Arabic she has dealt with the technical side of the publication of these books and of *Korot*. She even prepared for publication the text for one of our books on Jewish history in Scotland.

During these years in Israel, we had regular family trips to Glasgow which enabled me to keep my desk at the Centre for the History of Medicine and remain Chair of the Scottish Jewish Archives Centre. With some work on the medical aspects of Jews in the Polish Army I held the Edgar Astaire Fellowship awarded by the University of Edinburgh and I presented the results at the Scottish Jewish Archives Centre in Glasgow, the Royal College of Physicians and Surgeons of Glasgow and at a meeting of the World Fellowship of the Israel Medical Association in Haifa. At some conferences when presenting in Scottish medical topics I represented the University of Glasgow. At other times, and at Jewish academic events, I represented the Hebrew University.

A special visit was arranged in 2017 through a link, funded by the Erasmus Programme of the European Union, between the Hebrew University and the Paul Stradins University in Riga, Latvia. The exchange visit began with a short trip to Israel by Juris Salaks, Professor of Medical History and Ieva Libiete, Lecturer at the University's Institute of Medical History. We had a study day for them at the Hebrew University Medical Library and arranged a tour of the Old City of Jerusalem led by Helena Paavalainen, now a trained Israel Tour Guide. In return we had a visit to Riga. We saw the amazing new National Library and visited the resort town of Jurmala where we saw a Jewish-owned spa and rehabilitation centre. These spas in Jurmala had been very popular during the Soviet era, even attracting such leaders as Leonid Brezhnev and Nikita Kruschev but was now adjusting to more sophisticated modern demands. We also saw the Zanis Lipke Memorial Museum, opened in 2012, which showed how one couple managed to shelter some groups of Jews, up to a dozen at a time, between 1942 and 1944, before moving them to safe houses in the countryside.

A further interest has been in Jews and medicine in the Holocaust era. This began in the 1980s as I studied the response of the Scottish Royal Colleges to the influx of medical refugees from Nazism. Several hundred Jewish doctors, mainly from Germany but also a few from Poland and Austria, were able to enter British medicine with the Triple Qualification, the access to the British Medical Register provided by the Royal Colleges of Medicine and Surgery in Edinburgh and the Royal College of Medicine and Surgery in Glasgow. The refugee generation is now no longer with us but occasionally someone from the family of a refugee doctor makes contact. Recently, a couple met me at the gate to our apartment in Jerusalem and he told me that his grandparents had lived in our building. His uncle and her father had both obtained the Triple Qualification, one in 1936 and the other in 1939. I had the data to hand in minutes.

One of the biggest and most complex projects I have been involved in since coming to Israel helped chart further details of the Jewish story in Scotland. Neville Lamdan, Glasgow born and a former Israeli Ambassador, was now Director of the Israel Institute of Jewish Genealogy, which was putting the subject on an academic base. He had the idea of a complete demographic and genealogical study of the Scottish community to create a Family Tree of Scottish Jewry. A national study of this type had never been done before but it seemed worth doing and I agreed to partner Neville. We were to enjoy two enormous strokes of good luck without which the project would never have succeeded. One was the agreement of Michael Tobias, a second cousin on my mother's side of the family, to act as Principal Researcher. Michael is still Glasgow-based and is probably the most experienced and talented Jewish genealogist in the world and his work was painstakingly carried out and proved to be exactly what the project required. The other was the support of the National Heritage Lottery Fund which covered the shortfall from the other fundraising.

I agreed to write up the data for an easy to read and well-illustrated book, *The Jewish Experience in Scotland* (2016) which would serve as an introduction to the subject and explain the project in simple terms. I had also ended up being the Chief Editor of a more detailed and academic volume, *Two Hundred Years of Scottish Jewry* (2018),which described the complex details of the project and had a collection of essays which covered some of the themes it had generated. Sir Thomas Devine declared that 'no other immigrant community had ever been studied in such forensic detail'. I had editing assistance from both Professor Aubrey Newman and Professor Bernard Wasserstein, both of whom had strong Glasgow connections. Aubrey had spent many years with family in Glasgow while Bernard was in Glasgow while his father was on the university academic staff. Bernard and I were in the same year at the High School of Glasgow until the family left when his father took up a post at the University of Leicester.

Possibly the most successful of the books on the Jews in Scotland was *Jewish Glasgow: A Pictorial History* (2014). The idea had been conceived by Stephen Kliner, when he was President of the Glasgow Jewish Representative Council, but only came to fruition after we were both living in Israel. Stephen managed the project, raising the necessary funds and seeing the book through to publication. Harvey Kaplan provided the research and sourced the illustrations. Jacqueline Speyer, now living in Jerusalem, but known to us from Scotland as a gifted graphic designer, produced the layout while I wrote all the connecting narrative and sourced a collection of vignettes, mostly by the late Chaim Bermant and A.C. Jacobs. Bernard Wasserstein wrote the Foreword. We had two launch meetings, one in Glasgow and the second at *Bet HaTfutsot*, the Diaspora Museum in Tel Aviv, where a more than capacity crowd over-filled the auditorium, bought out all our stock and met up with friends and acquaintances they had not seen for years or even decades.

During all these years I was to collect and store all the family memorabilia being gathered in London, Jerusalem and in the Americas. At the same time, I began to organize my recollections of the stories of my grandfather and his children into a form that gradually came to be recorded. Finally, in the electronic era relatives around the world began to explore their Kagarlitsky heritage and made the contacts which have enabled the assorted notes to be collected into book form.

Conclusion

At the end of June 2003 we paid our first trip to Russia and Ukraine. It was the three hundredth anniversary of the founding of St. Petersburg and the city was guaranteed to look its best for its special birthday. Moscow would give us an opportunity to visit the capital of the Slavic world, to see the city of Anna and Iosef and maybe to meet up again with Boris. Kiev was the gateway to the places in Ukraine where the Kagarlitsky family began. We booked our hotels through Intourist and our visas arrived fairly quickly.

We loved the beauty of St. Petersburg with its summer 24-hour long daylight and happily strolled alongside its canals and boulevards. We visited the spectacular Hermitage Museum and admired the fabulous collections of Russian and international art. We also saw the signs of Jewish revival after more than 70 years of Communism, with kosher restaurants and restored synagogues and schools. One of the kosher restaurants at that time was some distance from the city centre but was fortunately near a Metro station. I know the Russian alphabet well enough which was then essential for Metro travel as the station names were not in English characters. The restaurant was crowded with two very different looking groups. There were some teenage school pupils with their teachers, probably Chabad rabbis, and nearby were the parents, brought up in Soviet times, clearly totally unfamiliar with the rituals of the meal and the Mincha (afternoon) and Ma'ariv (evening) prayers. I also had a lucky escape in St. Petersburg, while walking along the famous Nevsky Prospekt, after being surrounded by a crowd of street children who were attempting to pick my pockets. Fortunately I emerged with my possessions intact. We had a warning from a passer-by to watch out for trouble. Irene shouted 'STOP' and the children ran.

We took the night train from St. Petersburg to Moscow and were at once drawn in to its lively and chaotic streets. There were drunks at the pavement sides and signs of poverty and wealth co-existing side by side. By the time we returned to Moscow, only a few years later, there were no drunks and no signs of poverty in the city centre which was now completely gentrified and home to the wealthy with their shops, cafés, hotels and restaurant testifying to the new lifestyle of the Russian rich. On Friday morning we visited the synagogue on Bolshaya Bronnaya to check out Shabbat arrangements. The courtyard was packed with the local poor waiting patiently for basic food supplies. This too had disappeared by the time of our next visit to the city.

Communication with Boris in 2003 was not easy. We had no access to the internet and the telephones in the street kiosks were not compatible with his mobile phone. Fortunately, our hotel, the Ukraina, a splendid relic of Stalin's grandiose Moscow building projects, had a variety of phone kiosks and eventually we managed to contact each other and arrange to meet at the statue of Pushkin, close to a Metro Station. We were able to talk over a pot of mint tea in a Moroccan café and marvel at the opportunity we two Kagarlitsky second cousins had to meet up again and review our lives since we had last met. Boris described his own upbringing in Moscow as part of an extended Kagarlitsky family with its intellectuals and scientists, and his memories of his grandmother who carried stories of her life in Glasgow so many decades earlier.

From Moscow the next stop was an even longer overnight train journey to Kiev which involved a passport and visa check. We had a two-bunk cabin complete with regular creature comforts – some toiletries and a bottle of kvass, the popular Russian rye-bread-based low alcohol beer, for each of us. I was later to try a kosher version of this drink in Israel, but it seemed to be a somewhat acquired taste. We did find, though, that the Russians had quickly adapted to the taste of Scotland's best-selling soft drink, Irn Bru, which we found to be widely available.

Kiev's lively Jewish life, even after the migration of so many of its population in the decade after the end of Communism, proved to be quite inspiring. We saw the food depots bringing food to the Jewish poor and the renovated synagogues. The Brodsky Synagogue in the city centre, returned to the community after years as a puppet theatre, was truly imposing and a kosher snack bar at its side provided Jewish Ukrainian food at minimal prices. The old synagogue in Podol, which functioned through the Communist years, still boasted a Heath Robinson style matzah bakery and had a functioning Yeshiva.

After exploring Kiev and visiting the site of the mass murder of Jews and others by the Nazis at Babi Yar (Babyn Yar) it was time to move south to Kovshevata. We hired a driver and a guide. We spoke to the guide the day before and outlined our itinerary. She mis-heard Kovshevata and thought we wanted to visit Korsun-Sevchenko, a favourite place for those interested in the tank battles of the Second World War. During January and

February 1944, an 80,000-man German force was encircled and destroyed by the Red Army there and the town has a museum of the history of the battle in an eighteenth-century palace.

Our first stop was Kagarlyk (Kaharlyk), the central town of the Kagarlitsky district, from where the family name was derived. The central square indicated its date of founding as 1142 and at one side was a wartime tank illustrating the sacrifice of Soviet citizenry in defeating the Nazis in some of great battles of the Second World War. Kagarlyk had suffered during the pogroms of 1919: a crowd of Jews awaited the White Russian troops to greet them in the traditional way with bread and salt. The greeting ceremony turned into a plundering and looting spree. Three Jewish men were killed, one of them murdered as he tried to protect his wife from rape. The pogrom continued for several weeks and did not stop until most of the Jewish population left town.

Many wartime battles, on the way to Stalingrad, crossed the Jewish villages of the region destroying many of the village homes and the ancient

Where the family name began, Kagarlyk, June 2003.

Jewish cemeteries which lay just outside the towns. Once out of Kiev we travelled on the modern highway which links the capital with the southern city of Odessa, but as soon as we left the highway we could see that we were stepping back in time. The twenty-first century had not yet arrived in this part of Ukraine. The locals, dressed in peasant fashion of an earlier generation, went about their business on horses and carts.

The sign at the gateway to Kovsehvata (Kivshovata) said it all. We were back where the family had been formed and where great-grandfather Zev and grandfather Solomon were born more than a hundred years before. The views were beautiful with the hills, the fields and the lakes just as family legend recalled it. The Russian Orthodox church, newly restored, with its onion domes stood proudly on the highest hilltop. I remembered the picture of Kovshevata from 1920 showing the church and tried to replicate it. Unfortunately, while I did manage to get an image of the church and the hill-top my photograph was taken a little distance away on the other side of the hill.

Family from Moscow had visited Kovshevata in the 1960s and at that time there were locals who could point out the Kagarlitsky homes, but 40 years later there were none who could recall the stories from before the First World War. We did, however, become aware that the shadow of the Holocaust was commemorated in the village. Workers directed us to the ravine where the last Jews of Kovshevata had been murdered in September 1941. We came off the paved road, stopping at a house where a woman was drawing water from a well beside her mulberry trees, drawing enough for us to drink the cool, still, pure water. She indicated a rough path where barefoot children were scrambling about. Walking past some tethered animals, including one almost emaciated cow and a goat, we found ourselves in the eerie silence of a grass-covered ravine with trees on the surrounding hills. At the foot with some stone steps cut into the hillside below there was a small stone monument erected in Soviet times which referred specifically to the massacre of Jews by the Nazis. This had been a sensitive issue in Communist times when the suffering of the Jews was not allowed a voice separate from the experiences of the local population. This was exemplified at Kiev's Babi Yar, where mention that Jews had been targeted in the massacres was suppressed for a long time.

We could just about make out the words on the weathered stone, written in a simple Russian, and we stood for a while in silent contemplation about the evil which had come to this place. The local high school had taken a lead in understanding the past lives of its Jewish community and had instigated an almost unique oral history project covering the story of the final days of Jewish life there. A photograph album was prepared and a documentary film was being produced. There had been about 300 Jews still living in Kovshevata in September 1939 as the Second World War began. Most had managed to leave before the Nazis arrived in the area and an attempt was made to smuggle the remainder to somewhere safe, but the rescue was compromized and 44 Jews were murdered. The evacuated Jews did not return to Kovshevata after the war.

We later discovered that there are two Jewish cemeteries in Kovshevata. One, at the north-west edge of the village, which we visited, is now a field, owned by a farming co-operative and no gravestones have survived. The last funeral took place in 1941 before the arrival of the Germans in August. There is another cemetery on the southern outskirts, also surrounded by agricultural properties, where about twenty gravestones still stand and there is a mass grave. The municipality has made attempts to clear the cemetery of overgrown vegetation and pupils from the High School volunteer to help with regular maintenance. We discovered that a presentation about the Jewish community had taken place at the High School just a couple of years before our visit but a message to the school, written in Russian by a friend, went unanswered.

The pain of the past was crushing as we recalled the story of the bungled attempt at evacuating Kovshevata's last Jews and walked back to our car to make the return journey to Kiev, although not before we had visited nearby Boyarke, where Solomon's wife Golda had been born. The village was laid out with small wooden houses set back from the dusty unpaved roads which criss-crossed the settlement. It looked as if time had stood still since Golda had left more than a century before. Back on the highway we saw some stalls at the side of the road. We discovered that the workers in the nearby sugar factory had not been paid for some time and that they had decided to sell the sugar themselves to make up their wages. Further on, we found a similar stall selling tyres from another factory that had defaulted on its payments to its workers. We flew back to Glasgow, with a stopover in London. On the evening of our departure, Kiev's airport, which served a population of more than two million in a country of over forty million people, had only three international flights, to London, Tel Aviv and Moscow. When we passed through Borispol (Boryspil) ten years later on our way from Athens to Tbilisi it was as busy as any international airport.

Back in Glasgow we collected the photographs we had taken and began to consider again the family story and our place in Glasgow. The city was changing. From a leading centre of ship-building and heavy engineering it has reinvented itself as a financial hub and tourist destination, based on culture and the arts, and there are many signs of this rejuvenation. At the same time the Jewish community was declining in numbers. During the 1950s as I was growing up, Glasgow's Jewish community was at its peak with around 15,000 members and the following decade saw the start of a slow but persistent decline. The exodus of new graduates had been noticed by the great chronicler of Glasgow Jewish life Chaim Bermant from the middle of the 1950s as Glasgow University trained more graduates than the local economy could absorb. The Gorbals synagogues were beginning to amalgamate or to close but there were new synagogues developing in Newton Mearns, Giffnock and Clarkston which clearly represented the way of the future. Jewish institutions were also moving out of the Gorbals. In 1974 the Great Central Synagogue in South Portland Street, where so many family *barmitzvahs* and weddings were celebrated, finally closed. By then the active Jewish link with the Gorbals was at an end and a sense of nostalgia for its warmth and Jewish ambience gradually obscured the poverty and privation which many had suffered.

The Jewish newcomers to Scotland became fully engaged with Scottish society and came to contribute to its arts and culture, medicine and law, politics and philanthropy out of all proportion to their numbers. Chaim Bermant reflected on the similarities between Jews and Scots and noted that 'what is maddening to outsiders is the good conceit which both have of themselves is not entirely unjustified'.

I was already thinking about retirement planning when we returned from our Russian and Ukrainian trip. The 2001 Census showed that there were just around 5,000 Jews in Glasgow and our closest friends were also moving away. Eventually we found that there were more of our Glasgow friends in London. Our children, like most of their Jewish contemporaries, had left Glasgow to study, Eve and David in Manchester, Tamar in London and Rachel in Israel. Today, two are in London and two in Israel and few of their friends returned to Scotland after university.

It had always been a dream to live in Jerusalem and our two Israeli sabbaticals had made the possibility more real. The year after our Beersheva visit in 2003 we had bought an apartment in Jerusalem and in 2009 finally made *aliya*, although retaining an apartment in Glasgow for family visits and enabling us to keep all the memorabilia of over 40 years of family life that we did not wish to part with. The Jews of Glasgow although much reduced in numbers still have a vitality and an array of institutions that would be envied by many larger communities. My attachment to Glasgow and Scotland of course continued through my continuing interest in its Jewish past, which I still happily chronicle. As noted, I was also to remain

Chair of the Scottish Jewish Archives Centre (SJAC) and to participate in setting up the Scottish Jewish Heritage Centre (SJHC) at the Garnethill Synagogue. We might be based in Jerusalem but as the saying goes – 'you can take the boy out of Glasgow, but you can't take Glasgow out of the boy'.

These demographic changes in Glasgow helped us reflect on the decisions made a century before which caused the family to leave Kovshevata scattering the family members around the world. Some of the movement was driven by events: Shuka and Lyuba seeking a place as far away from Russia as possible; Zelman and Chassia being sent to London; Sam and Ray Kagar feeling the economic pull of America and Motti, Clara, and for a time Ida and Jacob taking the Zionist path and bringing Zev with them; Iosef and Anna choosing to return to Moscow. Solomon and his family came to fulfil his manufacturing dreams in Scotland while some of his siblings and cousins were experiencing many challenges in Russia and not all survived Stalin. However, Solomon's arrival in Glasgow owed as much to chance as the movements of his siblings. He was ready to move to America in 1912 and it was only the intervention of Wolf Anton that persuaded him to try Glasgow first.

Solomon's generation was the last to be born in Kovshevata. The village's other Jews were also leaving, moving to Kiev and Odessa and on to Moscow, or heading for the New World while the last few Jews, trapped there when the Nazis arrived were massacred in 1941. The family story is one of movement. My father was born in London and I entered the world in Glasgow on 23 December 1947. Our children were all born in Scotland, but nine of our twelve grandchildren were born in London and three in Israel.

In Yuri Slezkine's *The Jewish Century,* he outlined three destinations for Jews fleeing from the *shtetls* of Tsarist Russia: New York, epitomizing the West, Palestine/Israel representing the Zionist dream and Moscow, where the *shtetl* Jews who saw the Soviet state as the legitimate place for their children's lives were concentrating. As Slezkine points out, no less than a million Jews left the *shtetls* for Moscow, St. Petersburg and Kiev, cities which were, for the most part, closed to them in Tsarist times – a movement almost rivalling the trans-Atlantic route. Each had its proponents in the Kagarlitsky family. Certainly, those who settled in Britain, Solomon, Shimmel and Zelman's wife and children, led comfortable and secure lives in a broadly welcoming society. For the Americans too, the choice of Sam, and also Ida after a decade in Tel Aviv and a bewildering array of Kagarlitsky cousins now known as Kagar, Karlin and Carl, their new life in the United States gave them the opportunity for social and cultural advancement. The

Argentinian family too have proved fairly resolute in their place in South America. Their country has had its share of chaos, dictatorship and antisemitism but the family there has prospered and found opportunities in the professions.

The Israel story has been mixed. After the deaths of Motti and Zev, and the departure of Ida and Jacob Rashal, only Clara was left of Zev's children in the Holy Land. For those who moved in recent times to Israel from the United Kingdom idealism and identifying with Zionism were the motivating factors. We have been joined in more recent years by many of Zev's family – the descendants of Reysie, Shuka, Shimmel, Solomon and Zelman who have all become well settled and successfully integrated into their own parts of Israeli society.

One memorable Jerusalem moment was the first Kol Nidrei during my chairmanship of the HaTzvi Yisrael Synagogue. Because of its location near the official homes of the President and Prime Minister both Shimon Peres and Benyamin Netanyahu were in the congregation to hear my message of welcome, in Hebrew, to all the worshippers. I was very nervous but felt that the evening represented the fulfilment of so many family dreams of past and present generations.

The Russian relatives have been leaving in significant numbers in the past 30 years and the close family is now represented there only by Boris, Irena and their children, although other more distant relatives remain. Boris and Irena remain committed to their lives in Russia, determined to raise their voices in the search for their own views of a fair and just society.

I had always intended to tell the family story in the detail it deserved but it was only the Coronavirus epidemic and the extra time confined to home that provided both the impetus and the hours to begin writing. We leave Zev's story with the image of him in his last years, a pious Jew dressed in the traditional frockcoat, even in the Tel Aviv heat, and wearing a large black skull cap (*kipa*), on his head. The children and grandchildren he is photographed with are dressed in the modern fashion and the men are bare-headed. The earlier picture we have of Zev, which appears on the cover, is quite different. The large *yarmulke* is missing, and he seems to be dressed in fashionable Russian clothing of the time. Zev's children, in the main, remained traditional Jews without his level of observance. As the family story has progressed there is a wide range of Jewish adherence, whether religious or ethnic, with others whose links lie beyond the Jewish world, but still recognize their Jewish origins. The shifting sands of family identity show many influences.

Left to right: Jacob, Ida and Rita, Zev, Yosef, Clara and Ruth, Tel Aviv, 1928.

The Kagarlitsky family story will continue and more information will emerge from many sources, including the digitization of dusty Ukrainian archives and the translation of Russian language family documents, but the story to date recalls the experiences of a resilient and international family.

Kenneth Collins
Jerusalem, January 2021

List of Illustrations

Map of the Ukraine.

The historical Family Tree – from 1740 down to Zev's generation.

The two family trees of Zev's Children and Grandchildren (first and second marriages).

Motti's certificate indicating 'previous residence in Petach Tikva'.

Rutenberg with his first employees: Motti is at the far left in the back row (10/6/1920).

Motti's watch, retrieved after the exhumation.

Motti's Funeral: Rutenberg is on the left of the picture wearing a dark jacket and pith helmet.

Nikolaev Zionists c. 1904. Zelman is in the back row third from left.

Article by Zelman in Hebrew from *Hed HaZman*, on Palestine and Egypt. His surname is spelt Kaharlitsky in the Ukrainian style (7/4/1910).

Portrait of Sir Emmanuel Kaye (National Portrait Gallery).

Three generations of Zev's family, grand-daughter Mona and great-grandchildren Anita, Jeffrey and Kenneth, with Benno Schotz's mahogany sculpture of Zev's daughter Ura. (Kelvingrove Art Galleries and Museum, Glasgow, August 1996).

Motti with sister Ura and cousin Anna (left) in Glasgow, 1920.

Emmanuel and Ura at Dinard, August 1939.

Report in local Marseille newspaper of the Righteous Gentile Award to Rosanne Romagnan, June 1991.

List of Illustrations

First page of Motti's letter to Anna sent from Jerusalem prior to her departure for Moscow.

The author with Boris and Goscha Kagarlitsky at Newark Lodge (the Jewish Old Age Home for Scotland), Glasgow, 1988.

Alla's photograph of Alf and Zev, Tel Aviv, 1928.

Alf Collins poses for a New Year card, Tel Aviv, September 1928.

Collins family get-together around 1950 to welcome Sam Kagar and daughter Sylvia from America.

Ze'ev Amzalem with one of his artworks.

Collage of Rashal products from Palestine and the United States of America.

A rare surviving picture of Gudis (1888-1921).

Motti with Ida and Alik (in military uniform), 1917.

The first Glasgow Collins workshop, Gorbals, 1912.

Solomon, Golda and children with Ura, Kennishead, Glasgow 1922.

Nithsdale Lodge, 204 Nithsdale Road, Pollokshields, Glasgow.

Where the family name began, Kagarlyk, June 2003.

Left to right: Jacob, Ida and Rita, Zev, Yosef, Clara and Ruth, Tel Aviv, 1928.

About the Author

Kenneth Collins was a general practitioner in Glasgow for over 30 years. He has served as President of the Glasgow Jewish Representative Council and Chairman of the Scottish Council of Jewish Communities. He a founder of the Scottish Jewish Archives Centre and has been its Chairman since 1987. He is currently Senior Research Fellow at the Centre for the History of Medicine at the University of Glasgow and Visiting Professor, History of Medicine, Hebrew University of Jerusalem. He was Editor of *Vesalius: Journal of the International Society of the History of Medicine* from 2009 to 2017 and is Co-Editor of *Korot: Journal of the Israel Society of the History of Medicine and Science.* His books include *Second City Jewry: the Jews of Glasgow in the Age of Expansion* (1990), *The Jewish Experience in Scotland* (2016) and *Be Well! Jewish Immigrant Health and Welfare in Glasgow, 1860-1920* (2001). He was Chief Editor of *Two Hundred Years of Scottish Jewry* (2018) and has been an editor of books on Jewish medical history and Jewish medical ethics. He is Joint Editor of *Medicine: from Biblical Canaan to Modern Israel* also published by Vallentine Mitchell. He is married to Irene (née Taylor) and they have four children and twelve grandchildren.